ONE HAND FOR YOURSELF,

ONE FOR THE SHIP

ALSO BY TRISTAN JONES:

Aka

Dutch Treat

A Steady Trade, a Boyhood at Sea

Heart of Oak

The Incredible Voyage

Saga of a Wayward Sailor

* *Adrift*

Ice!

* *Yarns*

Outward Leg

The Improbable Voyage

Somewheres East of Suez

To Venture Further

* *Seagulls in My Soup*

* Published by Sheridan House

One Hand for Yourself, One for the Ship

THE ESSENTIALS OF SINGLE-HANDED SAILING

Tristan Jones

S SHERIDAN HOUSE

First paperback edition 1990 by
Sheridan House Inc.
145 Palisade Street
Dobbs Ferry, NY 10522

Reprinted 1992, 1996

First published 1982 by
Macmillan Publishing Co.

Material in the chapters on a new mast and on
anchoring was reprinted by permission of
Larry Pardey.

Illustrations by the author

Library of Congress Cataloging-in-Publication Data

Jones, Tristan, 1924-1995
        One hand for yourself, one for the ship
        Bibliography: p.
        Includes index.
        1. Sailing, Single-handed.   I. Title.
        GV811.J66 1982 797.1'24   82-14797

Printed in the United States of America

ISBN   0-924486-03-1

To all who asked the questions . . .

to all who gave the answers.

And to the doctors, nurses, and staff of

St. Vincent's Hospital, New York.

Contents

Author's Note

This book is by no means intended to be a comprehensive treatise on the technicalities of small-craft sailing or on long-distance voyaging. There are a number of very experienced voyager-authors, such as Eric Hiscock, whose personalities are more suited to, and who are far more adept at, detailed, technical writing than I.

Rather, *One Hand for Yourself* is mainly a collection of thoughts on subjects that have not, I feel, been sufficiently touched upon or stressed in small-craft texts to date. As with everything else, the pace of progress in small-craft design, building, and fitting-out has increased so much in recent years that it is almost impossible to keep track with it. Some of the ideas expressed in this book will be considered old-fashioned in some quarters, but I know that at sea, in rough weather without a fortune to spend on the latest state-of-the-art hull and equipment, nothing is really old-fashioned except jumping to conclusions. The only thing that matters then is "will it get the boat from A to B safely?"

This book is meant to be an appetizer for the person who is not too well off, and yet who is attracted to long-distance voyaging. There will be some yachtsmen who will not agree with some of what I have written here, and many who will. It is a case of "different ships, different longsplices," as it always has been and always will be. One thing that will never be argued, though: The most important entities in any boat are the *people onboard*.

Fear God, beware of fire and keep good company.

—SIR FRANCIS DRAKE, "Instructions to
Captains of the Fleet Before
Rounding Cape Horn, 1578"

And I must beg of you to grant me a favor: if . . . you
hear me using the words which I have been in the habit of
using in the market place, at the tables of the money
changers, or anywhere else, I would ask you not to be
surprised, and not to interrupt me on this account. . . .
I would have you regard me as if I were really a stranger,
whom you would excuse if he spoke in his native tongue,
and after the fashion of his country. Am I making an
unfair request of you? Never mind the manner, which
may or may not be good; but think only of the truth of
my words, and give heed to that.

—SOCRATES before the Court of Athens;
PLATO, *Apology*

Afrad pob afraid. (Everything unnecessary is waste.)

—OLD WELSH PROVERB

ONE HAND FOR YOURSELF,

ONE FOR THE SHIP

The Wind of the Sea

THE oil-based system in which the advanced nations live today is sooner or later doomed. As the world's oil is used up and so becomes more expensive and wasteful, so other systems of generating motive and electrical power will be developed. Atomic, wind-driven, coal-powered, and hydrological plants on earth and ultraviolet-ray systems out in space will supplement, then replace the oil-driven internal combustion engines of present-day transport, generating stations, and big-ship propulsion units.

The individual transport vehicle with internal combustion engine, such as the automobile and the small power boat, will become more expensive to operate. Gasoline-powered cars will probably be replaced by electrically driven models or mass transit. Oil-driven pleasure boats will become a thing of the past. From the point of view of oil and fumes pollution of the air and the sea this might not be such a bad thing, but looked at from the point of view of individual control of and initiative in one's movement on the face of the earth and the waters, it will be a loss to mankind.

Three sure means of free motion will be left to the individual: walking, cycling and sailing. When all the superhighways are broken tracks of concrete, there will still remain, at least for the next couple of generations, some areas of the hills and the deserts to wander in comparative freedom. And the sea. The wind of the sea will still be free.

The good lord saw fit to make walking easy for most of us. He gave most of us two legs with feet on the extremities and solid earth. Only He can walk on water, so in His wisdom He saw fit to make sure that if we want to wander the oceans of the world we must use our wits and make ourselves the means to do so. We *Homo sapiens* being what we are, if we are prevented by force of circumstances from doing something one way, we are going to find another way to do it. Roaming around freely is one of the basic needs of common man, especially in youth. Deprived of the freedom to wander, man

I

often becomes frustrated, bored, dulled; a moron, a machine, an automaton, although there are exceptions to any rule, of course. Soon one of the only areas of free movement will be the sea. That is, if enough people become interested enough to prevent the bureaucrats from legislating private seafaring out of existence. This they will try to do in the name of safety, supposedly to protect citizens from their own foolishness and ignorance. All that happens eventually, of course, will be that so many rules and regulations will be passed into law that freedom will be lost altogether. So it is up to the individual to forestall the bureaucrats and make sure he knows as much as he can about small-craft handling and navigation before he puts out to sea.

The more people have become attracted to the sea and to voyaging, the more the middle-men have initiated and increased their operations: the boat dealers, the marina operators, the gadget manufacturers. This has not always been a bad thing; in fact, it is doubtful that weekend sailors and day sailors in many parts of the world could manage their craft without marinas and the services they provide. Likewise, responsible boat dealers ensure that people who are not too knowledgeable about boats are to an extent protected from being stuck with unseaworthy vessels. The gadget manufacturers provide often completely unnecessary trinkets and toys, but sometimes the tools and appliances they turn up are very useful, and the market they sustain maintains an outlet for good ideas.

Mass boat-building has now become the general rule. This, too, has its advantages and disadvantages. Some of the craft turned out by the more responsible companies are well thought-out and constructed; others are dummies; a few are outright dangerous. If the bureaucrats must interfere with boating, it is in this area, the quality of boat construction by the builders, that they should direct their efforts. They should come down very heavily indeed on shoddy workmanship, and they should make a law that every craft sold should be provided with a detailed specification of all the materials used in the construction. After all, we get the ingredients of canned food listed on the label, why not those of a boat?

Out of the millions who will take to the sea in the rising generation, some thousands will, at one time or another, consider making a long-distance voyage. By that I mean a passage of over a thousand miles touching a continent other than that in which the voyage started. For some this will remain a supposedly impossible dream, through force of individual circumstances outside their control. For others it will be an impossible dream because the will, the inner spark of determination will not be present, or because they will be unwilling to give up the supposed conveniences and comforts of modern shore-side life, and they will spend their lives inventing excuses to themselves for this. For others it will be an impossible dream for economic reasons, because they imagine that they will never be able to afford a sailing craft and all the necessary equipment needed to cross an ocean. But this, too, is an excuse for lack of will. I myself, and many other voyagers I have known over the years, have never been financially well off, but we have been so devoted to our calling that no sacrifice has been too great in order to obtain the wherewithal to get out to sea. I have shoveled coal in a department store boiler-room; I have mixed concrete on a French building site; I have painted and varnished the gin palaces of the rich; I have delivered other people's craft, some in unbelievably unseaworthy states; I have skimped and saved and even starved to obtain or maintain my craft and my freedom to roam where and when I wanted to. Some of the ways in which I managed to stay free are described in my books *The Incredible Voyage, Ice!*, *Saga of a Wayward Sailor*, *Adrift*, and *A Steady Trade*.

An ocean voyager, and especially a single-hander, must be a Jack of all trades. He must be his own carpenter, sail-maker, electrician, cook, doctor, navigator, mechanic and sometimes lawyer. He has to have an open mind to learn anything. Very often in foreign ports some of his skills can be turned to good use working onboard other people's craft, solving their problems. A good electrician and electronics man, a good diesel mechanic, a good sailor, is very often worth his weight in gold in many areas where yachts congregate, whilst a good carpenter is a treasure. Ashore, in most parts of the world a bricklayer, carpenter, electrician, scaffold erector, or plumber can always depend on being able to make money. Dentists are usually allowed to practice in most Third World countries, whereas visiting doctors and lawyers are usually not. When it comes to earning money in Third World countries, or even in many advanced countries, the blue-collar man definitely has the advantage over the professional types. So the first thing I advise anyone who is thinking of long-distance voyaging is to learn one of the construction trades.

Writing is another way of earning money whilst aboard; but the writer's task is onerous onboard a small vessel. It is impossible to write anything onboard a small sailing craft at sea. There is too much movement, too much going on (contrary to the average landsman's

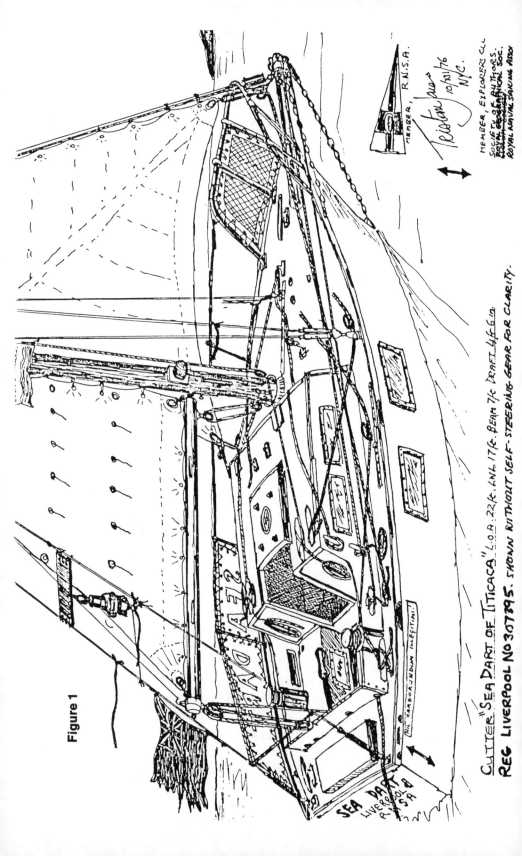

Figure 1

CUTTER "SEA DART OF TITICACA". L.O.A. 22ft. L.W.L. 17ft. BEAM 7ft. DRAFT 4ft 6in.
REG. LIVERPOOL No 307895. SHOWN WITHOUT SELF-STEERING GEAR FOR CLARITY.

MEMBER, EXPLORERS CLUB
SOCIETY OF AUTHORS.
ROYAL GEOGRAPHICAL SOC.
ROYAL NAVAL SAILING ASSN

Tristan Jones
10/XI/76
N/c.

R.N.S.A.

belief that one is idle at sea!), and a sailing writer has to have a vocation. Another drawback is that payment for a work might take as long as a year. Besides, good writing demands research, and this can only be done properly when the mariner is shore-based after the voyage is done.

Once a suitable vessel is obtained and made oceanworthy, once all the basics are onboard and all the necessary food and equipment are stowed away, the really difficult part of the voyage, for the impecunious person anyway, is over. Abroad, there are a number of ways to save money: for example, by purchasing the main stocks of canned and dried foods at duty-free stores; by feeding off the land, as the locals do, and by catching food by fishing and hunting. In this way the total food bill for one person for one month can be kept down to something like thirty-five dollars. Try to make all your own repairs, as well. In general, forget about trading. For one thing, your craft will probably not be big enough to carry a paying cargo and for another, the Customs would usually make it unprofitable.

Forget also about smuggling drugs. You might get away with a little once, but the sailor's world is terribly small and the bush telegraph incredibly swift, and the people you deal with shore-side would probably betray you. There's the moral aspect, too; you have to live with yourself for a long time, and the sea is not kind to folks with bad consciences.

Rather than starve or go in for illegal activities, it is worth considering leaving your vessel (in good, trustworthy hands, of course) and returning home for a few months to refill your coffers. This would mean that you would have to retain the price of an air ticket home at any time during your voyage. That might be enough for you to sail to some country where you could earn money anyway without leaving your boat (and it's marvelous how much money living onboard can save!). This is a problem only you can solve, according to the circumstances.

Will the effort demanded be worth the trouble? Each person, individually, must answer that question. For me I can say yes, a great big unqualified yes. I have had bad times, uncomfortable, sometimes even very dangerous times, and I have made a lot of sacrifices. How many times have I dreamed of being able to go and see a good play, or sit in a library and read, or watch a horse race, or even just be in my own house in my own armchair by a fireside? But the rewards have far outweighed the sacrifices: being so close to nature, watching the workings of the universe, seeing the real wonders of the real world, the different cultures and customs, and meeting up with many wonderful people, many other ocean voyagers, the most magically *alive* people on the face of the globe.

Women need have no qualms about becoming ocean sailors, and single-handed ones at that. Ocean sailors have never, to my knowledge, treated women as anything but equals. Their respect for human life would not allow otherwise. A number of remarkable ocean passages have been made by women alone, and the list grows every year: Ann Davidson, Edith Baumann, Ingeborg von Heister, Nicolette Milnes-Walker, Sharon Sites Adams, Marie-Claude Fauroux, Naomi James, Teresa Remiszewska, Ann Michailoff, and my favorite lady sailor, Clare Francis. Women do not go in for building their own craft so much as men, but they need not concern themselves; I've never built a boat myself, either.

Prepare for Sea

RECORDED single-handed ocean voyaging by private individuals in small craft began roughly a hundred years ago. Immediately there spring to mind such stalwarts as Howard Blackburn, the Canadian fisherman, who single-handed the Atlantic after losing all his fingers on the Newfoundland banks; the immortal Joshua Slocum (also a Nova Scotian, by the way, even though he did sail under the Stars and Stripes) and Captain Voss, who sailed around most of the world in a canoe, going crazy in the process, inventing the sea anchor, and being accused of murder in Australia.

Between the end of the nineteenth century and World War I there was a lull in small-craft voyaging, except for Ernest Shackleton's brave rescue voyage across the Southern Ocean, and the trial of the last case of cannibalism to be held in England. This crime took place in the South Atlantic; the accused were the captain and mate of a large sailing yacht that foundered while being delivered from Cowes to Australia. They took to the long boat and on board it ate the unfortunate cabin boy.

After World War I came Connor O'Brien and *Saorse*, and the redoubtable Alain Gerbault in his *Firecrest*. There were quite a few ocean passages in the twenties and thirties, but most of them were ill-recorded and went unsung. World War II brought another complete stoppage to small-craft voyaging, with the one remarkable exception of the Argentinian Vito Dumas, who sailed around the world through the "Roaring Forties" during the roaring early '40s.

In the fifties more and more small craft started to cross the oceans. I remember seeing the 10.8m (35 ft. 3 in.) blood-red hull of *Samuel Pepys* in Bermuda back in 1948 and saying to myself, "By gum, *that's* for me!"

I don't know about the States, but in Europe and especially England, in the fifties and even well into the sixties, the average long-distance voyager was (a) a pretty rare bird and (b) scratching his rear-end financially. He usually did all his own fitting-out and maintenance. This bred a small group of extraordinary men. Intelligent, ingenious, and courageous they were, and wily to the point of animal cunning. They usually had a sense of humor that made a Wilkinson's Sword blade look like a bricklayer's trowel. If one of their craft came in through the Verrazano Channel tomorrow, all the world would wonder, not only at the vessel, but at the man himself. Their favorite saying was "It's not the ships, it's the bloody men in 'em!" They were the direct descendants of Blackburn and Slocum and Gerbault, and for a glorious twenty years they held the ring, doing the thing for the pure joy of doing it.

Then in the middle 1960s came the sponsored voyager. While he made invaluable progress in the development of materials and techniques, he also brought a kind of commercialism into sailing that even now threatens to turn what should be a living dream into just another rat race. But, thank God, I see signs of the old amateur spirit creeping back. I see people taking off across the oceans just for the sake of *doing it*. It is to those kindred spirits that my words, my hopes, and my heart are directed.

The first concern of the single-hander will be choosing a boat. The size of the boat depends on a number of factors, the main one being the amount of money initially available to buy or build her and then to maintain her. Nowadays, with inflation rampant, the maintenance cost should also be of paramount consideration. This cost tends to rise rather gently in proportion to the size of the boat, until a waterline length of 36 feet is reached. Then there is a flattening out until 39 feet; but from there it just shoots up like a rocket. Therefore, it would appear that for folk of modest resources intending to sail in company, the ideal size of craft is around 38 feet. This is certainly large enough to accommodate four people and the necessary victuals and gear for any ocean crossing. For the single-hander, this is a bit too big; he would be better to go for 26 to 30 feet. Anything smaller will be uncomfortable and terribly wearing after a couple of weeks' bouncing around in the ocean. I should know, for my *Sea Dart* was only 16 feet 5 inches on the waterline. The movement in her, going to windward, was like being on top of a double-decker bus accelerating to 40 miles an hour while jerking to a stop every three seconds or so. Going off the wind, in any kind of weather, was like being on a roller coaster run amok.

In average ocean conditions, the 30-foot craft rises quite nicely to the swells and is large enough to be moderately comfortable. At the same time, her canvas is not too much for one person to handle.

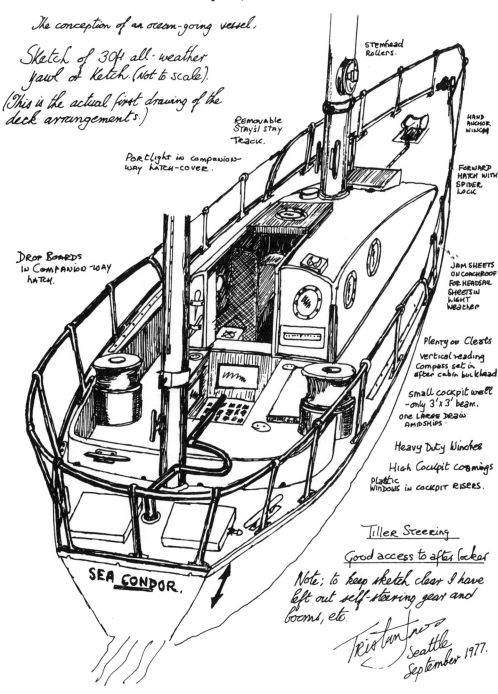

The conception of an ocean-going vessel.

Sketch of 30ft all-weather yawl or ketch. (Not to scale.)
(This is the actual first drawing of the deck arrangements.)

Stemhead Rollers.

HAND ANCHOR WINCH

Removable Stays'l stay Track.

FORWARD HATCH WITH SPIDER LOCK

Portlight in companion-way hatch-cover.

JAM SHEETS ON COACHROOF FOR HEADSAIL SHEETS IN LIGHT WEATHER

DROP BOARDS IN COMPANION-WAY HATCH.

Plenty of Cleats

vertical reading Compass set in after cabin bulkhead

small cockpit well - only 3' x 3' beam. ONE LARGE DRAIN AMIDSHIPS.

Heavy Duty Winches

High Cockpit coamings

plastic WINDOWS IN COCKPIT RISERS.

SEA CONDOR.

Tiller Steering

Good access to after locker

Note: to keep sketch clear I have left out self-steering gear and booms, etc.

Tristan Jones
Seattle
September 1977.

Figure 2

Incidentally, while on this subject, I reckon that the largest sail an average man can handle alone is 450 square feet. Anything bigger and he's asking for trouble.

Having found your boat at the right size and price, the next consideration is seaworthiness. Here, if you haven't been apprenticed in a first-class boatyard, you should engage a surveyor. He will go over the hull structure and fittings with a fine tooth comb and make his report. If you cannot afford a survey, then you should wait until you can. To a good sailor, patience is not just a virtue, it's an absolute necessity. I'd rather lose a leg than my patience. (After writing this I *did* lose a leg! My patience remains.)

If the boat you are buying has done a fair bit of sailing, you must be very suspicious of the rigging fittings, and especially the masthead fitting and turnbuckle gear. If there's any doubt about them, send them to the makers for a test. Even stainless steel develops metal fatigue, and sometimes it may have an internal fracture not evident from the outside.

Given that the hull and gear are sound, the next consideration is stiffness. The boat should be able to carry a fair amount of sail in a strong wind without heeling over too far. At the same time, she should be able to steer herself, especially when close-hauled, but ideally even with the wind on the quarter. This is a blessing if you don't have a wind-vane steerer or if you do and it goes on the blink. It means that you can leave the wheel or the tiller long enough to make yourself a meal or even to have a short nap.

Another important point is speed. To a great extent speed is a factor of the waterline depth. You don't want a racer, but when considering the amount of food and water stowed, it is much more comforting to cross the Pacific Ocean at five knots than at four. When you are clawing your way off a lee shore in a gale, windward sailing ability, stiffness and speed are all-important.

The boat must also be buoyant. By that I mean she shouldn't crash through the seas, she should ride over them without taking too much water on deck, even when heavily laden, which of course she will be at the start of an ocean crossing.

It goes without saying that the boat must be easy to steer on all points of sailing and that she must not carry too much weather helm. You should be able to steer her on any point of sailing, in a 15-knot breeze, with just one finger on the helm. Buoyancy and balance are in many ways mixed up with one another. Some designers, to give added buoyancy, give too much freeboard; this increases windage,

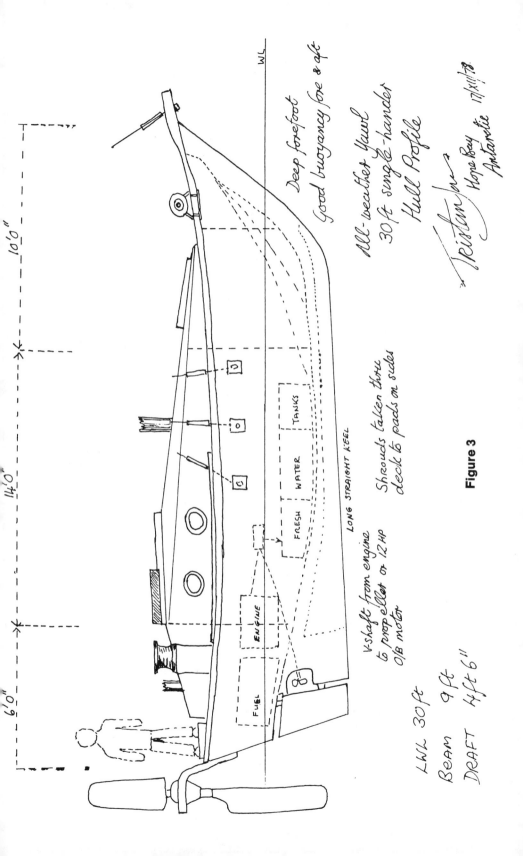

Deep forefoot
Good buoyancy fore & aft

All-weather Yawl
30 ft snug 2-hander
Hull Profile

Tristan Jones → Hope Bay
Antarctic 17/XII/73

WL

LONG STRAIGHT KEEL

Shrouds taken thro'
deck to pads on sides

V-shaft from engine
to propeller or 12 HP
O/B motor

TANKS
FRESH WATER
ENGINE
FUEL

LWL 30 ft
Beam 9 ft
DRAFT 4 ft 6"

10' 0"
14' 0"
6' 0"

Figure 3

making a boat a cow when going into the wind and also making the hull look ugly. If a boat looks ugly, she usually is also bad tempered. The important thing is to have good freeboard fore and aft at the ends of the boat, so that she lifts at the bow and stern. For this reason, she should preferably not be "reverse sheer." Neither should she have a canoe stern. These pointed sterns are supposed to part the seas so they don't break onboard, but that's a load of poppycock. My old *Cresswell* had a canoe stern, and she took enough seas onboard to float the QE II during the time I had her. All a canoe stern does is enable a lifeboat to maneuver stern first when necessary. The only other thing it does is reduce buoyancy, and who needs that?

The next virtue that your ocean boat must have, if you are to remain happy, is *comfort*. By that I don't mean red plush on the toilet seat, I mean she must not be a roller or a jerker. This is something peculiar to any individual vessel, and I have seen two craft, both exactly the same size and design, both loaded the same, with one sitting there without budging while the other wallowed around like a drunken porpoise.

If you are heading for the tropics, the boat must have excellent ventilation, to allow a good breeze to blow through the cabin. The deck should be insulated to prevent too much heat entering; otherwise you will find yourself existing in utter misery, when all around you the world looks like a Caribbean holiday advertisement. Incidentally, while on the subject of habitability, I once conducted an experiment, over a period of two years, to find the best color to use below in a small craft. I tried at least fifteen shades, and the one that came out tops was pale green. It was the most restful on the eyes and the least conducive to seasickness. This was not the way it affected just me, as I was taking a lot of people out on day-charters in the Mediterranean at the time. Ever since then I have used pale green paint inside a boat. Too much varnish below is depressing, although a little touch here and there is all right and adds a bit of class, if you need it.

There should be a table down below at least 27 inches by 20 inches, big enough for a chart to be laid out. The fiddles should be 2 inches deep.

The berths should be at least 6 feet long.

The galley stove should be kerosene-run. This is the only fuel available everywhere in the world. Electric lights are best because they do not give off much heat, which is important in the tropics, but there should also be kerosene lamps, in case of power failure.

When planning accommodations, the most important thing is good stowage. In this respect it is far better to have a lot of little lockers. Then anything you have to find can be got to easily, instead of having to dig it out from under a pile of other items.

ELECTROLYSIS   When it comes to the hull, the best preventive for electrolysis is not zinc pads, which are usually fitted somewhere near the propeller, but magnesium alloy sacrificial pads which do a much better job, if you can afford them. Carry at least one set of spare pads. They usually last a couple of years.

I get the impression that many boats are over-powered. This, of course, wastes fuel and the space needed to carry it. A sailing vessel, if she is to have power at all, should stock enough fuel to move her at a minimum of 2 knots against a 20-knot wind for two hours. Again, before the engineers start throwing their wrenches at me, this is a minimum requirement. I am not one of these elitists who look down their noses at engines, but I am pointing out that too much power means too much space wasted, and space comes directly after patience in the order of important assets in an ocean sailing craft. Many a time the power is used merely because of lack of patience, anyway. Whatever the power unit, it should be able to be started by hand. The diesel engine is by far the best, simply because it has no electrics, at least in the actual function of power production. Gasoline is highly volatile, and volatility being the opposite of patience, there shouldn't be any on board. Fuel range is a case of 'to each his own,' but I would say that a boat cruising the tropics and possibly crossing the doldrums would need 600 sea miles. But since it's not always possible to find the room for that amount, I will stick to my guns and my minimum requirements as outlined above.

The engine-cooling water intake pipe should be fitted with a branch of flexible hose, ending in a suction strainer. This makes a fine emergency bilge pump in case of dire emergency. If an electric bilge pump is carried, it must not be trusted to run forever. At least one large-capacity hand bilge pump must be fitted. Of these, the finest of all for dependability and ease of maintenance and repair is the Whale diaphragm pump. I would have two of these and a few metal or plastic buckets.

One of the most frequent questions asked of me is "What about type of sailing rig?" Here again, it's a matter of one man's meat being another man's poison. My favorite rig, for all-around use, is the yawl. The reason is that it heaves-to better. With a reefed-down mizzen

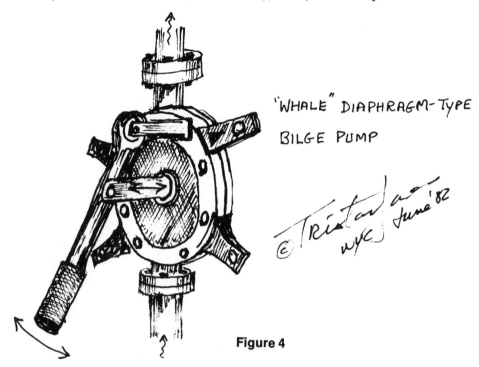

"WHALE" DIAPHRAGM-TYPE
BILGE PUMP

© Tristan *nyc* June '82

Figure 4

hauled in tight and everything else snugged down, a yawl will lie with one bow onto the most tremendous seas, with no need for sea anchors or any other kind of fancy and very dangerous gear straining outside the vessel.

A yawl's mainsail is big enough to move the hull in light airs, while it is small enough to be handled without too much effort, grief, and pain. The mizzen sail doesn't entirely block the wind off the main-sail when the boat is sailing downwind, and when she's on a broad reach she can carry a mizzen staysail and really thrust along like a steam train.

With a yawl, if you get one of those very sudden, bitchy tropical squalls, as, for example, in the so-called Bermuda Triangle, you just hand the main and there you are, still going like the clappers, yet in sailing trim with a genoa, stay'sl and mizzen up.

All right, you say, but surely you can do the same with a ketch? True, but with the damned great mizzen boom sticking out it's almost impossible to fit a wind-vane steerer, and it makes life miserable when you have to moor stern-to to a jetty, which you must do in many parts of the world.

A sloop is more efficient going to windward. She steers easier be-

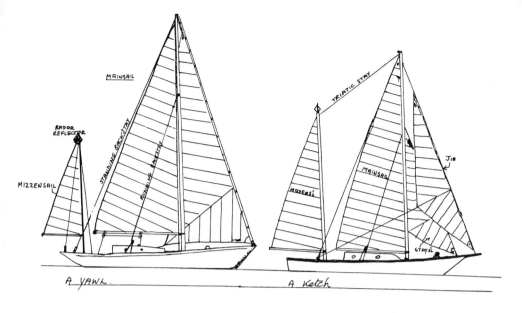

A YAWL.   A Ketch

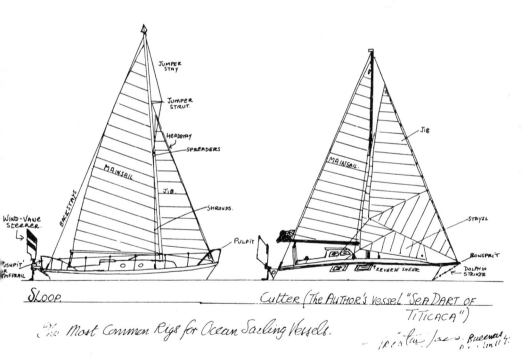

SLOOP.   Cutter (The Author's Vessel "Sea Dart of Titicaca")

The Most Common Rigs for Ocean Sailing Vessels.

Figure 5

cause the mast can be stepped practically anywhere you want it, to balance the boat. But then, most ocean sailing is done downwind anyway. And once that one mast is gone, you've got nothing to hang a sail from. A mizzen mast, no matter if it is only one-third the height of the main, is very handy indeed for fixing up a jury-rig good enough to get you in.

When you look at your vessel's rig, bear in mind that she is going to be sailing more and farther in one week than the average coastal pleasure craft will sail in a year. For weeks, months, years, she will be continually moving, and your life will be a relentless struggle against sail, line, and hull *chafe*.

Inspect the rigging screw pins for signs of wear. If the boat has done any amount of sailing, these may have become reduced in size. If so, they should be replaced. The bolts on the bow and stern stay fittings should also be carefully checked.

These days you will probably have stainless steel wire standing rigging. If you have, check that there is no kinking caused by the wire having been rove around a thimble that is too small. All the thimbles on stainless steel wire should be generous in size. The sails will chafe against the rigging when the boat is running free, so *baggy wrinkle* (pads made of old rope), should be made up and fitted to the standing rig, although this increases windage aloft. I prefer to use insulation tape, which is then served with small stuff and varnished over the top. And that's about the only varnishing I ever do! Bear in mind also that no bronze should come anywhere near stainless steel. If it does, the steel will be destroyed by the corrosive interaction between the two metals.

If the rigging screws (turnbuckles) are the open type (and they are the best type), have them tested by the makers. When that's been done, protect them with anhydrous lanoline. This is better than grease, but it doesn't lubricate, so it's no good trying to protect any moving parts, such as in a winch, with lanoline. There you must use good-quality grease.

Where the headsail sheets pass the standing rigging, they will chafe unless you protect them by wrapping insulation tape, served, around the stays, or split wooden rollers if you can get them. At the outer ends of the spreaders there should be chafing pads. There are some very fancy and expensive plastic ones on the market, but I use tennis balls, which are simply laced onto the stays above and below the spreaders. At the inboard end of the spreaders, be careful that the bolts holding them to the tangs on the mast are not worn.

Mainsheet chafe is a problem to which there is only one solution: Have the mainsheet block running on a horse track high enough to keep the sheet from chafing on the guard rails. A high horse behind the helmsman, with a weathercloth laced below it, is fine protection for anyone when it's blowing seven bells from astern.

Dacron rope is the best for running rigging. It will outlast any other kind. Nylon is fine for mainsheet and for anchor lines, but it is too awkward for general use.

For tropical sailing, the sails are best colored—a light blue or brown is very good. Otherwise the reflected glare can be bad enough to cause damage to the eyes. The working sails should not be too heavy, or they will lose the wind when the boat is ghosting in light airs.

The bottom six and a half feet or so of the mainsail should be laced to the mast; this makes for easier reefing, as the slides don't have to be taken out of the track. For a long-distance cruiser, there should be no roach on the main. If there is, you must have battens, and battens are an invention of the devil. Besides, if there is a roach, the topping lift will continually foul it, causing tremendous chafe on the leach over the weeks of movement. The best types of sail are hand-sewn dacron, as the thread does not stand proud of the seams, as it does on a machine-sewn sail. The best type of cut is debatable, but I prefer miter-cut, because if the sail rips the main part can still be used.

All the headsails should have a stainless steel wire, insulated with vinyl, in the luff. This will make them set much better and prevent sag, which in turn causes chafe.

Of course, being a pessimist, you will have reefing cringles and eyelets in the mainsail, even if roller reefing is fitted.

The storm sails, the trysail, and the spitfire jib should be roped all around for safety. Only the bowline (along the luff) needs to be heavy.

The batteries that are charged by the engine, if fitted, should have nickel/iron cells, which are supposed to last much longer than any other type. All electric terminals should be greased with petroleum jelly. The electric navigation lights should be backed up with kerosene lamps, in case of power failure and to save electric drain at sea.

The sailing yacht's white masthead light is confusing to other vessels if shown on its own. It is far better to have a kerosene dioptic lens light lower down in the boat. This casts a beam a matter of five sea miles or so in normal conditions and doesn't swing about as wildly as the masthead light.

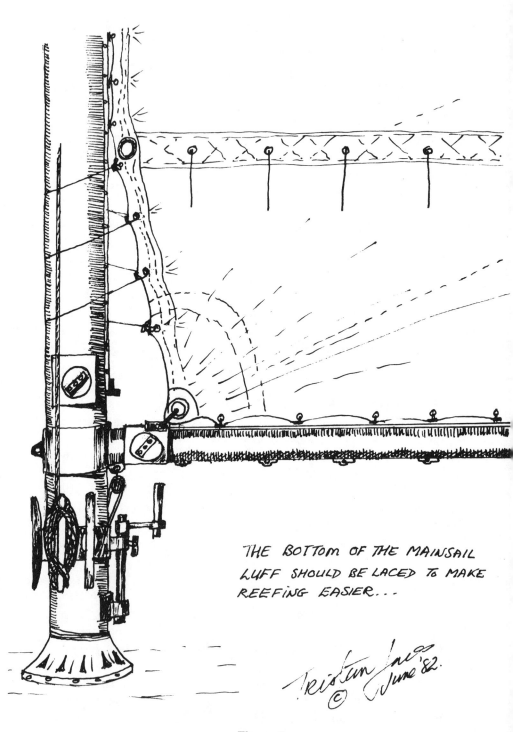

THE BOTTOM OF THE MAINSAIL
LUFF SHOULD BE LACED TO MAKE
REEFING EASIER...

Figure 6

Another useful electrical gadget is the echo-sounder. This can be much more convenient than the sounding lead, but do not depend on it too much when cruising near coral, for coral heads poke up very suddenly. In any case, even if you carry a sounder, make sure you also have a sounding lead in case of power failure.

The cooking stove should burn kerosene and be fitted on pivots fore and aft. The pivots should be at the same level as the burners; otherwise there will be a pendulum motion and a scalded and weary cook.

If a radio is carried, the receiver should have earphones, as it is sometimes almost impossible (in bad weather conditions, with the clanging and bashing of the hull through the water, and the wind whistling in the rigging aloft) to hear a weak signal.

Don't accept a compass deviation more than one year old in a boat which has not done much sailing. Get the compass swung again before you commence your voyage and note the deviations.

An electric refrigerator is a blessing as long as there is power to run it, but you should equip your ship with a power failure in mind. Remember that an icebox is almost as useless as it is bulky and ice lasts only a few days in the tropics.

As a guide to fridgeless storing, I give my rations list for a solo Atlantic crossing (one man, eighty days), in Chapter 17.

Freud Was Not a Sailor

THERE's an old saying in Britain, where I hail from: "There's nought so strange as folks." One of the biggest wonders of human nature is its infinite variety.

At one end of the scale you have the shy, introverted wallflower, and at the other end there's the blustering, swashbuckling extrovert. In between, an array of nature's marvels to behold. And so it is with sailing folk. There's no special type. Shakespeare himself would have been hard pressed to delineate the range of different characters that can be found on any waterfront or in any good-sized yacht club or marina.

One of the obvious results of sailing over a period of time, however, is the formation, or reinforcement, of certain traits in the psyche. Among these, I would put (in my order of importance) patience, compromise, the ability to get down to brass tacks (clarity of thought on immediate problems and swift calculation of priorities), humor,—even at your own expense—fairness, precision when it is necessary, generosity when it's not, determination, and understanding, not only of your own weaknesses but also of other people's.

If anyone asked me why I thought people took off single-handed on long voyages in small craft, I would answer that probably they were seeking any or all of the above virtues in their own nature. If they continue to sail alone, it is because they are content with what they have found inside themselves.

The psychology of the average single-hander is impossible to define in general terms, because each person is different and so each one must be taken separately.

In my case it was purely and simply a matter of logistics. In other words, either I could not afford to feed a crew, or my itinerary was so risky that no one else would come, or my vessel was too small to carry the stores and water needed for more than one person on the voyage, or the extra weight would impede progress. I have, on other occasions, probably sailed with as many other people as any man alive, and yet I can think of only two of those hundreds of people that I would not sail with again on a voyage of any duration. The reason I would not sail with the two exceptions was that they consciously, and against instructions, put other people's lives in jeopardy. Not only that, but after the danger was over they adamantly refused to admit that they had been wrong. Stupidity in an intelligent person is unforgivable, and at sea downright dangerous.

My own attitude toward the sea is basically practical. I want to go somewhere; my home and my vehicle is a boat, which sails on the sea, which leads to wherever I want to go. I have had people direct some very loaded questions at me, loaded with the implications that I am some special kind of creature who, like a hermit, wants only to get away from his fellowmen and the problems inherent in modern life. That's completely wrong. There's nothing I like better than good company, telling and listening to yarns, and there's nothing I admire more than man's achievements in every field of the tremendous struggle to reach the present stage of civilization.

Sure, we've got our problems. But if we had no problems, there wouldn't be the challenge of finding the solutions.

I've seen the so-called idyllic existence of the so-called noble savage. No thanks! Give me Picadilly Circus or Times Square any day, not to mention the Louvre, the Sistine Chapel, hot and cold running water, television, automobiles, telephones, and all the rest of the paraphernalia of modern life that a whole generation of misguided and certainly inexperienced people have been so busily criticizing for the past twenty years or so!

But let's get back to the single-handers I have known. What would I say was their general trait? First and foremost—and I'm talking about after they have completed long voyages, not necessarily before —the striking thing in all cases has been their intrinsic courtesy. It is as if, having been out of human company for extended periods, they have come to realize the value of each and every human being, no matter what that person's attitude to them. In particular spring to mind Sir Percy Wynn Harris, Frank Casper and Tom Follet, Edward Alcard, and Steve Dolby, who sailed almost blind from Australia via Good Hope to New York and gave up his circumnavigation in his tiny *Ghost Rider* only at my insistence that he was too good a lad to commit suicide, and anyway, it wouldn't be seaman-like. Then there's Bernard Moitessier and Loike Fougeron, Frenchmen, and Zbigniew Puchalski, a Pole, and Sven Lundin, a Swede, and Kensaku Nomoto, a Japanese, and several Dutchmen and Germans;

it didn't matter what their country of origin, they all have in common a great courtesy, and it isn't put on, as it often is with landlubbers and which is immediately clear to the single-hander or any ocean small-boat voyager. These people reach a stage at which they often know what another person is going to say before he says it.

In my experience, *déjà vu* ("seeing" things before they happen or appear) has been very common, and I have often known what was coming long before it appeared, or before I rounded a point, even when I had no prior information on whatever it was that did eventually turn up. I think it is possible that everyone has this sixth sense, but alone at sea it is highly pronounced once it has developed. Other single-handers have mentioned the same thing to me.

Being alone is not the same thing as being lonely. I can feel more alone on the New York streets than I ever would in mid-Atlantic. In fact, when one is alone, awareness of other people, not only loved ones and friends, but even the slightest acquaintances, is very pronounced. I have felt closer to them, alone in mid-ocean, than I sometimes have while being in the same room with them. Love and friendship have nothing whatsoever to do with geographical position or distance. As my old skipper Tansy Lee used to say when we were sitting in some dock, waiting for cargo, "Absinthe makes the 'eart grow fonder."

Anyone contemplating single-handing an ocean should like at least some of his own traits and be able to generously forgive the ones he doesn't like, or at least make allowances for them and not let them interfere with the well-being of the boat and her skipper. If he tends to be lazy, then he should be lazy about the right things (I direct my own few tendencies to laziness toward varnish work and small things like peeling potatoes; I just pop them in the pot, skin and all). It pays to be sloppy in a few, comparatively unimportant ways, because a perfectionist would be hell to live with, even if he is yourself. Very boring! And if you bore yourself, don't single-hand. Always make sure you've got someone else to bore—as long at it's not me.

With respect to religion, I have found that it has mostly been very difficult to converse on that topic with single-handers, and they nearly always shy off the subject. Eventually I realized, looking back on my own experience, that this is because they shy off it even with themselves. I consider this the healthiest thing to do.

I have for years thought that if I were formally religious I would probably become a Moslem, or, even better, a Jew, because I have found that in Israel at least, they have a good old booze-up in the synagogue at some ceremonies. That would suit me fine, and I don't at all mean that in a disparaging way.

In my own case I have never had the so-called racing spirit. I've never felt that I wanted to outdo anyone else, and apart from preventing the food and water from running out, fast passages never meant much to me. True, I went for the vertical record, where I seemed to wind up being first at a number of things, but the underlying motive behind that voyage was merely to point out the stupidity of racing round and round, faster and faster. In this day and age, it seems that very few people will take notice of you unless you break some meaningless record, so I set out to make the most ridiculous record of all. Anyone who single-hands to achieve anything but the passage and his own satisfaction, unless it is a race against other single-handers over a reasonable distance, is wasting his time and should take up goldfish swallowing or doughnut eating. He will achieve the same result in much more comfortable surroundings.

This seems to be the attitude of a number of solo sailors I have met. They are concerned with making a good passage, not so much with outdoing anyone else. I realize, of course, that there is a great sport in racing under sail, and I appreciate the technological advances that racing has brought about. I don't want to knock racing. I'm just saying that no single-hander should take off on a transatlantic voyage with the idea of beating Jimmy Blogg's time in a smaller boat.

Fear is probably the single-hander's greatest hazard. It can lie in wait to ambush him at the times when he might least welcome it. But fear is only Nature's way of overcoming man's inherent intelligence. Nature is wily when she wants to be, and the way to deal with fear is to remember that it interferes with man's place in the scheme of things as a logical, crafty, scheming, calculating son of a bitch who won't let Nature take his mind over. Fear is a nuisance; it clogs up the brain, and it doesn't do a thing for the boat, nor for the successful conclusion of the passage. It belongs with all the other vices that Nature seems to have thrust on us to prevent our reaching the infinity, which is our right and which we are going to reach anyway, unless we let fear foul up the winch-sheets.

Concern is another thing altogether. That is facing up to the reality of any given situation. Worry, often confused with concern, is Nature's way of getting her foot in the door so that fear can come in, bringing panic with her. Concern is worry without fear. Concern is the hallmark of a good seaman: concern about himself, his ship, other people, and the situation with which he is confronted. Concern is the harbinger of solutions, the defeater of fear.

J. R. L. Anderson, in his excellent summing-up of solo voyagers in the book *The Ulysses Factor*, says that the common denominator of single-handers is an instinct that derives from the need to explore alone. I agree, but each person has his or her own areas of exploration, both within the self and in the world at large. Some people do it to prove themselves. Some do it for nationalistic reasons. Some for material gain (the racing people, in the main, but by no means always). Some do it to "escape a humdrum life." Some to sort themselves out (though I cannot imagine why anyone would go to sea to do that). And some for the pure poetry of it, and these latter I'm with, all the way. *Because it's there.* That's the most human reason of all.

When Donald Crowhurst went mad, during the single-handed 1969 Round-the-World race, I was out in *Barbara* looking for him in mid-Atlantic, as it was well known that he had been faking his positions. He had made the mistake of undertaking a voyage for all the wrong reasons. When he set out, he trusted neither himself nor his craft—that is plain from his logs—and the whole thing had deteriorated into a lunatic playing God, even though his voyage was quite an achievement for a man with his slight experience. It reinforced my intense disdain for all these highly publicized, commercially sponsored stunts and made me even more determined to cast as strong a light as I could on the rapidly developing rat race by going for the vertical record, which would confound the lot of them by being absolute and unbeatable.

Above all, a single-hander should be a seaman. He should try to get as much experience as he can with other boats and people before setting off alone. I know that there have been some very lucky beginners, but there have also been a vast number of unlucky ones. I sailed for five years as crew before taking off alone for the Arctic, and during those five years I learned to handle a small craft under all conditions. I learned to be my own carpenter, plumber, mechanic, sailmaker, cook, navigator, wire-splicer, and general dog's body. I also learned a lot about human nature, including my own.

Quite a few of the single-handers I have known, transferring to craft other than their own, would be utterly lost as far as running the vessel was concerned. The best training, I think, is to gain experience in various craft without engines. This instills, for example, a wariness about lee shores that one would find it difficult, almost impossible, to obtain, in powered craft. There are some single-handers who take great pride in the fact that everything they have done they have done completely on their own. That's foolish, because we are all part of the whole, and I consider myself to be part of a vast company of sailors who stretch back to the dawn of time. To their patiently gained knowledge I have perhaps added a few meager scraps.

Some people are natural-born seamen. You can tell that by the way they move on board a small craft. Others are clod-hoppers, and I have nothing but admiration when these people eventually, patiently, turn themselves into sailors.

A good seaman, when he boards another vessel, has his eyes everywhere—at the comfort, or lack of it, at the gadgets and fancy gear. But he is watching the rigging, the deck fittings, the way the gear is stowed, the way the wires are spliced and the lines coiled. Whatever he does, he is always learning.

In my experience, the age of discretion and responsibility at sea is reached at about twenty-four. Younger than that, unless the person has actually been raised throughout most of his/her childhood in an oceangoing vessel making long voyages, there just has not been enough time to absorb the knowledge and experience that ought to be in hand, or rather, between the ears. And if there is, then there hasn't been enough time to gain knowledge and experience in the ways of this wicked world—for example, to deal with corrupt officialdom in many of the outlying parts of the globe, or to deal with vexing and serious emotional problems that crop up from time to time. Of course, there are exceptions, but they are rare.

Anyway, I think that anyone younger than twenty-four who goes off on his/her own sailing for months on end is wasting time, what with all the shore-side attractions for youth.

On the occasions when I have sailed with Western youngsters, especially Americans, I have been astonished at the change in their attitude to age and experience when things came to a disturbing head. This is in contrast to the usual disdain, sometimes amounting to a complete lack of communication, often shown in port. I don't blame the kids for this, at least not for all of it. I blame the older people for having let this happen. This generation-gap business, because that is what it is, is a load of codswallop artificially engendered by the marketplace hucksters. Don't get me wrong, I don't want to identify with youth in the matter of social preferences, though I think some of the stuff they like is excellent; a lot of it is so much ullage. It's just that I would like them to know all the stuff that I learned from people who were sailing before I was a gleam in my old man's eye. Advice is invaluable, and they will need it one day.

A small craft in the ocean is, or can be, a benevolent dictatorship. The skipper's brain is the vessel's brain, and he must give up his soul to her, regardless of his own feelings or inclinations. If he cannot do that, he has no business being a skipper.

As skipper it is my duty to complete a passage with the vessel and crew in good order, to be aware of budding problems, and to be ready to cope with them. In someone else's boat at sea I list my responsibilities in the following order: first, to God and the vessel; second, to my crew, and to the people in any other vessel in distress; third, to the owner of the vessel.

When I am single-handed, in my own boat, the order of responsibility remains the same.

Thus, I have led you to realize, I hope, that the skipper of a crewed oceangoing vessel should have all the virtues (and, I hope, none of the vices) of the experienced single-hander. He should never ask anyone to do anything he cannot, or would not, do himself.

A good skipper must be a good seaman. He must anticipate any emergency or defect that might arise, not only in his boat, but also in his crew. A small example: If heavy weather is expected, it is his responsibility to see that all the gear is sound and lashed. It is his responsibility to see that all his crew has a good hefty meal; that they are in good spirits, and that they will be safe, with life-lines worn by the active, while the unneeded hands are sent down below to rest before the blow. If the worst happens and the boat sustains heavy damage, it is his responsibility to prevent panic if it seems to be rising, and to make the decision whether to abandon ship.

When it comes to crewmen, I have sailed with a lot. Some were very experienced, some complete greenhorns. I cannot say that I prefer either, except on a short passage, where the greenhorn has no time to learn anything. In that case the experienced hand is much more welcome. On a short passage (and by that I mean up to, say, ten days), personalities do not matter much. But when it comes to an ocean crossing, where you're going to be confined together for up to three months, personality counts a great deal. In that case I would far rather be with a beginner who doesn't know the sharp end from the blunt end but who has a stable, balanced nature, than with a hotshot winner of the Trans-Atlantic Single-handed Race who is a neurotic know-it-all.

But again, as with so many other things in ocean passage-making, it is a matter of personal preferences. The two best mates I have had, out of any number, were Peter Kelly, a Manx fisherman, and Conrad Jelinek, a London truck driver. In both cases they were highly intelligent, and in both cases we could at times go for days on end without more than a few words—to do with the running of the vessel —passing between us.

Women make good crew. Good women sailors are, I have found, physically more enduring than men, though they are not as strong. If a female takes to the sea, she is very good for as long as her emotions will allow her to be. In my experience this is for about eighteen months. I am also recalling female crews on other long-distance craft. Women's natural needs being what they are, it seems to me that most of them have a basic nesting instinct to stay in one place, if only for a while. The emotional strain of continually being on the move shows up either in the first three weeks, or between one year and eighteen months after departing the homeland. There is a period when they seem to go to pieces emotionally, though a few get over this. I would say that no woman should cruise continually for more than a year without having a rest, even if it is only a couple of months in one port, just long enough to establish fresh roots, however tenuous, and make some friends among other people. It's a hell of a strain for a female to be out there, and the ones who I have seen on passages around the world are among the people I most admire.

I have seen any number of marriages and alliances broken up simply because the husband or lover failed to see the innate female need for security above all things. The men would talk to the women until they were blue in the face about how fine the vessel was, about the attractions of warm winds, blue ocean, and sunny skies, but what most of them never understood was the very nature of femininity itself, which yearns for security.

My point is that the strength and security in a boat, apparent to the male, are by no means always so to the female. She has an affinity for earth, not water. You have only to see her, after a long ocean passage, scrunching her bare toes in the sand, lingeringly touching stray flower blossoms, gazing at children, to know this. If humans are descended from animals who left the sea, I'll bet that the first one to straggle ashore, wobbling on its flimsy fins, was a female.

Lastly, children. In the past ten years or so, some ocean voyagers have raised families during long passages. I have met some of these kids, and they are admirable. I think they will be very fine adults, but it's too early yet to know for certain. Wouldn't it be great if the first person to reach the stars was the child of an ocean roamer?

Single-Handed Sailing—the Art

USING THE AUXILIARY ENGINE Contrary to what the sailing elitists would have us believe, I maintain that the most useful item onboard a sailing craft entering or leaving harbor is a good, dependable auxiliary engine. This is the case especially when the boat is single-handed. I couldn't begin to guess how many engineless single-handers have made the offing of some haven, only to find that local wind and weather conditions made it impossible to enter, perhaps through a tricky entry passage; or how many have been becalmed when approaching land after a long ocean passage and had to sit out for days waiting for a breeze to enter, with the food and water running low.

However, I qualify this. There's nothing handier than a good dependable engine as long as the vessel is navigated and handled as if the engine were not good and dependable, or as if there were no engine at all.

For example, if you are making an entry into a harbor, or a coral atoll, or a river mouth, start your engine, but always make sure either that your sails are hoisted or that they are ready to hoist at a moment's notice. In a single-hander, have them hoisted anyway. It's better to flap the sails a little than to run aground and risk losing the boat. If the engine stops, you're prepared.

Never stand in to a lee shore if it is in the least avoidable, with the idea that if the onshore wind increases the engine will get you off. Once out of haven, always navigate as if you had no engine.

I have seen sailing vessels entering port under power through a crowded anchorage with their sail covers on. This takes place frequently in the West Indies and Mediterranean charter-boat havens. I suppose the idea is to look ship-shape and "smart." There they come, with the diesel engine running and everyone in his place, ready to anchor or moor . . . and the sails would take about ten minutes to get ready to hoist. Watching them is enough to make an ocean sailor take up roller-skating.

Being really smart and really ship-shape is being ready for any emergency; the more so in crowded roadsteads, where other vessels might be involved in the results of unpreparedness.

WEIGHING ANCHOR   One of the most difficult operations when single-handed, is, at times, breaking out the anchor. Here, an auxiliary engine is a great help, because you simply haul up to the rode, belay the anchor line, and motor the hook out of the ground. Then, when the anchor is free you take way off the boat and go back on the foredeck to haul it in, making sure that there are no vessels to your lee with which you might collide, as the boat drifts whilst you bring the hook onboard and cat it. Don't lash it down right away, in case the engine stops before you get the headsail up.

Under sail only, getting in the anchor is a different kettle of fish. If the wind is anything but light you probably won't be able to haul up to the rode, unless you are built like King Kong (and incidentally very few single-handers are). Here, it is a case of beating up to the anchor in short tacks. I use my No. 3 jib for this, as it is cut high and misses swiping my ear when I'm up forward hauling in the rode. I lead the sheet fag-end forward, after sheeting in the main, and control the boards at the same time as I am taking in the anchor line and chain. This is not the circus it sounds, as the boat brings herself about every time she pulls up short on the anchor line. As soon as the boat drops off on the opposite tack, the anchor line slackens off; then I haul in like mad. Watch out you don't get your fingers trapped when the anchor line tautens up, though, after the boat has sailed up to it again.

If the anchor has really dug in well—for example, over soft, sludgy mud—you may have to bend the anchor line around the main winch in order to break it out, and if it is obstinate, even bend a block and tackle onto the anchor line just below water level with a rolling hitch and break it out in that manner. In extremely obstinate cases it might even be necessary to get help from other vessels or ashore. But in any case, a single-hander always has a tripping line on his anchor and this, led to the winch and hauled mightily, will usually break out the most willful hook.

There is no shame in getting outside help. I've done it a hundred times. There are some things that are completely beyond the strength of one human being; that's why the good Lord sent along other boat's crews and dockside loafers. In most parts of the world, at least among small-boat sailors, help is generally given willingly. If it isn't, then stare at them hard, as if you know that the same thing might happen to *them* one day. If worse comes to worst, offer them a drink.

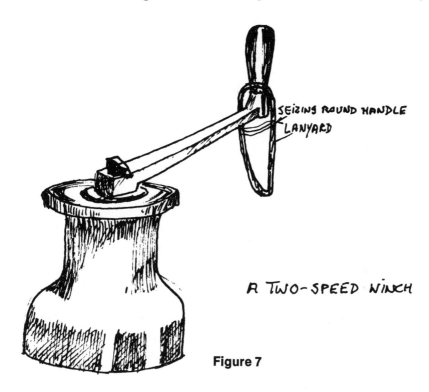

SEIZING ROUND HANDLE
LANYARD

A TWO-SPEED WINCH

Figure 7

My general-use anchor is a CQR, as I consider this the best type, for a given weight, for all-around use. I will use a Danforth only for a temporary anchoring or for a kedge anchor, when mooring between two anchors. I would never use it where strong squalls might be expected, or where the ground is rock or coral. It is apt to twist out of shape.

Apart from its excellent holding and breaking-out qualities, the CQR anchor is easy to get onboard and stow. It can even be locked into a fitting on the stem-head and left in place. I do this in quiet waters, but when I'm bashing away to windward I feel much more comfortable with it soundly lashed down on deck to the eye-straps provided. When the boat pitches in heavy seas, the less the sea has to crash against, the better.

For anchoring in hard weather areas, I carry a big sixty-pound "Fisherman" or Yachtsman's anchor. This is the old-fashioned type with two great flukes on it, which will hold against a hurricane in sand and weed. Getting this onboard is sometimes a heavy job, especially if it is festooned with half a ton of weed or mud. I do this by rigging up one of the running poles on a topping lift and fore-and-after guys, leading the anchor line through a block on the end of the pole, and winching home. If it is too heavy even for the winch, then to break the anchor out I rig a block and tackle, with a rolling hitch to the anchor line; this extra power generally will do the trick. If I have been anchored in mud, then, when the anchor is first broken out, I make the anchor line fast, then rock the boat by shifting my weight quickly from side to side. This tends to loosen the mud and lighten the load as the mud falls off the anchor.

After the auxiliary engine, I would say that the next best help for a single-hander is a good hefty winch. The number of jobs this can help ease is amazing, from hauling up an anchor to kedging off a grounded vessel. Also, good block and tackle are a must, as they are worth at least the strength of one extra crew member. For a fuller discussion on anchors and ground tackle, see Chapter 11.

DOCKING AND MOORING   When entering a strange haven, the best thing to do is to anchor off first, and then, when you are sure the anchor is holding and the sails are stowed, go ashore in the dinghy and find out what the local scene is with regard to docking alongside or mooring. In many countries, and especially in commercial and fishing ports, for a small pleasure craft to haul up right away alongside without permission is regarded as the nadir of bad manners. That's for starters. Apart from this, in many countries the harbors are not as well maintained as they might be in, for example, the United States, and God only knows what sunken vessels and other obstructions might be lying in wait for you at the base of the mole, ready to poke through your boat's bottom as the tide goes out.

Once you have been ashore and made friends with the local officials and hands, and found out where it is safe to come alongside or moor, it is time to consider which to do. If there is a good, convenient mooring, always choose this rather than an alongside berth, because in most commercial ports and fishing havens, especially in "nonadvanced" areas, going alongside means getting rats and insects onboard, to say nothing of unwanted two-legged visitors. If you are at a mooring you will still get visitors, but they will in most cases be people either involved with the haven operations or interested in voyaging. It's up to you, but my advice is to welcome them and be wary.

If there is no mooring and you are not allowed, or it is not advisable, to remain at anchor, then you must think about how to get alongside. If the wind is blowing *offshore*, it is a matter of beating up to the jetty and, when within a few feet, dropping the jib, the halyard of which is ready to let go as you dash forward, and, before the boat drifts off to leeward too much, getting a heaving line ashore. Then the bow is hauled in, but not too close in case there are wakes from passing craft that might cause damage. While the stern is still a fair way out, drop the kedge anchor over the counter on a slack line, then run a mooring line from the stern to the jetty and haul the boat in alongside with a bow and stern line. Before she touches the jetty pilings, haul in taut on the kedge anchor line. This will hold her off for two purposes. It will stop crawling insects and rats getting on-board, discourage other casual visitors and hold the boat out from the pilings, where she might bump hard if there are wakes from passing vessels. The wind being offshore when you go alongside, it will hold the boat off anyway. The wind might change, though, and you will be prepared for this with the kedge anchor out.

With the wind blowing *onshore*, sail up under short sail parallel to the jetty, to a point about six times the boat's length off, on a broad reach and anchor. Dowse all sail and the boat will then swing stern onto the jetty. Slowly ease out the anchor line until the stern is within heaving-line distance of the jetty, and get the line ashore. Put fenders over the side, then pass a line from the bow to the jetty. Bring the anchor line amidships and slowly ease it out to bring the boat along-side. Once within a few feet of the jetty, a short line should be led from the stern and secured with a rolling hitch to the anchor line. This will keep the boat parallel to the jetty, yet held off by the anchor.

Always make sure you have a trip line and buoy on the kedge, as otherwise you will have some irate fishing-boat skipper breathing fire and brimstone down your neck as his mate vainly tries to dis-entangle your kedge anchor line from his propeller.

If you can get permission to moor stern-on to the jetty, this is a far easier and perhaps safer operation in the long run. Here you anchor off in the same way, pay out the anchor line until the stern is a few feet from the jetty, then tie up with a mooring line from each quarter. But be careful of the self-steering gear. When it comes to this, I would rather moor bow-on to the jetty. Not only does it pre-clude any damage to the self-steerer, but it gives a lot more privacy onboard. In this case the anchor is paid off over the stern.

With the wind blowing *parallel* to the dock, here again it is a question of tacking up to a point about six boats' length out from the jetty and anchoring. Then take lines ashore in the dinghy, one from the stern and one from the bow. Then the boat can be warped into place.

There has been a lot of stuff written about going alongside under sail. Don't do it, unless you know the harbor like the wrinkles on your old mum's face. If you do, you are asking for trouble. In a lot of countries you might, if you have caused damage to another craft, even find yourself in jail until the damage has been either paid for or made good.

Go alongside using the traditional old sailing-ship way; that is, anchor and warp in. That's what lines and dinghies are for. There is certainly no loss of face involved, because, in fact, anchoring and warping is much more seamanlike than horsing around under sail, busting your bow-sprit and other people's peace of mind.

If there is no one around on the jetty when you get within heaving-line distance, then belay the anchor line and take your own lines ashore.

By this you will see that, in fact, docking and mooring under sail is not, in fact, the single-hander's way, because here he has to depend on other people being around to take his lines. If he anchors and warps, he need depend on no one else, and he can make a good, safe, steady job without any fuss and palaver. And that's what it's all about.

Safety for the Single-Hander

On deck, in any kind of seaway, always make sure you are tied to the boat, even if this is on a long line.

Always move about the boat carefully, and always think out any course of action before you make it.

Always try to move slowly, and always stay as low as you can.

When you are leaving or approaching land, or when there are other vessels around, always wear a lifejacket in heavy weather. There's not much point in this once you are out and free, especially off the shipping lanes, unless you are a confirmed optimist.

I hold old-fashioned views on rescue at sea. I do not intend to proselytize, but I should explain them. Whether you agree with me or not is your own business.

Nobody has the right to expect to be rescued if his vessel is in trouble, or if he has lost his boat, or if he has been washed overboard. These matters must be guarded against *before* the event. The hazard or danger must be fought through. Long and hard thought must be given to this before disaster occurs. The most effective means of safety at sea are the efficient preparation of the vessel herself and of the means of her navigation, *before the voyage commences.* Conclusions reached in dangerous situations must be calmly considered and they must be *decisive.* There must be no vacillation when a decision has been made. My rules for the long-distance voyager are these:

One: Know as much as you can about where you are going before you set out.

Two: Once your mind is made up on a course of action, carry it through to the best of your ability.

Three: *Never* depend on help from outside the vessel.

Always keep your deck(s) as clean and as clear as possible. They should either be covered with a nonskid material, or painted with nonskid paint. If you cannot get this, then mix some light sand with paint and use that. This includes the cabin sole.

No walking surface should be varnished. This includes hatch covers and companionway steps.

Any obstructions on deck should either be coated with luminous paint or wrapped with luminous tape, this for night work. The stays and shrouds should have a wrapping of luminous tape at hand height, so they can be clearly seen and grabbed when making your way along the deck in the dark.

Secure the headsail clews to the sheets with bowline hitches. Do not use snap-shackles, unless you are in the habit of sailing whilst wearing a World War II soldier's helmet or have a good supply of bandages and aspirin.

Never walk on a sail, especially dacron; it is very slippery.

Always tow a line to trip the self-steering gear. This should have a luminous painted buoy on its fag end.

Make sure you have sufficient hull-pumping capacity; that is, at least two hand pumps, one operable from deck without opening any lockers. Hook up your engine-cooling water suction system to pump the bilge when required.

All the guard-rail cables and lines should be of the highest-quality materials and regularly inspected. The top rail should be well above knee level. The stanchions should not be more than three feet apart and should be well secured below decks. Pelican hooks should not be used at all on the guard-rails, as they are liable to strain and break.

Always have a radar reflector rigged, day and night. This need not be a fancy piece of expensive sculpture; a bashed-in biscuit tin will do the job just as well. In fact, I have had reports from ships that a biscuit tin gives off a better echo, because the specially made octahedral type, which is usually rigged pointing upward, loses a lot of the radar beam, whilst the flat top of the tin gives off a great blurb of a return.

Make sure you can see what you are doing at all times. When you are entering a haven, do so with a high-cut headsail. If you use a spray dodger, make sure the windows are big enough to be able to get a good all-around view. Have red lights for the chart table and binnacle at night, so you don't lose your night vision. The best type of main compass has a revolving grid over it, with the grid lines marked in luminous paint. The north point on the compass disc is also painted luminous. You set the course by sliding around the grid so that the north point is lined up inside the grid lines when the boat's head is on course. It is very easy to see, in the dark, whether or not a proper heading is being made.

If you wear glasses, make sure they are properly secured around your neck, and always stow at least two spare pairs.

Never carry a sharp knife. There should be only one or two really sharp knives onboard, and these should be kept in special stowages, so that each time you need one there is a conscious effort involved in reaching it, which triggers the warning mechanism in the back of your skull—be careful! If you must carry a knife, it need not be too sharp. If the reasons for this are not obvious to you, stay ashore.

If you cannot get the booms set high, then make sure that you always keep low. After a while this will become second nature.

Your dinghy should be compartmentalized. I prefer rubber Avon craft, which are extremely tough. For a single-hander you will need a seven- or nine-footer. Make sure that there is always a portable fresh-water supply handy to put into the dinghy, along with concentrated food and fishing tackle. This dinghy emergency tackle should be kept somewhere near the companionway. There should be sufficient concentrated food to last for at least thirty days. There should be a length of canvas (preferably orange) handy to form a shade (nylon or dacron is useless for this, as the sun's rays penetrate these materials). There should be a notebook, with two pencils attached, in which each day's noon position has been entered, so that if the worst happens you will at least know where you are. Not only should the last day's noon position be entered, but also the declination of the sun. Then an approximate latitude can be gained, in case there is not sufficient time to get the navigation tables into the dinghy.

At night, at sea, always wear a shirt and trousers, in case of having to abandon ship. Sunburn can kill.

Although I have little faith in electronic gear, I would advise carrying an EPIRB—an emergency locator radio beacon. This is a device that, when triggered, gives off a continuous SOS signal for about seventy-two hours. It is quite small and can be taken along in the dinghy.

Always make sure that your visual distress signals, such as flares and pistol rockets, are kept dry and renewed when the expiration date is reached. Take these along if you abandon ship.

Always have at least two emergency flashlights ready, and check them often. The rubber ones are best, because they float.

A small kit of fishing tackle may save your life.

SAFETY DOWN BELOW If you can, always do your cooking in a pressure cooker. This can be locked shut, and if it jumps off the stove will lessen the risk of being scalded, but watch out for steam, as the weight will jerk off.

Try never to stand in front of the galley stove when it is in use. The safety belt for use in the galley should be rigged to one side of the stove.

Even when the boat's movement is not too lively, when you turn in, always rig the lee-boards on the bunk. The movement may increase without your being aware.

Never fill a cup or a bowl with hot liquids. A half-full cup is better than a scalded hand. Remember, one hand out of commission means half the crew laid up.

A wall can opener is safer to use than a hand-operated one.

Have plenty of hand-holds around the cabin.

If you use butane gas, always switch it off at the bottle when the stove is not in use.

At sea you probably will not use the head, if you have one, so turn off its sea-cocks. The same with the sink.

Shortening Sail Offshore

My own attitude to heavy weather is that I would be quite happy never again to experience a wind over 25 knots. If I could sail forever on a coast with the wind coming offshore and gentle seas, with cool, sunny days, starry, balmy nights, and a snug anchorage every evening at sunset, I would be more than content to do so.

But this is not the way of the world, especially the sea world. If we demand our passage, we must be prepared to pay our tolls. But we should not overpay, and this means being prepared for a blow. Properly built, maintained, and fitted out, any small sailing craft can usually stand much more than her human cargo. Yet every year scores of perfectly sound vessels are towed into port by the Coast Guard simply because the skippers had little or no idea how to handle a storm.

Then the sailor's first line of defense is to shorten sail. As a rough rule of thumb, this is in order when the lee rail goes under—and stays there. Or as the old salts put it: "The time to reef is when you first think about it." There is no shame in easing a ship.

JIFFY REEFING   Confronted with a wicked and unexpected hard blow, which may very well happen in tropical waters or where warm air meets a cool current, such as in the infamous and misnamed Devil's Triangle or off the northern coast of Brazil, there is nothing to beat jiffy reefing for shortening sail quickly.

With this system a hook is fitted at the main-boom gooseneck and the reef cringle is attached to it. The leech cringle is hauled down by means of a hefty line rove from an eye on the boom, through the leech cringle and forward through a block on the boom. In the case of high-aspect rigs—long, tall sails—there may be more than one jiffy reef, in which case each has its own cheek block on the boom.

The sequence for jiffy reefing is as follows:

1. Go forward to the mast after easing the mainsheet.
2. Take up the slack on the topping lift so it takes the weight of the boom.
3. Lower the main halyard until the tack cringle can be hooked onto the gooseneck.
4. Hoist the halyard until the luff is taut; belay the halyard.
5. Cast off the clew line from its cleat, haul it in taut, and belay it back on the cleat. A small winch would be best suited for this, to make the effort a bit less strenuous. The clew cringle should be snugged down hard against the boom.
6. Ease off the topping lift.
7. At your ease (or as we say, taking your time by the dockyard clock), tie up the loose bunt (or belly) of the sail with the slab reefing points.

ROLLER REEFING   In roller reefing, the sail is wound up around the boom, like a window shade. The trick is obtaining a good sail shape after reefing. Keep pulling the sail outboard along the boom so that it doesn't bunch up near the mast. It can help to fix battens along the boom to increase its diameter as the sail is rolled up. By easing the halyard a bit at a time to maintain tension, the sail can be rolled up tightly. If the boat is equipped with a reel winch, be sure to remove the handle before lowering the sail. A winch that runs away can fling the handle with lethal force.

The roller-reefing gear should be hefty and the after flange large enough in diameter to stop the luff of the sail from creeping forward and jamming up the operation. The reefing handle should lock into the reel and stay there until released. Finally, be sure to keep the mechanism lubricated religiously. There is nothing worse than standing by on deck with full main and a frozen reefing drum as a squall bears down on you.

Through-the-mast roller reefing is not recommended, as the advantage obtained (eliminating the wide gap between the tack and the mast when reefed) does not outweigh the extra hazard of a defect in gear which is not accessible. For the same reason I would not prefer internal halyards. Everything should be easily accessible.

Rather than have deep reefs, with the consequent misshaping of the sail, I would prefer to set a storm trysail. This is loose footed, and the boom need not be used. I would fit a short piece of track, which would lead the trysail over the bent mainsail through a switch onto the mainsail track.

One piece of equipment that can be invaluable when shortening sail is a topping lift, which is used to support the boom when the sail is lowered. Apart from its added usefulness as a spare halyard, the topping lift can also be used to lower the boom when heaving-to, to minimize rolling.

For the headsails, I rig downhauls to ease the problem of getting them down on deck, especially while the wind is still in them. My jib has extra-large hanks, and I lead the downhaul through them to a small block at the tack.

With twin headstays, there is not much trouble changing jibs, as one can be hanked on while the other is still aloft. The stays must be far enough apart for the hanks not to foul. With this setup, one sail can be hauled aloft while the other is still up, thus losing no way, but I prefer to lower one, hoist one—transferring the halyard. The lowered sail is led into its bag and hung up on the stay, bagged, ready to rehoist—if the weather is easing. If the wind is piping up and I am reducing sail, then I unhank the dowsed sail, after bagging it, and stow it down below, reducing windage.

Where I have only one headstay, then I hank the new sail onto the wire below the bottom hank of the flying sail. I lower the latter, and as it comes down unhank it, bag it, then up goes the new sail.

Roller-furling jibs are very handy, except that they are not generally (unless they are fitted with luff rods) reefing sails. If they are rolled up for a blow, it means that either you have a lot of windage forward and aloft, just where you don't need it, or you have the awkward task of getting the gear down and stowed below or on deck. If the sails are partly furled (reefed), they sag and develop a belly. If the roller-furling rod is grooved for lowering the sail, there are no hanks and the sail can be lost over the side, especially in rough weather.

Only twice have I ever sailed in the knowledge that the vessel was not prepared for any eventuality: once near the Greenland coast and once in the River Plate. In both cases I had sailed in unprepared states through force of circumstances; in both cases I had weighed the odds and decided that although not properly prepared for any foreseeable circumstances, *with luck* I would get away with it. In both cases I almost lost my vessel and my life. Luck, as far as a sailor and his craft go, does not exist. Discount it. Make your own luck by making sure the dice are loaded on your side. Most of you will get second chances, but don't count on being among the ones who do.

Once you are satisfied with your vessel and her gear, you will know the happiness of a sailor who is confident that his craft can meet with any weather, and that's about as near to Nirvana (given a good stock of grub and water on board) as a person can expect to get in this life—a voyager, at any rate.

Rigs
and Rigging

THE best type of rig depends on a number of factors. First, you yourself. What is the rig you can handle safely in all conditions? How active and strong are you? In this respect you can decide only by actually trying out different rigs. For anyone under twenty-five or over forty-five I would generalize and recommend a split rig (yawl), but someone who is spritely and active might go in for the simpler sloop or cutter rig. The reason for the split rig preference is that the sail areas, for a given size of hull, will be smaller. With a mizzen staysail you can crowd on sail and even outdo the sloop or cutter in total sail area.

My own preference for yawl over ketch rig is purely personal. It is because I have tended to sail in out-of-the-way areas, off the beaten track, and this means much windward work. The yawl, with her high center of effort and bigger mainsail, goes better to windward than the ketch, and I am willing to sacrifice the little extra speed I would have running downwind with the bigger ketch mizzen for the better beating qualities of the yawl. However, for a round-the-worlder following the usual Canaries-Barbados-Panama, Tuamotos-Australia passage, probably a ketch is better, especially if she is fitted with a good, simple, reliable diesel engine. She would need this for entering such places as atolls, where the wind might be (and usually is) blowing straight from the narrow entrance. The ketch has the advantage of being more comfortable in a seaway than a yawl, because the center of effort is lower, and so the rolling moment less. Also, if the worst happens and she is dismasted, it is easier to jury-rig the ketch, as she has a higher mizzen mast, and a forestay can be rigged directly from the mizzen truck to the bow, for a headsail.

The problems of ketches are, first, as mentioned, they are not too hot going to windward; second, the mizzen blankets the main when running dead downwind; third, ketches can be dogs in light airs, needing a good breeze to get moving; and last but not least, it is awkward, with that great boom sticking out aft, to rig a self-steering gear.

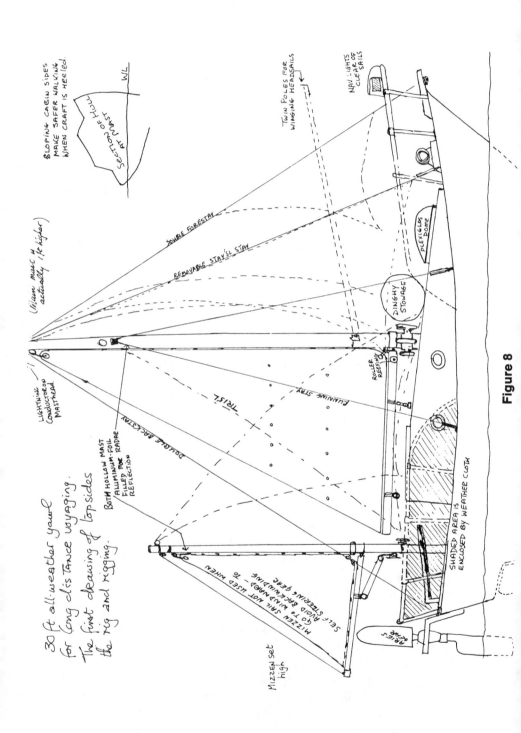

Figure 8

30 ft all-weather yawl for long distance voyaging. The first drawing of topsides the rig and rigging.

SLOPING CABIN SIDES MAKE SAFER WALKING WHEN CRAFT IS HEELED.

SECTION OF HULL AT WORST

W/L

LIGHTNING CONDUCTOR MASTHEAD

(Mizzen mast is actually 1 ft higher)

DOUBLE FORESTAY

REMOVABLE STAY'SL STAY

TWIN POLES FOR WINGING HEADSAILS

NAV. LIGHTS TO CLEAR OF SAILS

PLEXIGLAS DOME

DINGHY STOWAGE

ROLLER REEFING

RUNNING STAY

TRI'S'L

DOUBLE BACKSTAY

BOTH HOLLOW MAST ALUMINUM-FOIL FILLED FOR RADAR REFLECTION

MIZZEN SAIL NOT USED WHEN SELF-STEERING. AVOID BACKWINDING TO SELF-STEERING GEAR.

MIZZEN SET HIGH

ARIES

SHADED AREA IS ENCLOSED BY WEATHER CLOTH

Probably Sir Alec Rose's solution to this last problem was best; in *Lively Lady* he unshipped the mizzen boom and used the mizzen mast only to support a mizzen staysail. But there again, you may do that with a yawl, and have better windward ability.

My own vessel, *Sea Dart*, had a cutter rig. There is one big problem here. It means only one mast. In the event of a dismasting there may be nothing to hang a jury rig on, except perhaps a short stump with a running pole lashed from it skyward. The cutter rig is handy, and it means less cost and maintenance than a two-masted rig, and a cutter or sloop pitches less than a split rig. Going to windward, of course, the cutter or sloop will beat the pants off a yawl or ketch and also in light airs the high-aspect sails are great for catching what breeze there may be. In a strong blow, the cutter skipper just dowses the jib, reefs the main, and carries on under reefed main and staysail, still going reasonably efficiently to windward.

Generally, the staysail in a cutter is rigged on a boom, but this is a potential hazard to the single-hander; if it strikes him he might go flying over the side, if he doesn't break a leg; so the stay'sl is best left loose-footed for the solo sailor.

In any case, when you are beating to windward in confined waters single-handed, you would dowse the staysail and just use the jib and main; you won't lose much speed and will have only one set of sheets to handle.

In *Sea Dart* I have a removable staysail stay. This is hauled back flat against the mast when I am using the jib alone. In this position it does not interfere with the jib coming across when tacking.

All my halyards can be handled from the cockpit, and both headsails are fitted with downhauls, so I can lower the stay'sl, haul it down, and get it out of the way of the jib without having to dash forward with the boat out of control.

Another good, simple rig for the single-hander is the Chinese lug rig. This was greatly modified and brought up to date by "Blondie" Haslar, who is mentioned elsewhere in connection with his fine pioneering work on self-steering gears. The big advantage of this rig is that the sail can be handled completely from the cockpit or even from down below in the cabin, through the hatch.

The Chinese lug-sail has full-length battens and several sheets, which help to stop the sail from twisting out of shape and can be used successively as the sail is reefed. The sail is balanced, with its leading edge forward of the mast; this keeps the center of effort toward the luff. This is important, as otherwise when the boat is run-

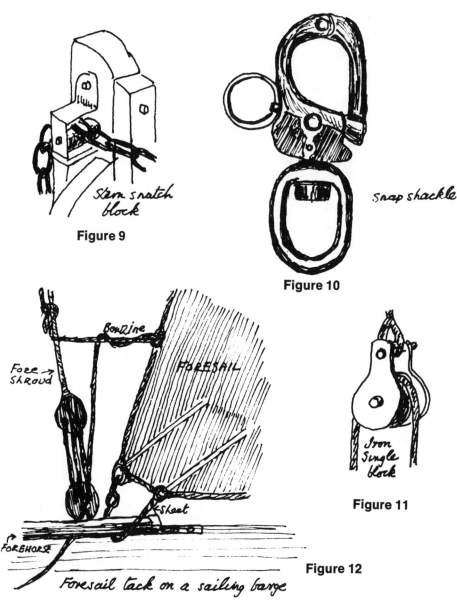

Stem snatch block

Figure 9

snap shackle

Figure 10

BowLine

FORESAIL

Fore → Shroud

Sheet

FOREHORSE

Foresail tack on a sailing barge

Iron Single block

Figure 11

Figure 12

ning free the center of effort would be off center of the vessel, causing tremendous weather helm.

The sail is controlled by four lines. To reef the lug-sail, the halyard is started, the battens drop down onto the boom, held in place by lazy-jacks, and the battens are held down by hauling in on the down-haul and the sheets.

For running downwind the Chinese lug-sail is probably the handiest, the easiest, the least trouble-prone of all rigs. It can be hauled up and lowered, reefed and unreefed a hundred times without the skipper's once having to go forward.

But, as with people, so with rigs; there are many advantages, but there are disadvantages too. The first is that the lug-sail is inefficient at going to windward. You will be lucky if you get closer than fifty degrees off the wind, and that only in dead flat water. In light airs, forget sailing and get the fishing lines out. You'll have to, or start the engine. Lug-sail-rigged vessels need a good stiff breeze to get moving. On some lug-rigs, such as Blondie used in his famous Folkboat *Jester*, there is no standing rigging; and the mast tends to whip around like a conductor's baton. I would either have a very short stump of a mast, or at least provide some kind of standing rigging, even if it was loosely stayed, to prevent too serious whip and the risk of dismasting.

When it comes to multihull rigs; I personally don't like them. I think the danger of a capsize is too great for a single-hander, with the exception perhaps of the Wharram design, which has no doghouse spread over the platform deck. Instead, James Wharram provides only slats, which allow the wind, should it get under the 'tween-hulls platform, to blow right through, and thus lose its capsize-tending force. But here again, comfort is sacrificed to safety, and the living accommodations in the two hulls are poky, even to me, and that is saying something. The windward ability of the multihulls I have sailed in, without engine assistance, was about on par with that of Grand Central Station. Especially when they were loaded down, as they must be for a long passage. Without an engine they didn't go to windward; with an engine they generally didn't sail to windward because of the weight of the engine. I cannot speak for all multihulls, nor would I; I can only comment on my own experiences some years ago. Multihulls may have improved, but I should need to be convinced of it before I took a lone voyage in one.

Where solo sailors are concerned, schooners seem to belong on the lids of biscuit boxes and tea caddies, along with stage coaches and crinolined ladies. They are usually very laborsome and need a large crew.

With any type of rigging, a bowsprit is useful for increasing the sail area and also can be a help in balancing the rig. But it is outside the hull and so is another point of vulnerability. I expect that more damage is done to other craft, when maneuvering in confined waters, by bowsprits than by anything else. If you do have a bowsprit, then the jib should be hanked to a running jib stay. This saves having to go out onto the bowsprit to hank on the sail—a perilous practice in any kind of weather.

Never take a long passage without a topping lift. Apart from always having a spare halyard readily available, in case the others jam, a topping lift is needed for topping up the boom when hove to, to minimize rolling, and also to "top-up" the mainsail when on a broad reach, so that the wind doesn't hold it and you can lower the sail. With roller reefing you need a topping lift to control the boom angle when reefing, otherwise it will drop as sail is shortened, and the boom swinging around can cause a lot of damage to structure and deck fittings.

MASTS   The weakest spars are wooden and hollow. Next, in increasing order of strength, come solid wooden masts, but that means a lot of weight aloft. Third come hollow metal spars. The strongest masts are fiberglass, which can whip around like crazy without breaking.

When it comes to mast height, this depends, I think, on the areas to be sailed. In the mostly steady wind conditions of the Trade Wind belt, a fairly high rig can be carried with a reasonable expectancy of safety. By fairly high I mean up to 20 percent higher, above deck level, than the LOA of the vessel. But I voyage a lot in out-of-the-way areas, north and south of the Trade Wind belt, sometimes far north and south, where heavy weather may be more the rule than the exception. For this reason, on my projected thirty-footer, I ask for a mast no higher above deck level than the LOA of the boat. This gives me a hoist of about 28 feet, and a mainsail area of about 175 square feet. I will willingly sacrifice speed for safety. I know that there are big tough guys who will scoff at this puny sail; but there's a bigger, tougher wind out there, and its argument impresses me much more than theirs. In any case, the staysail genoa and the main genoa will provide sufficient pulling power to make up for the low-aspect rig. My masts will be heavily stayed with 1 × 19 wire and Norseman wire-rope swage-type terminals to minimize the risk of dismasting.

The mizzen mast would be about two feet higher than the hoist of the sail. This is to give a better angle for a jury stay, in case the main mast goes over the side, or when the mast needs to be lowered.

With internal halyards, at the masthead there should be at least three sheaves, with the center one standing proud of the mast. This is for the main halyard, which otherwise will score the mast. The others are for the genoa and the topping lift; and the topping lift should be a spare main halyard. That way, if the main halyard sheave jams, you have a comparatively painless alternative. But for simplicity, all my halyards will be run outside the masts.

Around the base of the main mast I would have belaying pins set in a sturdy rail supported on strong stanchions. Belaying pins are more efficient than cleats, because the line belayed on them can be freed immediately by withdrawing the pin from the rail. Also, the space between the rail and the mast makes a fine stowage for items such as sail covers, bucket, strops, etc., though these would be stowed below in heavy weather. I advocate all halyards, sheets, and downhauls being led back to the cockpit, but this is for areas where the weather is changeable. In steady conditions, such as are found in the Trade Belt, the halyards would be belayed to the belaying pins, and so kept clear of the deck. You might run for days on end without needing to touch a halyard.

I would not have internal halyards because of the lack of accessibility. Instead, I would have a double block at the masthead and a single block and a shackle on the head of the mainsail. This would make hoisting much easier. There would be a downhaul rigged on the mainsail head so that the sail could be hauled down against the bite of the double block. The blocks would be wooden with metal straps; preferably teak cheeks and stainless steel straps and roller-pins. I do not like rubber-sheathed blocks because if the lead of the halyard is slightly off center to the sheave, the sheathing rubs away in time, and can, in fact, fail.

I would not use Teflon blocks aloft where they are not easily got at or where, as with the main halyard in the Trade Belt, they are not likely to be freshened often, because without regular use they seize up, or at least get very stiff, whereas wooden blocks can go six months without being looked at.

The halyard blocks would all be of the swiveling type.

My main halyard would be braided nylon. It stretches under strain, but there is little grief involved in going forward now and again to give an extra pinch on the winch. The reason for rope rather than wire is that I am going to be living in the boat, and the sound of stainless steel wire clattering against an aluminum, wood, or fiberglass mast is enough to make a bishop burn his Bible after a few weeks of the "Devil's Tattoo," as we call it. Also, of course, a rope halyard is much easier to renew than a wire. The halyard will be a half-inch diameter, so the block would be a four-incher, based on the formula one inch of block to every eighth of an inch rope diameter. To accommodate these blocks the mast would, therefore, have to be about a foot or so higher than the sail-hoist.

Both my masts will be stepped on deck. This will make the task of taking the main mast down much easier. It is an important consideration when voyaging in out-of-the-way places, where perhaps a low bridge has to be passed, or where I might be wintering in very cold areas, with the risk of "black ice" forming on the standing rigging and threatening to capsize the vessel. The main mast would be stepped in a tabernacle and arranged so that it would lower in a forward direction, with the mizzen mast acting as a "stand-off sheer-leg."

The mizzen mast would be heavily stayed, with running backstays, first because the main mast would be raised and lowered by using the leverage obtained from the height of the mizzen truck, and also because I consider the mizzen to be a heavy-weather sail. It is vital that both masts are independently stayed, so that if one is lost, the other is still standing. I have never heard of a boat losing her mizzen mast, though I expect it has happened. Usually it's the main that goes over. Then a heavily supported mizzen, to which a jury outfit can be rigged, is worth its weight in gold.

Again, the mizzen halyard would be braid. The same set-up as the main, only using three-eighths rope and three inch blocks.

The headsail halyards would be braided nylon three-eighths for the stays'l and five-eighths for the genoa/jib/storms'l halyard.

While on masts, don't forget a lightning conductor. This can be led down to one of the outer stays and from there a length of heavy-duty battery cable available to be clamped to the stay and dropped over the side. I don't know if it would do any good in those very alarming tropical lightning storms, but at least it's some kind of comfort.

RUNNING RIGGING   All the sheets would be braided nylon for the main mizzen, jib, and trysail (though here I would simply transfer the main sheet to the trysail). The sheets for the stays'l, working jib, and No. 2 jib (Yankee) would be half-inch diameter, whilst those for the light genoa, light genoa staysail, and mizzen stays'l would be three-eighths.

I would stow enough spare line onboard to replace every sheet three times. This type of line, in these amounts, may appear to be an expensive proposition, but I would much rather invest the money in good, sound, hard-wearing running rigging than in fancy gadgets. So, I

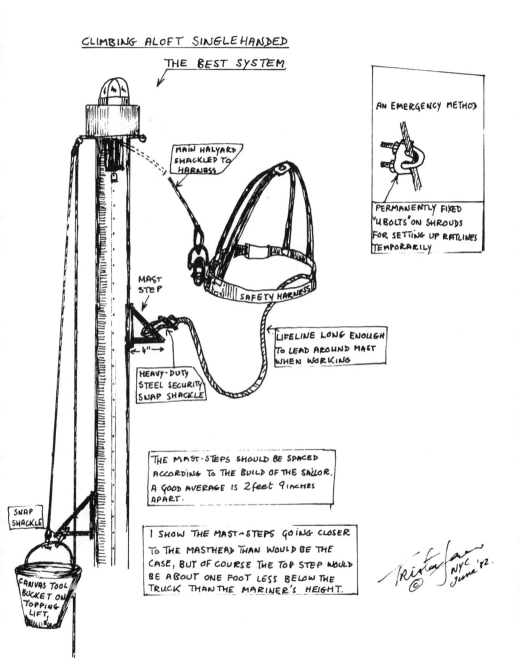

CLIMBING ALOFT SINGLEHANDED

THE BEST SYSTEM

AN EMERGENCY METHOD

PERMANENTLY FIXED "U BOLTS" ON SHROUDS FOR SETTING UP RATLINES TEMPORARILY

MAIN HALYARD SHACKLED TO HARNESS

SAFETY HARNESS

MAST STEP

4"

LIFELINE LONG ENOUGH TO LEAD AROUND MAST WHEN WORKING

HEAVY-DUTY STEEL SECURITY SNAP SHACKLE

THE MAST-STEPS SHOULD BE SPACED ACCORDING TO THE BUILD OF THE SAILOR. A GOOD AVERAGE IS 2 feet 9 inches APART.

I SHOW THE MAST-STEPS GOING CLOSER TO THE MASTHEAD THAN WOULD BE THE CASE, BUT OF COURSE THE TOP STEP WOULD BE ABOUT ONE FOOT LESS BELOW THE TRUCK THAN THE MARINER'S HEIGHT.

SNAP SHACKLE

CANVAS TOOL BUCKET ON TOPPING LIFT.

© NYC '72 June

Figure 13

will do without the wind-direction indicator and the off-course alarm. This will more than pay for the three sets of running rigging, which should last me for six years of hard use.

All the headsails would have foot-ropes on them, going through a single block on the foot of the sail and a double block on the deck in the case of the stays'l and on a bowsprit traveler in the case of the jib, etc. I know there will be criticisms about the heftiness and the ungainliness of these halyard setups, but I am out for simplicity, for strength, and for ease of replacement in hard weather conditions. I don't want to find myself at the masthead, swaying crazily on a bosun's chair, trying to unjam a wire halyard that has jumped off a sheave.

If I do have to go aloft in a bosun's chair, with a double purchase of the main halyard, I can haul myself up as I go, pulling the halyard downhaul through the thimble of the bosun's chair back, so that when I stop hoisting myself I can make a hitch on the thimble. I know that the double block means a tremendously long main halyard, but I want to be able to get the sail up even if I have a broken rib, or one arm out of action. I want to be able to get quickly at every part of the running rigging. With the luff of the sails hauled taut there will not be much clatter, even less if the masthead blocks are fitted on small "gallows" standing out from the mast.

I do not like permanently rigged ratlines, because this adds a good amount of windage in heavy weather. Instead, I prefer to rig up sturdy lines for when I need to get aloft to navigate. The ratlines are criss-crossed up the shrouds with rolling hitches over permanently fixed small U-bolts. These I can climb up, if need be. On the gaff-rigged *Cresswell* I used to climb up the parell rings.

All in all, the single-hander should avoid fancy gadgets and over-sophisticated gear, which, efficient as it may be for short-distance voyaging in advanced areas, and helpful as it may be when racing on Sydney Harbor or San Francisco Bay, may turn out to be difficult to maintain or inaccessible out in the ocean.

Let simplicity be you watchword.

Self-Steering—
Electronic and
Mechanical

NOWADAYS, the general run of offshore yachts are not very handy at steering themselves under sail, mainly because the designers aim to decrease the wetted area of the hull in the interest of increased speed. This tends to make the vessels very lively, so that they are always trying to come up into the wind. In the old days— and still with some traditionally designed hulls, such as the Colin Archers and the Tahiti Ketches, with their long, straight keels and deep forefoots—it was possible to set the sails, lash the tiller, and forget steering until the wind changed.

In steady ocean conditions, and especially when running down-wind, it is still possible to work out some means of steering by sail, but a lot of time and patience are needed to get it just right. And with some of the skimpier hulls, with their deep, skinny keels and skegs, I doubt if you could ever really trust sail steering. I know I wouldn't.

For these, as well as other, more obvious reasons, there have been developed, over the past two decades or so, various mechanical self-steerers and also electronic gadgets intended to serve the same purpose. There are also specially made sailing rigs, and the old time-proven working sail rigs.

No electrical or electronic self-steering device that I have sailed with has proved 100 percent dependable. They are certainly not economical; the battery drain, especially in heavy weather, when the boat is yawing heavily and the demand on steering gear is hard, is almost always unacceptable. It means that the engine must be run several hours a day to recharge the batteries, it means using precious fuel in midocean, and it means adding to the engine hours, which are mounting up steadily toward the next top-overhaul. Apart from this, transistors blow or burn out, and sea air attacks delicate contacts and switches, no matter how well they are protected. In nine-tenths of the ports of the world, the hope of finding someone who understands these things is about as realistic as the hope of getting Colonel Qaddafi to adopt the United States Constitution. For a vessel in which you are

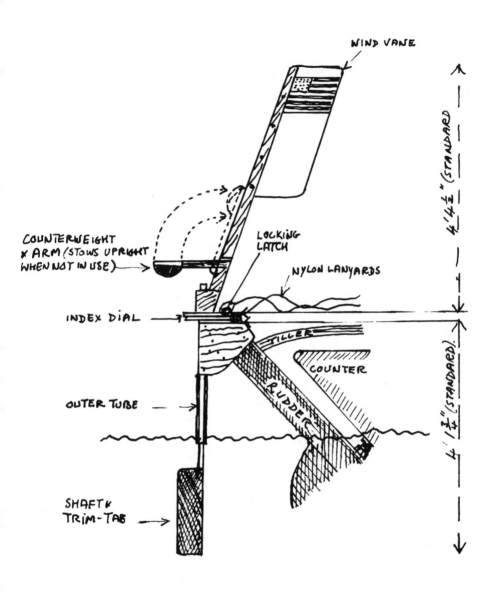

WIND VANE

COUNTERWEIGHT
& ARM (STOWS UPRIGHT
WHEN NOT IN USE)

LOCKING
LATCH

NYLON LANYARDS

INDEX DIAL

TILLER

COUNTER

RUDDER

OUTER TUBE

SHAFT &
TRIM-TAB

4'4½" (STANDARD)

4'1¼" (STANDARD).

"*QUARTER MASTER*" SELF-STEERING GEAR.
RECOMMENDED FOR CRAFT UP TO **28** feet LOA.,
WITH OUTBOARD RUDDERS.

Tristan Jones
NYC 1982.

Figure 14

contemplating several years of long-distance voyaging or cruising in the less advanced areas of the world, I say forget electronics, unless you yourself are a qualified electronics engineer.

For power boats, or for sailing vessels with plenty of electric capability, cruising in advanced areas, auto-pilots are probably a wonderful labor saver. But for the ocean roamer, don't be surprised if you are three thousand miles from the nearest workshop and the thing conks out, condemning you to spend hour upon weary hour, for days, or weeks, under the tyranny of the tiller, perhaps in bad conditions, with your speed slowing surprisingly, thus threatening the duration of your food and water supplies. Wind vane, yes; electronics, as an extra, perhaps!

Now, having roused the wrath and ire of every auto-pilot manufacturer twixt Valparaiso and Vladivostok, let's have a look at the wind vane systems. The beauty of these, of course, is that their power source is fairly constant, especially in the deep blue, and it is also free.

The wind has been harnessed to drive the boat for centuries, but it was only in the thirties that men started to think of using the wind to steer the boat. Marin-Marie, the French painter, first used a vane as an auxiliary to a homemade electrical auto-pilot on the first power boat ever to cross the Atlantic. That was *Arielle*, in 1936. Subsequently, several bright back-room boys in England put their eccentric minds to the problem, until World War II came along and put their thoughts to other, deadlier ideas for a few years.

In Britain, after WW II, several brilliant men turned their gaze once again on this fascinating idea. Mike Henderson, in *Mick the Miller*, made the first trim-tab gear. That was in 1954. Then in '56 Ian Major used a trim-tab gear in the Atlantic crossing of *Buttercup*. Whilst this was going on, from 1953 onward, the most famous of all the self-steering developers, Major "Blondie" Haslar, was working at it, first of all on a trim-tab design, then on a servo-pendulum model. Blondie was an ex-commando officer, renowned for paddling canoes into Bordeaux harbor, France, during the German occupation, and, with his dozen or so Royal Marines, attaching limpet mines to several German ships and blowing them to kingdom come. That was typical of him, intrepid in action, in thought, and in word.

The system that Blondie Haslar developed is still being manufactured in England by Gibbs, and I have seen it all over the world in any number of ocean craft. However, it is not my favorite, because it is not simple. There are too many parts to go wrong, too many bits of delicate mechanism. It is as accurate as any other, no doubt, but efficient simplicity is, at sea, the essence of seaworthiness.

The simplest gear is the all-above-water type, typified by the QME. However, although this rig works quite well on small craft, say, up to twenty-two feet, I am not going to recommend it for anything larger, simply because I have never met up with sailors who've handled a craft over that length who reported that it worked well in all conditions. The *Nuits San George* sloop, which I met with in '73, in Colon, Panama, was forty-two feet long. Her skipper was an extremely intelligent and able French architect, with many years of offshore cruising under his belt. He told me that the all-above-water gear he had shipped (a QME) was useless. This is but one instance of the negative reports I have had about this gear, and it is for this reason that I have never sailed with it. For small-craft cruising inshore waters, it is a cheap and fairly efficient answer to the problem of leaving the tiller for a short spell when sailing alone. Even then, I would only rig it in a vessel that was already well balanced. It seems that one of the problems with the all-above-water wind-vane gear is that for anything over twenty-two feet in length the wind vane has to be progressively larger in area, so that when you reach over thirty-five feet, to be really efficient and strong enough to affect the helm as it should do, the vane is much too large to be safe, and in fact in heavy weather it would constitute a hazard to the safety of the vessel. It would be well nigh impossible to rig a vane of sufficient size in anything but a masthead sloop or cutter with a high-aspect rig. In a yawl, mizzen, or schooner it would be havoc playing around with that enormous area of vane aft. I think, knowing me, that the first hard blow we came to, I would just hack it adrift and give it the deep six. In light airs, I do not think this type of gear would work at all.

We should now consider the first of the underwater-gear types of self-steerers. First, the vane-to-auxiliary-rudder type. This is the type I had onboard *Sea Dart*, which is seventeen feet on the waterline. However, I have tried it in a sloop of twenty-five feet LWL, off Buenos Aires, in moderate to heavy winds, and found that it was excellent, steering both my boat and the sloop within fifteen degrees of the course when running downwind, and within ten degrees when on a broad reach, five degrees when beating to windward. It is simple, having very few moving parts; it can be easily unshipped, and it requires very little maintenance. My own model was manufactured by Automate, in England, but a similar model is made in the United

States by James F. Ogg, in California. This is known as the Polaris. I cannot speak for the Polaris, never having used one yet, but I would recommend the Automate for use in any reasonably balanced boat up to twenty-six feet LWL.

One of the advantages of the vane-to-auxiliary-rudder type is that it is not fixed to the rudder below water, so no underwater maintenance is necessary. For a nonswimmer (like me) this is indeed a blessing. The other advantages to being able to haul the auxiliary rudder onboard easily are that you can eliminate that amount of drag below water level, when clawing off, or racing; also, when in harbor, you do not have another appendage aft to be damaged up against pilings or docks, or to look unsightly. But the biggest advantage of all, and the one that decided me on using it in *Sea Dart*, is that should the main rudder fail for any reason, the auxiliary rudder can be used in its stead. It is an inestimable comfort to know this when you are in the wild areas, or in heavy weather in midocean.

The way the Automate operates is simple. You simply gauge the amount of helm, after handling the tiller for a few minutes, lash it in the position most favorable to the course, clutch in the Automate, which is a mere push down on a lever at the base of the vane, and off you go. You then return to the tiller and make minor adjustments, if required, to the position it is lashed in.

A tip: Paint your ensign on the vane; this saves wear and tear on the fabric ones you have. Replacing these can become quite an expensive item in remote areas of the world, where the authorities insist on ensigns being in good condition when worn in harbor, which they must be.

The next type of vane self-steering gear on the list is the trim-tab type. These can be used in vessels up to sixty feet LWL, though of course the size of vane and counterweight will vary in different-size hulls. The main disadvantage of these is that the trim-tab is attached to the rudder. This causes such problems as getting lines snarled between the tab and the rudder, but with a swimmer around this can be easily solved. It is possible but difficult to use the trim-tab where the main rudder is hung inboard, and they are best used in outboard-hung rudders, such as we see on double-enders. The disadvantage here is that we are adding a delicate mechanism to an already vulnerable protruberance. This is especially of concern in restricted waters, such as harbors, and even more so where you must moor-to stern-on the jetty, as you must do in the Mediterranean, and in many marinas nowadays.

The operation of the trim-tab gear is simple. The vane turns the tab, which is hung on the after end of the rudder. The water flow on the forward side of the tab forces the rudder in the opposite direction, thus steering the boat. In light to moderate airs, the tiller is usually left free, but in strong winds the helm will be lashed, leaving the steering to the tab, just as with the Automate gear.

We now tackle the third vane-to-underwater system, the pendulum-servo mechanism. Among this type are included the Haslar gear, already mentioned, the Aries, the Gunning, and many others, but in my experience the finest, without any doubt, is the Aries.

The Aries is comparatively simple, heftily constructed, efficient, and practically maintenance free. The underwater pendulum can be hoisted out of the water to prevent the accumulation of marine growth. On the latest Aries it can be completely removed and stowed below. It is easy to clutch in and out, and to change the attitude of the vane to the wind, all these operations being easily done by lines to the cockpit. This obviates the hazardous exercise of having to climb outboard over the stern to do these things, as is sometimes necessary with other gears of this type. The Aries is made by Nick Franklin, Marine Gears Ltd., Cowes, Isle of Wight, England. Nick is a good sailor and a very human and practical man, and his delivery times and prices are good. If you anticipate any difficulty in fitting the Aries on the stern of your boat, just send Nick a drawing or photo of the stern and he will supply the right fittings. He seems to have a sixth sense about boat sterns. Mention my name, if you like.

With the Aries, as the boat turns off course, so the vane turns to head into the wind. The vane-turning motion is transmitted, through a toothed gear movement, to the horizontal axis of the pendulum, which is forced to swing to one side. This movement is transmitted, in turn, through a quadrant at the top of the pendulum, which pulls steering lines attached to the tiller or to the wheel-drum. In the Aries gear, the vane is a flip-flop; that is, it is working directly on the horizontal axis that operates the pendulum. This prevents damage by a swinging mizzen boom.

With the Gunning gear, I found that I had to fit different-size vanes for different-strength winds. This, after several days of shifting and strengthening winds, becomes tiresome. With the Aries, this is not so; the vane operates in wind speeds down to five knots, being very sensitive.

In a yawl, ketch, or schooner, it is always a problem to have a

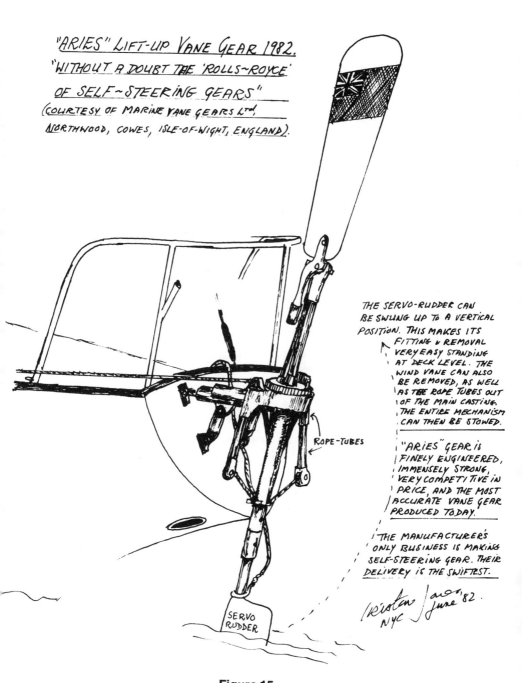

"ARIES" LIFT-UP VANE GEAR 1982.
"WITHOUT A DOUBT THE 'ROLLS-ROYCE'
OF SELF-STEERING GEARS"
(COURTESY OF MARINE VANE GEARS Ltd,
NORTHWOOD, COWES, ISLE-OF-WIGHT, ENGLAND).

ROPE-TUBES

THE SERVO-RUDDER CAN
BE SWUNG UP TO A VERTICAL
POSITION. THIS MAKES ITS
FITTING & REMOVAL
VERY EASY STANDING
AT DECK LEVEL. THE
WIND VANE CAN ALSO
BE REMOVED, AS WELL
AS THE ROPE TUBES OUT
OF THE MAIN CASTING.
THE ENTIRE MECHANISM
CAN THEN BE STOWED.

"ARIES" GEAR IS
FINELY ENGINEERED,
IMMENSELY STRONG,
VERY COMPETITIVE IN
PRICE, AND THE MOST
ACCURATE VANE GEAR
PRODUCED TODAY.

THE MANUFACTURER'S
ONLY BUSINESS IS MAKING
SELF-STEERING GEAR. THEIR
DELIVERY IS THE SWIFTEST.

Kristens Jarn, June '82.
NYC

SERVO
RUDDER

Figure 15

wind vane, other than the pendulum type, poking up aft, right in the way of the mizzen boom. It can't be helped, and the only solutions are either to have a longish boomkin aft, with the wind-vane gear sitting out on the end of it, well clear of the mizzen, or to vang the mizzen forward, thus preventing a sudden jibe, which might very well knock the vane right off, or at least seriously damage it. But considered alongside the great advantages that the wind-vane steerers give us, these are minor problems. One of the answers, for a long-distance vessel, is always to carry one or two spare vanes, made up to fit on the gear, in case of accidents.

The wind-vane steering gear saves an enormous amount of completely useless effort, boring, dreary, and deadly dull after the first few hours of steering. It saves long periods of exposure to the elements, the sun and the rain and the wind, which themselves can become extremely ennervating after a while. It makes time available to do all the necessary chores whilst underway, and to have time off simply to enjoy the scene, read a book, take a photo, darn a sock. It serves as faithfully, and probably more faithfully, at its task, than any person, and it eats no food nor drinks any water. Of all the developments in small craft, ever since man first hoisted a deerskin over a floating log, the self-steerer is the single most exciting. It allows a person to be creative whilst still making a passage. It is the emancipation of the slave-sailors from the tyranny of the tiller.

SELF-STEERING GEAR—SAFETY PRECAUTIONS   Whenever you are sailing, single-handed or not, with a self-steering gear operating, make sure you trail a line astern with a small cork or plastic buoy on the end so you can grab it if you go over the side. To this buoy should be led another, smaller line, by which the self-steering gear can be tripped. All the steering gears have a tripping mechanism, with the exception of the Automate. Because of this, on mine I stream a length of cod line from the inboard end of the rudder lever on the reducing lever mechanism. A good sharp pull on this will pull the auxiliary rudder broadside-on to the course, thus bringing the boat around into the wind. Then, once she is luffed, you can pull yourself on board. For the buoy line use half-inch nylon line with a breaking strain of five thousand pounds. For the tripping line use quarter-inch nylon line, breaking strain eleven hundred pounds, secured to the lifeline about twenty feet astern of the boat with a rolling hitch and slack in the tripping line so that there is little pull on the auxiliary rudder lever. In this way the line is streamed for an emergency, but it does not affect the operation of the steering gear until given a good hefty tug, which of course it will, with a body hanging on to it. The action, should the worst happen and you do fall over the side, is to grab the buoy line, which is streamed about sixty feet astern, and wrap it around you, under the armpits. This will not be easy if the boat is sailing at speed, but you will be surprised how comparatively easy tremendous efforts become when your life depends on them. Once the line is around you, haul your way along it, steadily and surely, to the steering-trip line, then hang on to that. The gear trips, the boat comes up into the wind, all standing, and you then climb back onboard over the stern, using the self-steering for great footholds. Then you severely chastise yourself, over a cup of hot cocoa, for being such a fool as to be topsides and not secured with your safety harness.

SELF-STEERING UNDER SAILS ONLY Self-steerers, being mechanical or electronic, are, by their very nature, subject to hard wear and tear, and thus to breakdowns. Therefore, we sailors being pessimists, it behooves us to study methods of making a vessel steer herself without the aid of mechanical gear or electric wizardry. We do this by rigging the sails, either specially made sails that will steer the boat downwind whilst the helm is left free, or our ordinary sails, adjusting them so that their sheets will operate the helm, thus steering the boat.

The big advantage of using sails for self-steering is that it avoids the necessity of buying expensive mechanical outfits, as the sails are needed anyway. The disadvantage is that sails are nowhere near as efficient as vane-steering gears. Many single-handers, over the last twenty years or more, have worked out their own methods of steering by sails alone, but the techniques are by no means new, for fishermen were using similar ploys centuries ago, by which they would set the sails to manage their boats whilst they tended nets. It is quite probable that the old Viking longships steered themselves for long periods, too; they certainly appear to have had that capability. We know that they used to return to Norway, for example, from the east coast of England, with a crew of only two. With the prevailing southwest winds, they would have been running free all the way back to that ragged, drizzly shore of theirs.

The Polynesians, too, seem to have used self-steering techniques in their ancient ocean migrations. Ibn Batuta, the great Arab explorer, reported back in the thirteenth century seeing two-man catamarans that had arrived in Zanzibar, from Indonesia. Here again, with their split squaresails, and the southeast monsoon driving them steadily, they would have been able to rig the helm.

But back to the late twentieth century, which, after all, is much more fascinating, if only because we're in it.

FENGER RIG   The usual type of specially made wingsails are boomed out on either standard spinnaker poles or specially made running poles, from the mainmast. It is advisable to have the poles angled out ten degrees forward from a line abeam of the mast in light to moderate winds and twenty-five to thirty degrees in strong winds, that is over thirty knots to thirty-five. In winds stronger than that I would not use this rig, unless I could reef down the wing sails.

The poles are also cocked up about thirty degrees from the horizontal to keep them from dipping into the ocean and preventing serious damage from the sails filling with seawater.

With this rig, the helm is left free, and it is simply a matter of watching for changes in the wind strength, so as to adjust the angle of the booms before the mast. In my experience with this rig, the boat tended to yaw quite heavily, up to fifty degrees each side of the course, and she rolled mightily. The solution to the rolling was to hoist a forty-five-pound Danforth anchor up the mast to the height of the spreaders and lash it there. This had the effect of raising the center of gravity, reducing the pendulum motion quite effectively.

The advantage of the Fenger system (named after a solo sailor of the thirties, who first thought it out) is that there is practically no chafe of the sails or the cordage. Everything is very stiff. Of course it only works with the wind well abaft the beam, but then, on the usual ocean runs, the wind usually is in that quarter. If it isn't, then we must take a look at "Tristan's System," which is a rig I have used in various types of vessels, sloops, cutters, yawls, ketches, and schooners. In any reasonably well balanced, not too cranky vessel, this will serve the purpose with the wind from anywhere abeam to dead astern on either tack.

TRISTAN'S SYSTEM   Here we use the staysail (or the jib, if we don't have a stay'sl; it doesn't work quite as well, but it will serve the purpose, giving us a track about fifty degrees each side of the course); we use the staysail and the main, whilst if we are in a mizzen-rigged vessel we hand that sail and forget it, at least until the wind blows hard enough for us to have to change rig to the next step, the "Eureka" system. In Tristan's System, the main is broad off to lee, foreguyed forward hard. Care must be taken that the main boom doesn't go dowsing itself in the sea. If it appears likely that it will, then it should be hauled up clear of the water with the topping lift. Don't worry too much about any sag or belly in the sail; in moderate to hard winds it will still serve its purpose, but you will have to look out for chafe on the shrouds and stays. Here, to prevent the sag, you can either reef the sail down a hand or two or lead small lines, one or two, back from the reef cringles to somewhere aft, so holding the sail off the stays.

The staysail or jib sheet is led aft, through a block, to the tiller, where it is secured. It pulls the tiller against a length of shock cord, which tries to pull the helm to leeward. You can use either shock cord or surgical tubing, which I prefer, as it is more sensitive.

The angle of the running pole, which holds out the stay'sl, should be about twenty-five to thirty degrees forward of the mast, and at this will work most efficiently with the pole angled at about sixty-five to seventy degrees from the direction of the apparent wind.

No special sails are required for this rig. The only extra equipment needed is a length of strong shock cord (which no boat should be without, anyway).

Should the main jibe (accidents happen in the best-regulated families), all you need to do is release the stay'sl sheet from the helm, put the helm hard over on the opposite side to the main, upon which, after a few seconds, the stay'sl will flog over and fill, bringing the boat right around (wearing her) and so getting the wind back on the after side of the main again. Then you set the gear up as before. But if care is taken with the angle of the stay'sl boom, a jibe should not happen, except by a very sudden shift in the wind, an unusual thing out in the ocean.

In winds above forty knots I would not run under this rig. I would dowse it and run under hand steering, reefed main and spitfire.

"EUREKA!" RIG For yawls and ketches, there is another heavy-weather rig that will steer the boat quite well. This I puzzled out whilst in the Indian Ocean in a thirty-eight-foot yawl, shallow draft, center board, whilst running with a northeast monsoon wind, about forty knots on my port quarter, from the Seychelles to Madagascar. Two of us had been hand-steering for two days, watch on, watch on, with the electronic auto pilot as dead as a dodo and us getting more than fed up. I decided we'd had enough, and, after flattening the mizzen broad off (we had been doing a steady six knots under genoa and mizzen), I then backed the genoa. After an hour's fiddling about, the Eureka is what came up. The boat lost about three-quarters of a knot of speed, but held the course quite well, not wandering off more than forty degrees, but always coming back, and we bucketed along very easily at five knots for six days under this easy and safe rig. It works with the wind anywhere from dead abeam to dead astern, though the farther aft the wind is, the more the yawing. The ideal course under the Eureka rig is with the wind broad on either quarter.

I had a reefing mizzen, and in the last two days of this passage we encountered a cyclone, with winds of well over sixty knots. With this rig, using the No. 2 jib and the reefed mizzen, we bowled along very comfortably. After two days, though, the cyclone increased, so I hoisted the spitfire, dowsed the mizzen, and ran before it, hand-steering for three days, until we fetched up in the lee of Cape Ambre. In subsequent rough passages in the Strait of Mozambique, however, again we used this rig, and again it stood up very well. The only possible chafe is where the mizzen is hard up against its shrouds (I wrapped and served old rags around the shrouds) and where the clew of the headsail is taken under the mainmast shrouds. Here I rigged up a line from the clew to a small block on the toerail forward, and this kept the clew clear of the mast.

The setting up of an efficient system of self-steering under sail by mizzen-rigged vessels had been for years a subject of great argument. To celebrate our figuring out of the Eureka System, my mate and I went ashore and downed a big bottle of the best champagne. In Majunga, at northwest Madagascar, at Madame Chapeau's, the biggest *Maison de joie* in the Indian Ocean. Well, you can't be dead on course all the time, now can you?

Accommodations

Fitting Out a Cabin for
Long-Distance Ocean Voyaging

Twenty-four years of full-time living in small craft have led me to the conclusion that at sea, in any but the balmiest weather, such craft must be the most awkward, most uncomfortable, and pokiest abodes in existence. But in harbor they can be the coziest, most welcoming, cheeriest dwellings in the world.

A typical ocean solo sailor's craft would at first sight probably give the uninitiated visitor the horrors when he steps onboard as she lays alongside or at anchor in port. There will usually not be a lick of varnish anywhere to be seen. There will be clothes in various states of wear and disrepair hanging all over the topsides. There will be an unfinished sail repair in full swing on the foredeck, the day's meal steaming away in the galley, and a bilge pump in bits in the cockpit. It will seem chaotic. But ask the skipper if you can borrow a number fourteen sail needle, or a one-inch thimble, or a pipe wrench or a three-eighths-inch shackle, and the alacrity with which the sought-after gear is located will indeed be a surprise.

A true sailor never leaves anything that is not in use out of its stowage. The single-hander is so particular about this that he might seem to be overfussy, until you realize the reason. Everything on board must be controlled.

STOWAGE One of the most important things below is good stowage. In this respect the best system is to have a lot of little lockers. Then anything you have to find can be got at easily, without having to dig it out from under a pile of other items.

The aim should be to keep the working gear of the boat—tools, sails, spares, lines—out of the main cabin. Sails, lines, and spares

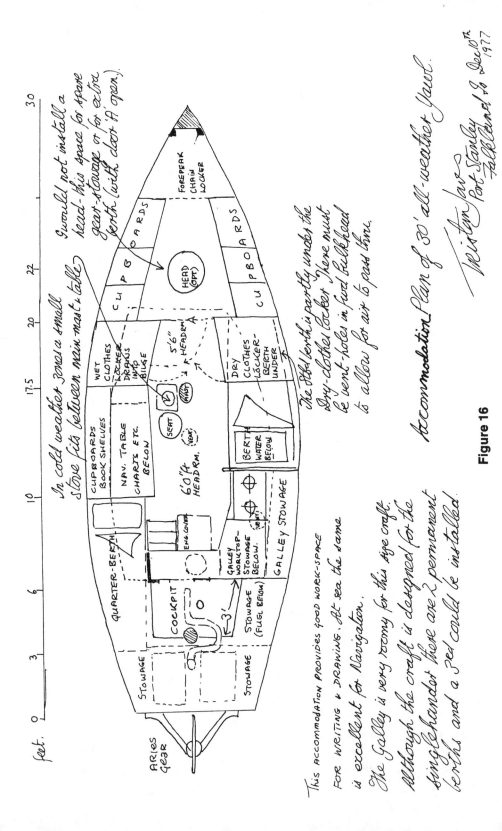

feet. 0   3   6   10   17.5   20   22   30

In cold weather stows a small stove fits between main mast & table

I would not install a head - this space for spare gear - stowage or for extra berth (with door 'A' open).

FOREPEAK CHAIN LOCKER

C L I P B O A R D S

HEAD (OPT)

CUPBOARDS

WET CLOTHES LOCKER DRAINS INTO BILGE

CUPBOARDS BOOK SHELVES

NAV. TABLE CHARTS ETC. BELOW

5'6" HEADRM A

MAST

SEAT

VENT

6'0½" HEADRM.

DRY CLOTHES LOCKER - BERTH UNDER

QUARTER-BERTH

ENG.COVRD

BERTH WATER BELOW

The Stbd. berth is partly under the dry-clothes locker. There must be vent-holes in fwd Bulkhead to allow for air to pass thru.

COCKPIT

3'

GALLEY WORKTOP - STOWAGE BELOW.

VENT

STOWAGE

STOWAGE (FUEL BELOW)

GALLEY STOWAGE

ARIES GEAR

This accommodation provides good work-space for writing & drawing. At sea the same is excellent for Navigation.
The Galley is very roomy for this size craft.
Although the craft is designed for the singlehander there are 2 permanent berths and a 3rd could be installed.

Accommodation Plan of 30' all-weather yawl.

Tristan Jones
Port Stanley
Falkland Is Dec 10th 1977

Figure 16

should be stowed up forward—the sails and lines ideally in the fore-peak, the spares in drawers in the section between the mast and the forepeak. Paint and other flammables should also go here. Tools should, if possible, be stowed in an after space, handy to the cockpit, which is where most work is done when in harbor. This leaves the main cabin clear for passage and the stowage of navigation equipment, charts, books, food, fresh water, and personal effects.

FRESH WATER In a vessel at sea it is vital that the fresh water supply be secure so that there will be no loss through leakage or waste, and the tanks should be accessible both inside and out.

Fresh water, being the most precious commodity on board the boat, should never be stored in one container. It should be in at least two tanks, even better four or more. Each tank must be fitted so that it can be isolated from all the others on the suction and filling systems. Apart from guarding against losing all the water, which would happen if only one tank were fitted and developed a leak, using a number of tanks breaks up the "free surface area" of the fresh water, which otherwise would affect the stability of the craft in rough conditions (see *Figure 17*).

At sea you should count on a consumption of two and a half gallons per week per person. This means that fresh water should not be used for some types of cooking or for washing dishes. Instead, sea water should be used, by either fitting a cock on the engine-cooling water inlet pipe, or by the much better bucket-over-the-side method.

The cockpit awning should be fitted up to catch rainwater, but this should never be added to good shore fresh water, because even out on the high seas rainwater is brackish and holds pollutants that cause it to go off after a while. Keep the rainwater in jerry cans and use it before the shore water. Rainwater is especially good for washing clothes. Sea water isn't much good for this because it never dries properly, so the clothes have to be rinsed in fresh water anyway. Of course, your only chance to have a shower is when it rains.

If an electric fresh water pump is fitted, there should also be a hand pump in case of power failure. There should be an arrangement for getting at the fresh water in case of failure of the hand pump, too. There should be hand-hole covers on each tank, tightly sealed yet easily removable and large enough to get your hand in with a pint mug in case it should be necessary to bail out the fresh water.

If the fresh water tanks are steel, there should be no brass or copper in contact with them, or there will be electrolysis problems,

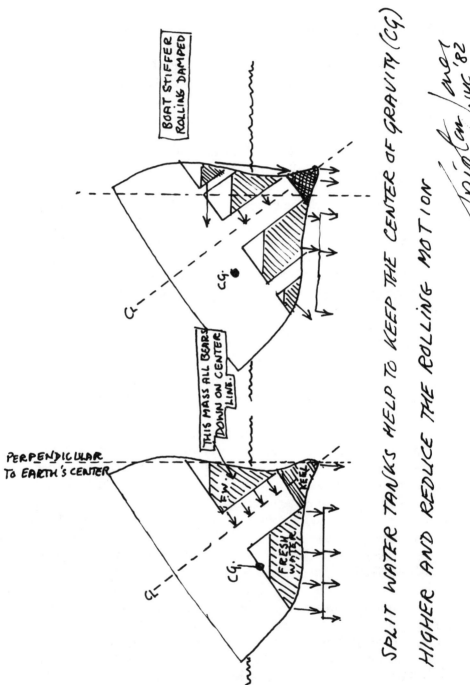

BOAT STIFFER ROLLING DAMPED

SPLIT WATER TANKS HELP TO KEEP THE CENTER OF GRAVITY (CG) HIGHER AND REDUCE THE ROLLING MOTION

C.G.

CG

THIS MASS ALL BEARS DOWN ON CENTER LINE.

PERPENDICULAR TO EARTH'S CENTER

C.G.

CG

F.W.

FRESH WATER

KEEL

Tristan Jones NYC '82

Figure 17

and the risk of losing all the fresh water in a tank, especially if it is in contact with the bilge.

In vessels with limited fresh water capacity, on an ocean crossing, a good idea is to install a ready-use tank. This can be a container large enough to carry one day's fresh water supply for the boat. The day's supply is pumped into it, and that amount only is used for that day. A clear plastic container installed above the galley sink, with a gravity-feed, positive shut-off faucet, is best, since the rate of usage is obvious at all times.

The reason I put the fresh water under the main cabin is that it will be kept from freezing in cold-weather areas. For the same purpose there must be a flow of air between the boat's side and the tank. Any insulation must be removable, and the space between the tank and the hull wide enough to enable the ship's side to be accessible in case of damage to the hull. This space need not be wasted, since it can be used for the stowage of canned food, well sealed in plastic bags to protect it from any bilge water that might slop up the sides in heavy weather.

Another advantage to placing the water tanks under the main cabin is that it is amidships, so a heavy mass is being stowed where it should be, and not toward the ends of the boat, where it would adversely affect buoyancy; buoyancy at the ends of the boat is almost as essential as a fresh water supply.

FOOD   An average adult needs about 5 pounds of food per day. For a six-week Atlantic crossing, this means 210 pounds of food. Add onto that an emergency margin of 25 percent, and the total is 262 pounds.

If we average out the weight of the bulk (the space it takes up) at 30 pounds to the cubic foot, we get a figure of 34 cubic feet of food stowage. About half of the food can be stowed in odd spaces (such as atop and alongside the water tanks), but the other half needs a stowage of its own. So there must be 16 cubic feet of food stowage space in or near the galley. Here, such items as flour, sugar, dried milk, tea, and cereal will be stowed, protected from damp and heat.

If a refrigerator is fitted, its bulk will have to come out of the 16 cubic feet. This leaves a parsimonious space for dried foods—one of the reasons I would not have a fridge on board. A portable icebox, perhaps, since when empty it can be stowed anywhere. A can of corned beef is many times more dependable than fifty thawing pork chops sitting in a fridge that depends on a compressor driven by an engine with the big-end gone in mid-Pacific.

The stowages for dried and/or perishable food stores must be protected from possible damage by bilge water slopping up in heavy weather or when the boat is heeled. The main galley stowage should be completely watertight. The dried food stowage must be a container separated from the ship's side, like the water tanks. Yet at the same time the hull behind the dried food stowage must be accessible. This is achieved by having a removable panel in an opening at the back of the box fastened against a rubber sealing gasket. Again, well-sealed cans of food can go in the space between the hull and the box.

The top of the dried food compartment becomes the galley working table and is topped with stainless steel or plastic. It has two-inch fiddles, removable when in harbor.

Below the stove I would have an oven for baking bread. It would not be used often, but the space would not be wasted when not in use because, being on gimbals, it would become a space where liquid (such as melted fat, reconstituted milk, etc.) could be safely stowed at sea with little fear of spillage. Bread does not bake properly in any kind of seaway, so when baking is being done, the movement of the boat would be gentle enough to trust the spillable liquids to the galley shelves. Otherwise, bake in a pressure cooker.

LOCKERS   The dry and wet clothes hanging lockers are just forward of the main mast, in a position close to the forward hatch. In harbor or in fine weather at sea, when not beating, these lockers can be aired by making provision for their doors to be held ajar. The dry clothes hanging locker would be sealed completely from the bilge below, whilst there would be drainage holes in the wet hanging space.

FURNITURE   No part of the internal furniture should be fitted so that it could not be unshipped or taken apart in a matter of a few seconds; at the same time, each part would be able to take a 200-pound weight colliding with it at speed. I know that unless this is very carefully thought out and constructed, it will detract from the aesthetic view of the accommodations. This is of minor import. I want to be able to get at any part of the hull from inside the vessel in a very short time without having to wield an ax. For example, the big navigation-cum-working table should be detachable from the hull by a series of sliding bolts. The same goes for the library shelves, in case I need to get at the ship's side in a hurry.

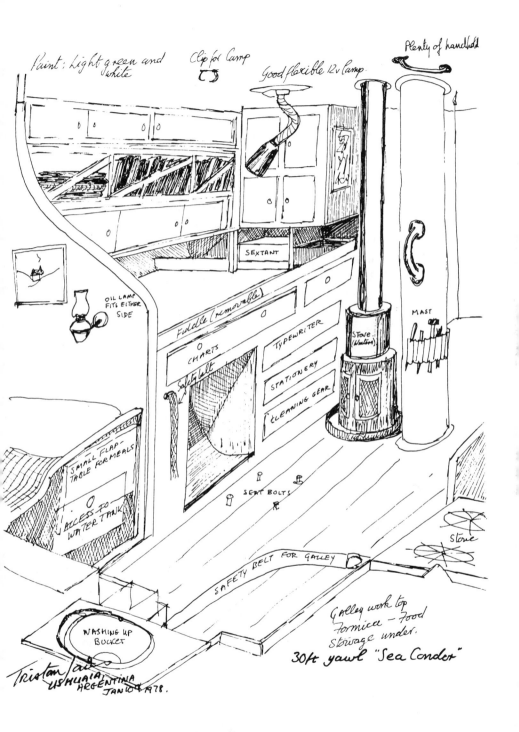

Figure 18

I don't have a center table because, being alone, I don't need a big table to eat on. The advantage to a single-hander in not having such a table is great, because it gives him plenty of clear passage when he is lugging big sailbags or anchors through the boat from the forepeak aft; also it means that he has immediate access to any part of the keel and garboard inside the boat. The advantages of this far outweigh the smallness of the eating table fitted either on the quarterberth or the ship-side berth. It seems to make the cabin twice as roomy. If you do expect to be rich enough to invite people on board for meals, then you might carry a folding table sturdy enough to rig up in the center of the cabin on those occasions, and seating that would be slung from fittings on the berths.

The working table is set against the ship's side, where normally a berth would be. The reason I have this huge (by boat standards) table is because I do a lot of writing when at anchor and a good amount of survey work when on remote coasts, so I need an extensive surface to work on. I have fitted a small eating table on the side of the quarter berth, and use the companionway steps as a seat for meals.

Drawers. All the drawers in the vessel should be of the lift-and-pull type. This eliminates the consequences of latches failing (see *Figure 19*).

Bunks. In a long-distance sailboat a lot of time is spent in bed, so the size of the bunks is important. The minimum length of berths should be about seven feet. The width of the berths should take into account the area to be sailed. In cold-weather areas the sleeper needs to be as tightly cozy as possible, so a width of three feet is fine. But in hot climates the wider the better, to allow plenty of air to flow around the body, and here I would say a width of three feet six inches. The foot of the berth need not be as wide as the head, of course, but this is desirable if it can be arranged.

I like to have two berths. This gives me the option of sleeping on the lee side of the boat regardless of what tack she is on, while if I do have company there is somewhere for him or her to sleep. With one of my berths on the quarter I would probably use that the most, since it doesn't need a lee-canvas or board and there is no risk of being thrown out in a heavy sea. In the tropics the quarter berth is a pleasure to sleep in, since I am near the helm, can look up through the companionway and can check the course by the stars at night without having to get up.

I personally find that the compass heading of the boat when she is

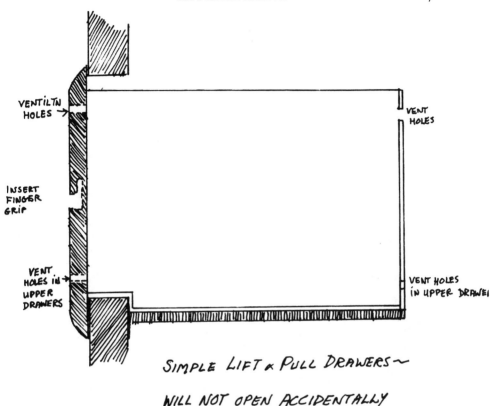

VENTILTN HOLES →

VENT HOLES

INSERT FINGER GRIP

VENT HOLES IN UPPER DRAWERS →

VENT HOLES IN UPPER DRAWEI

SIMPLE LIFT & PULL DRAWERS ~

WILL NOT OPEN ACCIDENTALLY

Tristan Jones NYC 1982.
ⓒ.

Figure 19

at anchor affects my sleeping a great deal, and I sleep much more soundly on a north or east heading that I do on a south or west in the Northern Hemisphere, and vice versa in the Southern. This is very handy when it wakes me through a change of course while on self-steering, or when the boat rides at two anchors and the keel passes over the mooring. But around the equator it is confusing, and for days I have been disoriented in my sleep. With berths that can be slept in either way, this problem is diminished.

VENTILATION   The problem with quarter berths is ventilation, so at the after end of mine I have a small watertight hatch, to allow a flow of air to come down through the companionway, along the top of my body to my feet, and out into the after compartment. In cold or heavy weather this hatch is shut.

In the tropics a good flow of cool air throughout the boat makes all the difference between comfort and purgatory, especially when lying at anchor, perhaps behind the lee of high land. I provide for this with a large hatch forward in the cabin, which opens from the after side when at sea and from the forward side when at anchor. In still or slight breeze anchorages, a windcatcher is led down to the hatch to pass the air down below. All the athwartship bulkheads have small hatches placed in their lower surfaces, which are opened when in harbor to allow a flow of fresh air to pass through them, so preventing mildew from forming on clothes, charts, etc.

LIGHT   I do not like large windows and/or ports in a cabin. They detract from the structural strength of the hull and topsides. If windows are fitted in the ship's side, as indeed they were in *Sea Dart*, they are subject to the hazard of being struck by floating or semi-submerged flotsam, especially in areas off the mouths of tropical rivers. In *Sea Dart* I blocked the windows up inboard with one-inch marine ply to reduce the hazard of a sudden sinking. After a while at sea, large windows below detract from a sense of security.

A lot of light below is not a luxury. It's a necessity. I have several hefty skylights—the small round pattern—set in the coachroof and the long narrow pattern close inboard on the side decks and foredeck, where there's less chance of slipping on them. The amount of light they cast below is surprising. I also have a Plexiglas semidome set into the companionway hatch cover, so that in heavy or wet weather I can see what is happening all around topsides without having to open the hatch cover. When the hatch is closed, this provides good lighting for the galley and the engine space.

Artificial Lighting. If electricity is available, I have three lights in the main cabin, each on a flexible fitting so they can be positioned at any angle. One is over the navigation table, one is over the galley, and one is just forward of the mast, where it has to be so made that once in position the light can be rigidly fixed at that angle. On each flexible fitting there should be two lights—one white for daytime use or when at anchor at night, the other red for nighttime use at sea, when I do not want to lose my night vision, even when I'm only making a cup of tea. The electrical system is ring-main—that is, one continuous cable running right around the boat with plugs positioned at conveniently accessible intervals, to which wandering leads can be connected should I want to get into any poky corners.

In the center line of the boat I have two or three fluorescent lights, which are economical on electricity, for use in arctic conditions when the skylights must be blocked off to preserve heat below.

Apart from the electric lights, I carry one big, high-power kerosene pressure lamp. In the tropics this is positioned at the top of the companionway ladder so it casts its brilliant light below and its heat rises up into the open night air. There are also at least two kerosene reading lamps set in gimbaled brackets, and several bulkhead fittings to which the lamp brackets can be shifted, to reposition the lamps. If I'm not using a berth, I don't need a light over it.

DECORATING THE CABIN I often go on board other people's craft and see inside the cabin several pictures of yachts at sea. I can never understand why anyone inside of a yacht wants to look at a picture of a yacht at sea. All he has to do is go topsides.

I sometimes get the impression that landlubbers look upon voyagers, especially single-handers, as philistines interested in nothing but back-splices and beer. This is simply not so. Alcard, Bardieaux, Moitessier, Tangvald—all these and many more could discuss any aspect of art for hours on end. I never met a true voyager who did not appreciate art in all its forms.

I personally find that a still life or a country or city scene is tranquilizing. Something with a house in it, or one of the old cathedrals. Horse racing scenes are, for some reason, attractive in a boat, at least to me. I can't imagine why, since I've rarely placed a bet in my life, except *with* my life. Cézanne's still lifes, mainly of fruit and wine, are peaceful when everything else around me is in an uproar of violence. In each of his works he hacks order out of chaos. Just the thing to look at after reefing the main.

Paint. Varnish, especially over extensive surfaces down below, is anathema to me. After several weeks it becomes as depressing as sitting in an undertaker's parlor.

Several years ago I realized that varnish is conducive to seasickness. I found that the surface coating least jarring on the nerves, and where the fewest effects of seasickness were felt, was pale green, flat pale green, with decks dark green. I have used this color paint down below for several years. Edward Lear was well on track when he wrote, "The owl and the pussycat went to sea in a beautiful pea-green boat."

HEAD   There are many different types, and the one I thoroughly recommend, without the slightest hesitation, is a fourteen-inch-diameter rubber bucket, with a good codline lanyard bent onto the handle. Anyone who has ever tried to unblock the mechanical type of head, with all its bends and valves, in a tiny little cupboard of a compartment whilst the boat is heaving to the ocean swells will know why. There is always somewhere on deck with enough privacy for the ablutions of even the shyest wilting lily. And if you can't stand the sight of someone doing this, you shouldn't be sailing with that person.

INSULATION   For cold-weather areas much can be done to alleviate the discomfort brought on by the weather. The deckhead and sides of the coachroof and the hull can be insulated. The cheapest way to do this is simply to get some aluminum foil from the supermarket and stick it up on these surfaces with glue. It's a lot cheaper than cork or other types of insulation material, it lessens the fire risk, and, when the boat gets back to a moderate or warm climate, the foil can be removed and with it the layer of smut that will, no matter how much you try to prevent it, emanate from the kerosene-burning lamps and stove.

I position the heating stove between the mast and the table, because the flow of air from the one dorade ventilator passes over the stove and so heats my working and sleeping space by convection current. There is no danger of falling onto the stove in rough weather, simply because I never have a heating stove working at sea. Out sailing, I close off all the ventilators except one, keep the hatch-board in and the cover closed except when in use, and depend on the cooking stove to take the edge off the bitter bite of wintry winds. At sea, the rest of it is good warm woolen clothing and blankets. In arctic conditions it does not pay to have too much kerosene vapor issuing into the cabin, since it contains a large amount of water. This settles on the inner sides of the weather surfaces, such as the deckhead and the hull and turns to ice when the heating stops. When the heating recommences, it melts, and soon everything in the boat is wet through. For this reason the main heating stove burns solid fuel, either charcoal or wood. Charcoal is best, because the water content is practically nil.

The ports and skylights, in very cold conditions, must be insulated from the inside, as glass allows a lot of heat to pass through very quickly. Here I have felt flaps to button over any skylights not in use. I have a fluorescent light on a wandering lead, so that I may read in my bunk whilst wrapped in blankets to save fuel.

GALLEY Shelves and cupboards have fiddles and sliding doors to prevent them from spilling their contents when shocks run through the boat. Cups hang clear of one another on hooks screwed into the deckhead above the galley working space.

Tableware. Most of the tableware I have seen is unfit for sea. Cups should be sturdy, pint-size mugs, broader at the base than at the rim. Most of the plates on the market are poorly designed for use at sea. The ideal boat's plate would be shaped like a dog's dinner bowl, with a wide outside base and a deep crater. It would have a rubber gasket on the bottom to prevent sliding when the boat keels over suddenly.

Spoons should have a deep bowl, like a ladle, and knives should not have pointed blades; they can be very dangerous if someone loses his balance whilst holding one.

The galley stove should be kerosene-burning and fitted on gimbals fore and aft. The gimbals should be at the same level as the burners, or there will be a pendulum motion and a neurotic and weary cook.

Kerosene is the safest cooking fuel because it can be obtained almost anywhere ashore and there is small risk of explosion or fire. But the burners, despite being fitted with self-pricking devices, still get blocked up, and there are a lot of little fiddling parts to them, so plenty of spares should be taken on board.

Although I have sailed in several boats with butane stoves, which are far easier than kerosene stoves to maintain and operate—also far cleaner—and although I personally have had no problems with butane, I still do not recommend butane for an ocean passage. There is always that nagging suspicion of a leak, always that sniffng around. I would certainly not depend for very long on any electrical sniffing device, and there is always the hassle of having to change from one connection to another whenever you change countries, though this is mainly not the case in Western Europe nowadays nor, I would presume, in the States. Still, it's that feeling in midocean, when the nearest land is over a thousand miles away, that you have a potential bomb sitting on deck.

A small diesel-run stove would be ideal, of course, especially for Arctic cruising, but for me it would have to be a gravity system, or a hand-pumped pressure system. I've seen too many problems in big

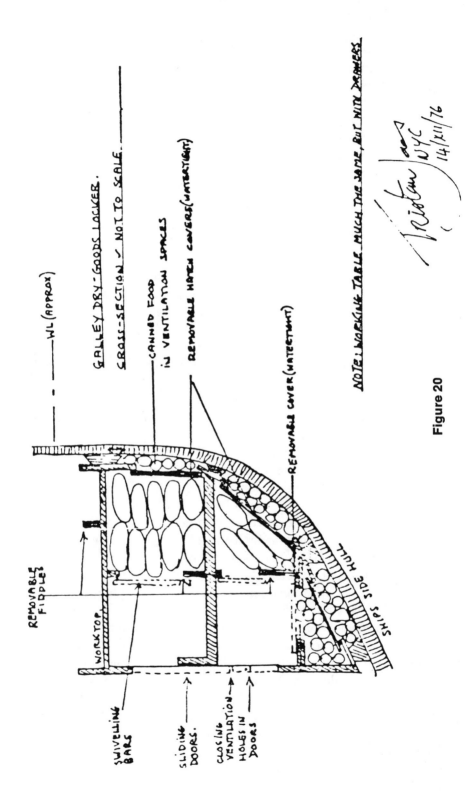

GALLEY DRY-GOODS LOCKER.
CROSS-SECTION ~ NOT TO SCALE.

WL (APPROX)

CANNED FOOD
IN VENTILATION SPACES

REMOVABLE HATCH COVERS (WATERTIGHT)

REMOVABLE COVER (WATERTIGHT)

SHIPS SIDE HULL

REMOVABLE
FIDDLES

WORKTOP.

SWIVELLING
BARS

SLIDING
DOORS.

CLOSING
VENTILATION
HOLES IN
DOORS

NOTE: WORKING TABLE MUCH THE SAME, BUT WITH DRAWERS

14/XII/76

Figure 20

yachts with electrically pumped diesel burners and electric blowers. Beware. Much of the time, as far as I could see, the crews ate uncooked meals.

Refrigerator. In my opinion, anyone who sets off on a four-year cruise with one will return home an expert in refrigeration repairs, but he won't know much about the places he has been to. Freeze-dried food does not need a fridge.

Keeping food hot. An efficient, cheap way of keeping food hot for long periods is to make a "hay-box." This method has been used among fishermen in northern waters for more than a century. The thin metal liner is made for a tight fit around the pressure cooker. It is placed in the hay-box body and lid, and then fine hay is compressed, as tightly as it will go, into the spaces around the outside of the thin metal frames. It can then be tacked into position using fine mesh, fine-gauge metal netting, if required, but it will be found in practice that after several days the few loose strands of hay will all have fallen out and the remainder will stay in place if the box is kept strapped down. Enough food for two or three sittings can be cooked very quickly in one session, thus saving a great amount of cooking fuel and, in the tropics, keeping the cabin from getting overheated, especially at midday. The method is to cook the food, with a pressure cooker according to the instructions given, and when it is done remove all steam over atmospheric pressure by releasing the weighted pressure valve. The lid is kept on. The pressure cooker is then placed in the hay-box and will continue to cook very gently for about six hours. It will keep hot for up to twenty hours.

In cold-weather areas the lid of the hay-box must be kept shut as much as possible.

In this manner a single-hander can cook all his food, for the following three meals, before breakfast.

If a smaller hay-box is made for the large Thermos flask, coffee or tea will stay piping hot for twenty-four hours and more.

The use of this simple appliance can cut kerosene consumption down by as much as 60 percent.

The thicker the box sides, the better, and of course the lid must be a close fit. Handles have to be riveted onto the top of the pressure cooker lid, as the regular handle must be removed to allow the pot to sink into the liner in the box.

MEDICAL SUPPLIES   All I ever carried in the way of medical gear was sufficient bandages and gauze for a sizable axe wound, splints, iodine,

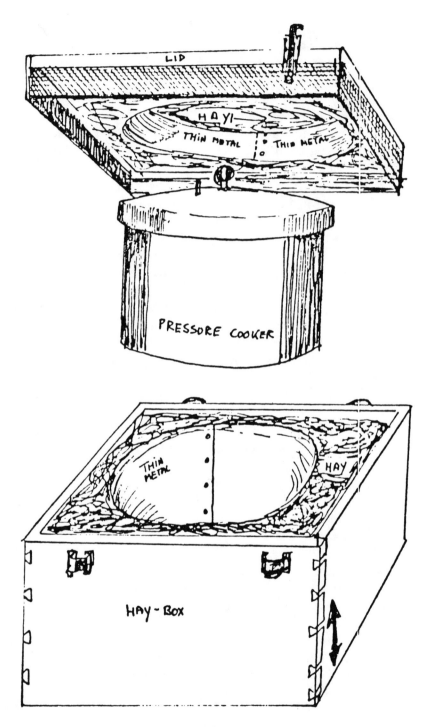

Figure 21

painkillers, burn ointment, a sewing kit with catgut, and scissors. Oh, yes, and a half bottle of Napoleon brandy, which proved very handy when on three occasions I had to take my own tooth out. If I'd been able to afford it, I would have visited a doctor and a dentist before any transoceanic passage. But if that is not possible, then anyone who doesn't feel in good health (I mean able to jog at least a mile without becoming out of breath), anyone who cannot do that and takes off on what might (but for the most part may not) be a strenuous passage is a fool. If he's on his own, he's taking a tremendous risk, which is unseamanlike.

Anyway, apart from the basic items of first aid and simple treatment of burns or fractures, I would only delve into anything else (having, of course, read up on simple surgery quite a lot) in case of life or death, where the subject, unless something is done quickly, is likely to die anyway. In that case, if I was absolutely sure that I could not get the person to a doctor, I would do whatever was necessary. Of course, if I did have a radio, then I would try to raise expert advice and follow instructions passed from whomever I was in contact with.

Apart from the teeth I was forced to extract myself with a pair of vise grips, a most painful experience, the only troubles I have had were broken ribs (on five occasions), an eye almost out of its socket, concussion from being hit by the boom (twice), and a broken arm from being thrown across the cockpit by a heavy sea (once). Also malaria, dysentery, etc.—the normal run of tropical ailments.

Before undertaking a transoceanic voyage alone, consult a doctor and read one of the excellent books available on the subject. Safe painkillers can be had on prescription, but you must be very careful of carrying drugs such as morphine or even amphetamines to some countries, where they may be used as an excuse to chuck you in jail and lose the key. If in doubt, inquire at those countries' consulates in your own land before departure, as to what is allowed.

Scraps of Navigation

ANY would-be long-distance voyager must learn as much as he can about navigation before he sets off. Not only celestial navigation, but also inshore and coastal pilotage, too.

Ocean navigation, even in the remotest waters of the world, is comparatively simple when compared with coastal pilotage, especially in the mainly unfrequented, often ill-charted, mostly unlit and unbuoyed coasts of many Third World countries. Voyages along the Red Sea, or the East African coasts, or the South American coast, for example, are many times more hazardous than any ocean crossing. Ask any ocean voyager, and I am sure he will tell you that he would rather cross the Atlantic than tackle the treacherous mouth of the River Amazon, the Newfoundland Banks, or the Strait of Gibraltar in winter.

The general rule is: Keep clear of the coasts unless it is unavoidable for the sake of reaching a destination. Where a coastal or inter-island passage is necessary, make sure that you have the corrected up-to-date charts and tidal information for the area. Get in as much practice, preferably with experienced skippers, in your own waters, as you can, before tackling strange coasts. In this way you will have much more interesting side trips on your way around the world, for you will have the confidence to undertake them. I would advise a winter passage along New England or the West Coast of the United States for starters.

A lot of people seem to imagine that sailing in the tropics is all blue skies, gentle winds, and waving palm trees. Often it is not so, by any means. It frequently entails very high winds, sudden squalls, uncharted reefs, unknown currents, very low visibility in heavy rain, and sometimes, for example on the coast of South America, fog, overcast skies, and open, unprotected roadsteads.

Probably more ocean-voyaging yachts have been lost in coastal and island waters than were ever lost out in the open sea. For this reason the average long-distance voyager keeps clear of the land whenever he can. But as you may have to go inshore, then it is up to you to know as much about pilotage as you can.

The subject of pilotage is so complex and involved that to go into it in detail would keep me occupied full time for the next five years, and even after that time I would have to bring myself up to date again. So I will deal with it in a very general way, presuming that you have made several coastal passages under sail in varying seasons and that you have read and digested thoroughly Chapman's *Piloting*, an excellent authority on the craft.

You will have noticed, on your passages in home waters, that the character of the sea bottom close to the shore is very often indicated by the lay of the land as it falls to the sea. When piloting in ill-charted waters, this "lay of the land" can be very useful indeed if you understand it. Steep hills close to the shore usually mean plenty of water close inshore. Steep, rocky hills with a broken-up appearance usually indicate the possibility of off-lying rocks. Gently rising hills often mean that the sea bottom falls away from the shore gently, with less probability of off-lying rocks. Vertical cliffs sometimes indicate that instead of deep water at their base, which would logically be expected, there is instead a fault in the rock structure, and the part that has subsided is, in fact, lying close to the base of the cliff in very shallow water.

Low-lying land and sandy beaches usually indicate shallow water close inshore, whilst marshland often means shallow water out some distance.

Volcanic shore and islands usually have very steep-to shores, with plenty of water right up to the coast, but beware of off-lying rocks and reefs.

Coral islands, on their windward side, usually are steep-to, but on the lee side there will be off-lying reefs and coral heads poking up very suddenly to ambush the unwary. In atolls there are usually one or two passages into the lagoon. They will be on the leeward side. They have been scored by the tidal currents over the centuries. Beware, coral grows at a rapid rate, and unfrequented coral shores and coasts should be approached carefully, if possible with the sun behind you to show up any hazards. No charts of unfrequented coral passages should be trusted, no matter how up-to-date they are. In some areas of the world a coral growth can expand out of all recognition in a matter of months.

Some people rig ratlines up the shrouds in order to get up high in the boat when conning into a tricky passage, but I do not like the extra windage aloft. I go as high as I can by the base of the mast, or even stand on the inboard end of the mainboom. That, in *Sea Dart*, got my eyes about double the height they would have been if I had remained in the cockpit, which was sufficient. My draft, however, was only four feet six inches.

If you can, always take note of your course when entering an ill-charted or tricky passage, by either taking bearings or noting the headings as you take soundings. That way you will find it easier to get out of the place again. And bear in mind you might have to leave at night, or when the sun is ahead.

There are some parts of the world where the nature of the sea bottom is severely affected, at irregular intervals, by underwater earthquakes (such as the north coast of Brazil). Here the charts may be hopelessly wrong even though they were brought up-to-date last week. If you see, in the pilot book for the area, that seaquakes are liable to occur, keep well clear of the coast and approach any destination on that coast at right angles, carefully sounding your way in. If you come to shallow water where it should not be according to the chart, feel your way along its edge on a course parallel to the coast (as a general rule in the Northern Hemisphere from south to north or east to west, in the Southern Hemisphere from north to south or west to east. Note, I stress this is only a general rule). If you do not find a passage, then either stand out to sea and make for another destination, or, if there are other small craft about, lay to and, when one approaches, signal for her assistance in finding your way in. If you have a radio transmitter, you can try calling up the local authorities on 2182 Khz, but let me warn you, in most Third World countries you can talk into the microphone until you are blue in the face, with no result. The chances of getting picked up or noticed are about 15 percent in Africa and 5 percent in South America, with the exceptions perhaps of Argentina and Chile. In South America do not follow directions given by local small craft, wait and follow them when they go in. They may try to send you astray so as to wreck and loot you. The exceptions are Brazil, Argentina, Chile, and the Guyanas.

In the Mediterranean there is little problem, as the waters are highly frequented and information, except for the Arab countries and Turkey, is well diffused and up-to-date. Radio assistance is ready, and location beacons are many.

Various items of pilotage and inshore navigation gear are essential.

THE LOG   There are many electronic logs on the market. I have no doubt that they are well made of the finest materials, by experts in the field, and that in the waters of advanced regions, such as the United States, Australia, and Europe, they are a fine aid to pilotage. A long-distance voyager should not trust them; they get sea atmosphere in them, transistors blow, they depend on the engine batteries for power. If you do have one, make sure you also have an ordinary old-fashioned taffrail log, a mechanical contrivance that is streamed over the stern, and keep it well oiled with sewing machine oil. In areas with weeds floating around, such as the Sargasso weed in the Gulf Stream, the log will have to be checked regularly, to make sure its propeller is not fouled by weed. An easy aid to this is to lay a four-inch length of yellow ribbon into the log line, between the strands. As the long line revolves, it whizzes the ribbon around, which shows up very well against the sea background even at night. Another hazard to the log is the shark or other big fish. They are attracted to the propeller as to a small fish, and I have had half a dozen log lines bitten through. For this reason you should always have at least three spare log lines and propellers for an ocean crossing, or in remote waters. The log must be calibrated over a known distance before departure.

Each noon, when the latitude is taken, the log is compared to the run between yesterday's noon and today's. Given good sights and considering the general feel of the boat's passage through the water during the past twenty-four hours, any discrepancy between the dead reckoning positions as indicated by the log mileage readings and the position as indicated by celestial sights will suggest a current and also indicate the direction in which it is running.

The log spinner should be taken in whenever the boat is becalmed or hove-to, to prevent the log line becoming jammed between the rudder and the keel, or wrapped around the propeller shaft. The way to take in a log line without having a tangle of line is easy, but I am always surprised by the number of people who do it wrong. This is the correct way:

1. Carefully detach the line's inboard-end hook from the log.
2. Stream the "inboard" end into the sea astern of the boat.
3. As the "inboard" end goes out, the "outboard" end (propeller) is hauled in until the propeller is in hand.
4. Haul in the line, coiling it up as it comes on board. There will be no tangle.
5. Make sure the line is dry before stowing it away.

COMPASSES   There should be at least two compasses on board: the main compass (which must be "swung" before undertaking a voyage, so you know the amount of deviation on any given course) and a hand-bearing compass, which can also do triple duty as (a) a dinghy compass, in case of shipwreck, and (b) a 'tween-decks compass, for checking the course when down below. But it is better, if you can afford it, to have four, each specifically designed for its own purpose. Keep clear of the rigging when using the compass from the same position on deck each time. There are many makes of hand-bearing compass, and one of the most popular kinds carries flashlight batteries in the handle to power a small light for night use. I have never known one of these lights to operate for more than a few months, but the battery case comes in handy for holding the compass when taking a bearing.

The best hand-bearing compass, in my estimation, is made in Finland. It is a tiny thing, which can be hidden in the palm of the hand. It is about the same shape and size as the old English penny (an inch diameter), but thicker. There is a small sight that pops up, and readings are taken through a slot in the edge, from a vertical-reading compass with luminous points.

The dinghy compass should, of course, always be stowed with the emergency dinghy kit, near the companionway. It should be checked from time to time with the main compass, as, being necessarily stowed perhaps near magnetic materials, its deviation may change.

DEPTH FINDER   This is important inshore, but even in the ocean it can be of use, indicating that the continental shelf has been crossed, though the change in sea rhythm should tell you. But again, a long-distance voyager should not overtrust electronic gear. Have two hand leads, properly marked, and practice their use. Hand leads have coir ropes, so always dry them out thoroughly after use, or they will rot.

WIND-DIRECTION INDICATOR   There are some admirable models on the market. There are usually electronic instruments, which are rigged at the mast truck. They therefore create windage and are liable to be blown off in any kind of a heavy blow. From the masthead, electric wires are led through the inside of the mast (nice and handy) to the console over the companionway hatch. Here the wind gauge with its chromium rim and sparkling glass or clear plastic window sits, for people on the jetty to wonder at and admire. At sea it sits, just waiting for someone in a hurry to poke the end of the running pole or a fluke of the hurricane hook right through the glass. And, being electronic, the chances of it's working for any length of time or of being attended to by anyone capable of repairing it in Third World areas are about the same as the chances of my being accepted into the Franciscan Fathers. No, the best wind indicators ever dreamed up are all three hanging on your head—one on either side of it and one just above your mouth. Practice using them and, barring accidents, they will never wear out or let you down. And they are free.

OFF-COURSE INDICATORS I imagine that if ever a special nursing home is established for the care of mentally disturbed ocean voyagers, it will be found that 90 percent of the patients are people who fitted an off-course indicator on board their vessels. When self-steering, which the vessel will be for most of the passage, she will be off course about 40 percent of the time. She will, in any kind of sea, be even *off* off course time and again, and to have this hooter or bell or whatever sounding off fifty times an hour, day and night, is a torture that only Lucifer himself could have thought out. If you must have one, shut the thing off and use the ones that the good Lord provided us with: the sense of the boat's movement, the slight or otherwise sound of the rigging and sails. You can become so attuned to these that even when you're fast asleep any significant change of course or weather will awaken you.

SAIL TRIM INDICATORS For ocean voyagers, unless racing, these too, are conversation pieces for visitors on board whilst cocktails are served when you're moored stern-to in Monaco. The best, most efficient ones are provided by the finest instrument maker of all time, and they are just below your forehead. Use 'em. Any skipper who doesn't know, at any given moment, how his sails are trimmed shouldn't be at sea in the first place, and certainly not alone.

I'm not saying that these instruments have no place in any sailboats. For racing craft, where every puff of wind, every extra tug on a sheet is vital, they must be excellent, if not indispensable, but in a cruising craft they are just so much extra burden of cost, fitting, and maintenance. It is better to put the money involved into extra winches and spare sailing gear, such as running rig and sails.

CHART TABLE INSTRUMENTS You need parallel rules—one long and one short—compasses, dividers—two sets—a small T-square, a setsquare, and plenty of soft-lead pencils. A handy thing, if you have room for it, is a small blackboard upon which temporary notations can be made. The chalk for this must be kept in an airtight can.

Another handy item is a plastic chart case, in which the chart can be folded, brought up into the cockpit, and worked on with marker pencils when you are piloting single-handed along a coast. This case keeps the chart from getting soggy or blown over the side and saves having to continually clamber down below to look at the chart. It should be weighted.

Any long-distance voyager should have on board the necessary charts for his next cruising area. He need not have all the charts for the whole cruise, because in many instances he will meet people who have been where he is bound for, and who are bound for where he has been, and often they can swap. This can save a lot of money. But in case this does not happen, he should always carry a recent List of Charts, so that he can order what he needs as he goes along. I always have the next two areas' charts on board, and order the third when the first area is reached. For example, if I were heading from, say, San Francisco to Australia, I would have the charts for Hawaii and Samoa and the islands in between that I might expect to pass close to or even call at. Then, when I reached Hawaii, if I met no one there who was bound for the West Coast of the United States from Australia, and would therefore swap charts with me, I would order charts for Australia from Hawaii, to be delivered to Samoa. In that way, with any luck the charts would be waiting for me when I reached my second area. Then, if I was a round-the-worlder, at Samoa I would order charts for the Indian Ocean, after first ascertaining whether it might be cheaper to obtain them in Australia.

Going into the unfrequented areas, such as the Aleutian islands or the African or South American coasts, you should have the charts for the whole area, as the chances of meeting another yacht are almost nil. In some areas you may wish to take a side trip but not have the time to await the delivery of charts for the area. In this case you may find another yacht, or a local yachtsman, who, whilst unable to let you have his charts, may let you trace them. This, carefully done to take in all the salient features and all the hazards, will also save a lot of waiting time and money.

With regard to obtaining local knowledge, advice from locals must be accepted with a grain of salt. The best sources are harbor pilots, fishermen and storekeepers (who don't want you wrecked; they'd lose a customer). In remote areas of the Third World, trust no one in this, especially not the police. Whilst on this matter, if you come across a fellow countryman in a very remote area alone, be wary. Some have valid reason to be where they are, others do not. Whatever happens, you don't want his political relations with the locals affecting yours. This might sound callous, but bear in mind that your first loyalty is to your vessel. Do nothing that might affect her well-being and safety, and your freedom.

NAVIGATOR'S CHECKLIST

Sextant
Chronometer
Stopwatch
Log
Spare propeller for log
Spare line(s) for log
Lubricating oil for log
Compasses (2)
Hand-bearing compass
Depthfinder
Binoculars
Hand lead and weight
Wind-direction indicator
Off-course indicator
Heel indicator
Sail trim indictor
Electronic hand calculator
Batteries for the above
Transoceanic radio receiver
Batteries for the above for two years
Radio direction finder
Batteries for the above
Parallel rules, short
Parallel rules, long
Chart compasses
Dividers (2)
T-square
Setsquare
Soft-lead pencils (not round)

Erasers
Small blackboard
Chalk in airtight container
Plastic chart case
Ball-point pens
Marker pencils
List of Charts
HO 249 Volumes 1, 2 and 3
Nautical Almanac
Tide tables
Pilot books (or sailing directions)
Star finder
World atlas
Chart paper (for constructing charts)
Logbook
Notebooks
Metric conversion tables
Ruler, inches and metric
Bowditch
Celestial Navigation for Yachtsmen by Mary Blewitt
Ocean Passages of the World, British Admiralty
Light List, U.S. Coast Guard
Radio Navigation Aids, Hydrographic Office
Reed's Nautical Almanac (for shipping routes information)

Celestial Navigation

For Spherical Triangulation Freaks

Celestial navigation is based on solving a spherical triangle.
The three corners, or vertices, of the triangle are:

1. P—the Pole, North or South, according to the hemisphere
2. Gp—the geographical position of the spot where a direct line from the heavenly body you are sighting (in this case the sun) passes into the Earth at the exact moment that the sight is made
3. 0—your position. As you don't know where you are, you *assume a position* near to where you *think* you are.

Now, from the above you can see that:

1. Gp-P equals 90 degrees minus Y 0 when the sun's declination is north, and Gp P equals 90 degrees plus Y 0 when the sun's declination is south (where Y 0 is the latitude of the Gp of the sun, i.e., declination). The declination is found in *The Nautical Almanac*.
2. 0-P equals 90 degrees minus X0 where X0 is the latitude of your assumed position
3. the angle Gp-P-0 equals the difference between the meridian of Gp and the meridian of 0. This is the local hour angle (LHA). It is always measured westerly from you. It is sometimes an outside angle as in *Figure 22* and sometimes an inside angle as in *Figure 23*. The meridian of Gp is the longitude of Gp, and it is found in *The Nautical Almanac*. The meridian of 0 is the longitude of your assumed position; you choose this for yourself as shown later.

Now, if two sides and the angle Gp-P-0 are known to you, the other side and the other two angles can be calculated and you can obtain:

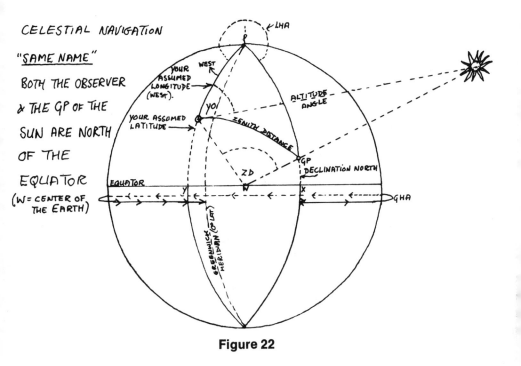

CELESTIAL NAVIGATION

"SAME NAME"

BOTH THE OBSERVER & THE GP OF THE SUN ARE NORTH OF THE EQUATOR

(W = CENTER OF THE EARTH)

LHA

YOUR ASSUMED LONGITUDE (WEST).

WEST

ALTITUDE ANGLE

YOUR ASSUMED LATITUDE

YO

ZENITH DISTANCE

GP

DECLINATION NORTH

ZD

EQUATOR

Y

W

X

GHA

GREENWICH MERIDIAN (OF LAT)

Figure 22

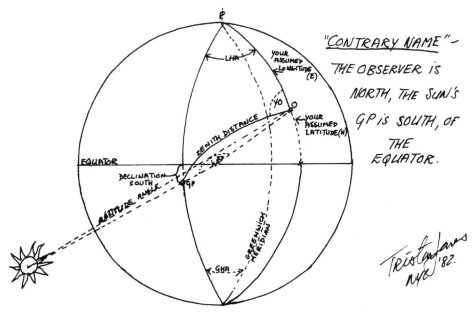

P

LHA

YOUR ASSUMED LONGITUDE (E)

YO

YOUR ASSUMED LATITUDE (N)

ZENITH DISTANCE

EQUATOR

DECLINATION SOUTH

GP

ALTITUDE ANGLE

GHA

GREENWICH MERIDIANS

"CONTRARY NAME" — THE OBSERVER IS NORTH, THE SUN'S GP is SOUTH, OF THE EQUATOR.

Tristan Jones NYC '82.

Figure 23

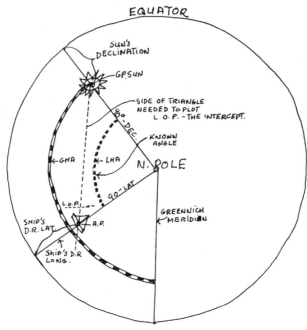

The assumed longitude applied to the Sun's G.H.A. renders the LHA. The two known lengths of the triangle which we know before solving the triangle are: 90° - Latitude and 90° - Sun's dec. The one angle we know is the L.H.A. With these two sides and one angle the tables give us an easy way of solving the third side, the *Intercept*.

Figure 24

1. angle P-0-Gp. This angle is the azimuth (true direction) of the sun's Gp from your assumed position. This gives you the *direction* of the Gp.
2. the side Gp-0 equals the zenith distance (ZD). Now take it as gospel that the altitude of the sun is 90 degrees minus the zenith distance if you are actually at your assumed position. If you are not at that position, then the sum of the altitude and the ZD will be more or less than 90 degrees, and that difference is called the intercept. The intercept tells you how much nearer or farther than the sun's Gp you are from your assumed position. In other words, the intercept tells you your distance from the Gp.

So we need to find 90 degrees minus Gp0, "The Calculated Altitude" (Hc), P-0-Gp, and the azimuth (Z). These the HO 249 tables provide.

Celestial Navigation in Plain English
For the Reasonable Man

To work out sextant sights, certain sums must be done. There are now pocket calculators on the market to do these sums, but any long-distance navigator must know how to do them in his head, and know not only how to do them but why he does them. If you can afford a computer to do the navigational calculations take one, but don't get into the habit of using it every time you take a sight. Use the computer one day, the next day do it yourself. That way you will stay in practice and so tend to make fewer errors if and when the computer conks out.

After a few months of daily practice, a good navigator can turn out a line of position (LOP) in about three minutes from the time of taking the sight. I doubt if it can be done much faster with a computer, and anyway, what's the hurry? In a small craft sailing at five or six knots out in the ocean, I doubt if it makes much difference if you know your line of position at 1043 or at 1047. And what are you going to do with the four minutes you've saved? Well, I suppose you could take another sight and time yourself and see if you could save four and a quarter minutes this time, and so on, ad infinitum, flying round in ever-diminishing circles, like a hoodlumbird.

I very often find myself looking forward to sight-taking time, savoring the prospect of spending some time finding out where I am. The sense of achievement in fixing a position is never lost, no matter how many times you do it. It is as I imagine a sculptor or a painter feels when he steps back and looks at his finished work. An extraordinary feeling. No wonder it's called the *art* of navigation. I can't imagine letting computers take what is left of the art away from us.

The first item of gear necessary for celestial navigation is a sextant. This does not have to be a very fancy one. Years ago, and in many cases even still, there was a sort of mystique among ship's officers about sextants. The way some of them secreted them and handled their instrument you'd have thought it was the Ark of the Covenant itself. This is a throwback to the days when crews were always potentially mutinous. If the mutineers had any sense at all they wouldn't, couldn't, kill the navigator. Sure, you must handle your sextant with great care, but it is after all only a tool, not something with which to frighten the living daylights out of some young apprentice anxious for promotion.

There is nothing mysterious or complicated about a sextant. It is simply an instrument for measuring the angle between one mass and another. That's all. It's a bit more delicate than a ruler or a set of compasses, but basically it serves the same purpose. It's a measuring device.

Usually the sextant is used for measuring the angle between a planet or a star and the horizon. It can also be used for measuring the angle between two points or objects horizontally.

In a small sailing craft the movement at sea is generally quite jerky, so it may take some time for you to obtain an acceptable sight. For this reason, the small-craft sextant should be light in weight, as the types of sextants used in big ships are too heavy. They make the arms tired after trying to shoot in a seaway for a few minutes. So it's best to get a lightweight sextant right from the start.

Plath makes a very good, solid-frame, aluminum sextant with a micrometer arc movement, at a reasonable price considering its accuracy, and that is my favorite. It is possible to hold up the aluminum Plath for as long as fifteen minutes without tiring, and very accurate positions can be obtained. Now, in any craft under sixty feet LOA, accuracy is most difficult to achieve, except in flat, calm conditions. This is no fault of the navigator; it is due to the movement of the vessel, which means that the angle between him, the sun, and the horizon is continually changing.

By accuracy I mean within a minute of the true angle. The general result obtained by an experienced navigator in normal ocean conditions, say, with a twenty-five-knot wind and steady sea, with the boat running before the wind, is within five to eight minutes of accuracy. An occasional voyager, upon making his departure on the open sea, may be content with an LOP anywhere up to fifteen miles from his actual position, but this should improve after a few days, and he should then obtain a line of position about three to eight miles from the actual. This error is not serious out in the ocean, because from the deck of a thirty-five footer, standing up, the navigator can see the horizon all around him at five miles' distance. His total width of vision is therefore ten miles, and his sights are putting him somewhere in the area of his circle of sight.

On your first voyage out, after sailing for a week or so without seeing any other craft, you might become a bit anxious as to whether your calculations are correct. As long as you are making the calculations in the correct order and manner, don't worry. The discrepancy between the log and your noon fixes might be caused by a current.

If you do pass close to a ship and manage to ask her for a position, it will probably vary from yours by a few miles, perhaps a bit more. Don't fret. Unless she's using a satellite system or Loran, her position by sextant for that day (out in the ocean) has perhaps been obtained by little Billy Bloggs, the junior officer, on *his* first trip out, and he is probably dying to ask you for a position to compare with his own before the first officer gets up on the bridge to bawl him out. Or the ship may pass you the result of her last fix, which might have been an hour or two before, and she's making fifteen knots.

Keep the mirrors clean of salt and lightly oil the arc every few days.

Check the sextant regularly, for increased index error especially. This tends to not make itself apparent. The others soon show up.

To check the index error:

1. Shoot the sun with the sextant set at zero. You will see two images of the sun. Bring the two images together, one above the other, until their edges touch. (If the two suns are not exactly one below the other, the sextant has side error and should be adjusted.)
2. Read the sextant scale.
3. Shoot again, this time with the images reversed.
4. Read the sextant again.

One reading will be on the plus scale, one on the minus. The lesser is taken from the greater and halved. The resulting figure is the index error, to be subtracted from observed altitudes if the greater figure was on the plus scale, added if it was on the minus scale. The two readings, if added together, should come to about sixty-four minutes. A sum much greater than this indicates that the sextant should be adjusted professionally.

A quicker way to read off index error is to shoot the horizon and adjust the scale so that both images of the horizon coincide. The reading on the scale is the index error, and it is applied to the Hs exactly as read on the sextant angle scale. (Hs is the symbol for the angle of the sun as taken by the sextant before any corrections are made.)

With an efficient long-range radio receiver it is not strictly necessary to have a chronometer on board, as there are radio stations that continually broadcast accurate time signals. However, I would not advise anyone to attempt an ocean crossing without a good chronometer for two reasons. One is that the radio might fail and the other is that in some parts of the oceans, especially in the Southern Hemisphere, there are extensive radio blind spots where nothing can be received.

The only reason for not having a chronometer is if you are able to work out lunar distances by obtaining the time from the angle between the moon and other known bodies. This is an esoteric, rather complicated exercise practiced by only a very few people nowadays, though it used to be the method of obtaining confirmation of the chronometer rate in the days of sailing ships, before radio. The only other ocean voyager I know of who uses this method is Frank Casper, but then he's the guy who found an error in the United States Navy's computer-calculated *Nautical Almanac!* And got a letter of thanks for his trouble.

There are wristwatches that claim to be also chronometers, they probably are if they are never worn on the wrist. The real chronometers are kept gimbaled and balanced in their own boxes, and their rate (or discrepancy between the time they show and the exact time as obtained from the radio) is noted at regular intervals, usually in the evening of each day, when reception is best, so that if the radio fails this rate of loss or gain daily is known and can then be gauged. It is no good taking the rate for a week and forgetting it, because the rate can change with just the effect of temperature change, or even the change in movement of the vessel.

If the worst happens and both the radio and the chronometer cease to operate, then, as you know your latitude, keep to it by taking the highest altitude of the sun daily, and head for a destination on that latitude. This, of course, is the old, time-honored system of "sailing down the latitude," which the sailing ships used to use before chronometers were common. They gauged the longitude from the distance run on the log. The chronometer should never be moved from its box except when absolutely necessary. The time should be taken from it, or from the radio, and transferred to a stopwatch.

The stopwatch or deckwatch I use is the ordinary sporting type, though I like the large kind, on a chain, which I fix to me. It is, after a while, easy to hold the stopwatch, with the stopping knob under the thumb, in the same hand that holds the sextant frame whilst the other works the arc. In company with a crew, of course, this operation is much easier, one can take the sight whilst the others note the time, but single-handed, after some practice, you can become pretty accurate at doing both, within a fraction of a second.

Remember, when you start off alone, to concentrate on the time first and note it down first. The angle on the arc will keep still, but the second hand of the stopwatch won't.

Two books are used in working the sights:

1. *The Nautical Almanac* is issued by the United States Navy each year and covers a twelve-month period. *The Nautical Almanac* tables tell you what is the geographical position (Gp) of a number of heavenly bodies at any second of any day of the period covered by the almanac. These bodies are the sun, the moon, the planets Venus, Mars, Jupiter and Saturn, and fifty-seven stars.
2. *HO 249 Sight Tables*
   Volume 2 for latitudes above forty degrees, and *Volume 3* for latitudes below forty degrees. This advises you of the difference between your assumed position and your actual position, based on the angle of the sun to the horizon, which you have obtained with your sextant.

These two books may be obtained at any good yacht chandler or nautical bookstore.

Starting off with the basics, forget all you have learned about the earth and the other planets traveling around the sun, or about the movement of the stars in relation to each other. Imagine the earth as a fixed body in space and every other body in space traveling around it, some faster than others, more or less in an east-to-west direction. One of these bodies traveling around the earth is the sun.

If you draw a straight line from the sun to the center of the earth, the point at which that line passes through the surface of the earth is the sun's geographical position (Gp). *The Nautical Almanac* tells us where this Gp is. The problem is for you to find out the distance and direction from the Gp to you. Once you know those two factors, then you know where your line of position is.

For your dead-reckoning calculations you assume a position. You denote the position by giving it a latitude and a longitude. Applying the figure you obtain from *The Nautical Almanac* to the figure you obtained from the HO 249, the result will give you a *line of position*

(LOP). Assuming that your sight has been accurate, you must be somewhere on that line. But you do not know where on the line you are. You need to find out where you are on the LOP. You need a *fix*. You need a second line, crossing the first LOP. During the daytime it is impossible to get this second line quickly from taking another angle of the sun because the sun moves so slowly; therefore, the LOP obtained from a second sight of the sun would be almost parallel with the first LOP.

If it is early or late enough in the day for the moon, planets or stars to be out, then a sight can soon be taken on a different celestial body. Once that is done and a second line, at an angle to the first line, is drawn, you will know that where they join is where you are.

But if only the sun is out, you will have to wait for a period of at least an hour to obtain another LOP at an angle to the first. Here again, the point where the two LOPs intersect is your position. Of course, if you have moved your position during the period between taking sights of the sun, then that distance and course that you have moved will have to be applied to the chart with the dividers and the parallel rules; the point where that line crosses the second LOP is your position. This is what is known as a "running fix." Most fixes obtained in celestial navigation are of this type.

In order to find out the geographical position of the sun, it is necessary for you to know the exact time of day. This can be obtained either from an accurate chronometer or from a reasonably accurate watch adjusted to a recent radio station time signal.

All geographical positions are given as east or west of the Greenwich Meridian (zero degrees longitude). Zero degrees latitude is the Equator. At the Equator one minute of degree equals one nautical mile on the earth's surface. Therefore, a vessel's position is given in degrees and minutes of latitude and longitude. For small craft the use of seconds of degree is not considered necessary.

The latitude of the geographical position of the sun is called its declination (dec.). The longitude of the geographical position of the sun is called its Greenwich hour angle (GHA).

The Greenwich hour angle of a heavenly body is the distance between that body's geographical position and the Greenwich Meridian. The declination of a body is the distance between its geographical position (north or south of the Equator) and the Equator. The GHA of a body changes rapidly, the dec. changes slowly.

Sextant Sight Calculations—the Exercise

Read and absorb this one sentence at a time, and refer back to this after you have mastered the drill.

Take the sun sight and mark the *exact* time of the sight. Any watch error must be applied before the time of the sight is entered into your calculations.

Enter *The Nautical Almanac*. Obtain the GHA and the dec. of the body. You now know its geographical position.

Apply the corrections for the sight. The sight that you obtained on the sextant scale is known as the Hs. Once the corrections have been applied to the angle you obtained on the sextant, it is known as the Ho (angle observed). These corrections are always the index error and the allowance for the observer's altitude (dip.). There are also other corrections, which differ according to the celestial body sighted. For instance, the semidiameter (SD) is applied in the case of the sun, the HP in the case of the moon.

Mark down the assumed position of your craft at the time when you took the sight. This is known as the AP. The assumed latitude (aLa) is marked down so that when applied to the GHA the result is a whole integral degree (whole degree with no extra minutes).

You now obtain the local hour angle (LHA). This is done by applying the assumed longitude to the Greenwich hour angle.

Enter the *HO 249 Sight Tables* at the page that corresponds with your assumed latitude. Then find the section that gives you figures relating to the sun's present declination. Go to the page within the subsection that is headed "Declination Same Name as Latitude." This is if you and the sun's Gp are both in the same North or South hemisphere. The opposite is "Contrary Name." From the appropriate LHA reading you will obtain the calculated altitude (Hc), the differential (d), and the azimuth (Z). The calculated altitude is the declination of the sun as it would be if your assumed position has been correct. The differential (d) is the key to the interpolation at the back of the Sight Tables. This will be either added or subtracted, according to the sign given in the tables. The azimuth gives you the exact direction to draw a line, the azimuth line, from your assumed position, upon which will be the LOP. The LOP is a line drawn perpendicular to the azimuth line. The distance along the azimuth line to the LOP is called the intercept (int.). The intercept is the difference between your Ho and the Hc. In other words, it is the difference between your assumed position as indicated by the sextant and your true position as indicated by the tables. When the Ho is smaller than the Hc, you are farther away from the sun than you had assumed. Therefore, the intercept is designated as "away." If the Ho is greater than the Hc, it is "toward."

Therefore, having drawn the azimuth line, if the intercept is "toward" the sun, you measure the distance along it and draw a line perpendicular to it. This is your line of position (LOP). *You are somewhere on the LOP.*

The Drill (Sun Sights) in Twenty-four Easy Steps

A. Sextant Angle and Time (after taking a sun sight)

1. First, mark down your dead-reckoning position in longitude and latitude. You may do this lightly on the chart.
2. Mark down the approximate time as shown by the ship's clock.
3. Mark down the approximate bearing of the sun.
4. Mark down your approximate height above sea level.
5. Take the sextant sight, making sure you get the exact time. This can be done by using a stopwatch, started at a certain minute show on the chronometer or from Radio WWV.
6. Write down the sextant angle (Hs) and the *exact* time of the sight.
7. Add the sun's main correction (obtain this from table on front page of *The Nautical Almanac*).
8. Apply the index error (ic). This can be either added or subtracted, according to the peculiarities of the sextant. You should find out what these peculiarities are before setting sail.
9. Apply the dip. This is shorthand for the height-of-eye correction, and it is usually subtracted from the sextant angle. The amount to subtract can be found from the table on the front page of *The Nautical Almanac*.
10. Apply the semidiameter (SD) of the sun. This is found from the bottom of the daily pages of *The Nautical Almanac* and is added if you shoot the lower edge of the sun on the horizon, which is the usual method.
11. You have now obtained the observed angle (Ho). Mark it down.
12. Apply the watch error. This means you must find out what the *correct* time was when you took the sight.

B. *The Nautical Almanac*

13. Go to *The Nautical Almanac* daily page and find out the Greenwich hour angle (GHA) of the sun. Mark it down.
14. Go to the minutes and seconds (of time) (yellow) page of *The Nautical Almanac* to find out the increment (the number of degrees, minutes, and seconds to add to the GHA). This will give you the actual GHA of the sun.
15. Now choose an assumed latitude (nearest whole degree to your D.R. latitude and assumed longitude, which, when applied to GHA, will give a whole degree. Mark the AP lightly on the chart.
16. If you are east of the GHA, then add your assumed longitude. If you are west of the GHA, subtract your assumed longitude. The assumed longitude should be such as to give you a local hour angle (LHA) in whole degrees.
17. Find out from *The Nautical Almanac* day page the declination of the sun at the time you took the sight and apply the "d" correction, given in the yellow pages at the back of the almanac. This will give you the true declination of the sun.

C. *HO 249* to Solve the Triangle

18. Go to the HO 249 page that is the same as your assumed latitude and to the line on that page that shows the sun's declination. From that line extract the unadjusted calculated altitude (Hc). (See *Note 1* below.)
19. From the same line in HO 249 extract the "d" correction. Go to Table 5 to find out the interpolation.
20. Apply the interpolation to the Hc previously obtained and obtain the adjusted Hc, adding or subtracting according to the sign of "d" (difference).
21. Apply the observed altitude (Ho) to the calculated altitude (Hc); this will give you the intercept.
22. Remember, if the Ho is smaller than the Hc, then the intercept is designated as *away* from the sun. If the Ho is greater than the Hc, the Intercept is *toward* the sun. (The intercept tells you how far along the azimuth you must draw the line of position.)

D. Chart. To Draw The Line of Position.

23. From the appropriate line in HO 249 obtain the azimuth (Z). This will give you the direction in which to draw the azimuth line from

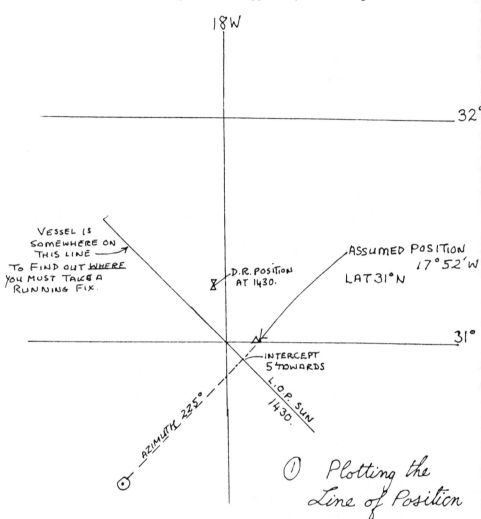

Figure 25

your assumed position. (See *Note 2* below.) A line drawn perpendicular to the azimuth line is your line of position. It is *not*
your position. *It is part of a circle around the sun's Gp upon
which you are positioned.*

24. In order to obtain a fix it is necessary for you to obtain another
sight and, taking into account your vessel's movement between
sights, obtain two LOPs crossed by a course. Where the course
and the second LOP join is your position. This is a *fix.*

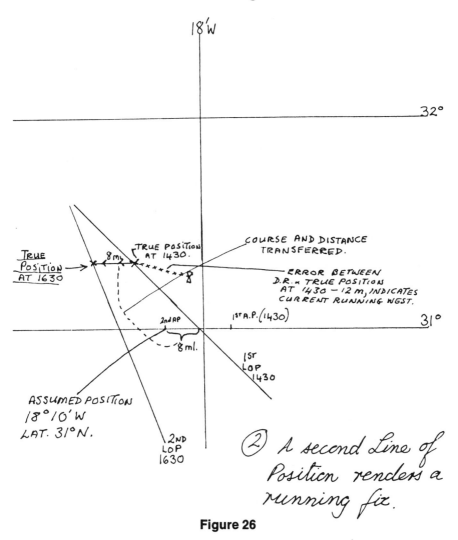

Figure 26

Note 1: If your latitude is in the same hemisphere as the sun's declination, then the HO 249 page will be headed "Same Name." If the boat is in the opposite hemisphere to the sun's declination, then the page will be headed "Contrary Name."

Note 2: Z must be corrected to find Zn (true azimuth). This is explained on the bottom of each page of HO 249 tables. In the Northern Hemisphere, if LHA is greater than 180 degrees, Z = Zn. If LHA is less than 180 degrees, Zn = 360 degrees minus Z. All azimuths are *true* bearings.

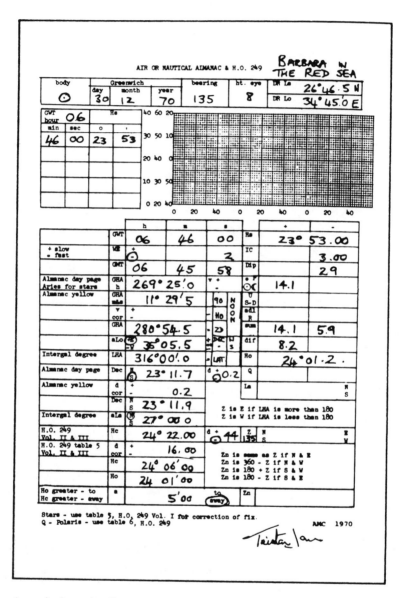

A typical navigation working sheet from *Barbara*, showing the working out of a sun sight on the thirtieth of December 1970 in the northern part of the Red Sea.

Figure 27

Sun Sights at Noon—"Finding your Latitude by Meridian Passage"

In plain English this means shooting the sun at the exact time that its geographical position (Gp) passes over your longitude. It stands to reason that when this happens the sun must be either: (a) exactly true north of you, (b) exactly true south of you, or (c) exactly over your head, at a ninety-degree angle to the horizon, and (d) that it is local noon.

In the case of (a) or (b), the line of position you obtain must be a latitude running true east and west, either north or south of the equator or on the equator itself. It cannot be anything else.

In the case of (c), you are extremely lucky. It has happened to me very few times. If your observed angle is ninety degrees, then the declination of the sun, listed in *The Nautical Almanac* for local noon, is your latitude. In the cases of (a) and (b), the calculations are slightly more complicated.

Only *The Nautical Almanac* is used.

1. To take a noon sight you don't even need the exact time. Just keep shooting the sun over the noontime period. It will rise steadily, then hover for a minute or two, then start to descend. The highest reading is the noon sight.
2. Apply the corrections to the noon-sight sextant altitude (Hs) to obtain the observed altitude (Ho), exactly as when taking an ordinary sun sight. This means adding the main correction, adding or subtracting the index error, subtracting the dip., and adding or subtracting the semidiameter (SD).
3. Write down 90.00   90.00
4. Below that write down the observed altitude (Ho).   − Ho
5. Subtract the Ho from 90.00 to give zenith distance (this means the distance from you to the sun's Gp).   = ZD.
6. Next go to the daily pages of *The Nautical Almanac* and find out the declination of the sun for noon today. If the sun is in the same North or South Hemisphere as you are, then add the declination to ZD (if contrary subtract).   ± dec.
7. The answer is your latitude.   = lat.

THE PLANETS   The planets used are Venus, Saturn, Jupiter and Mars, in order of brightness. Venus is brilliant and moves faster than bright stars with which she might be confused. Mars is a reddish color. But if there is any doubt in your mind as to which planet you are looking at, identify the nearest navigation star to the planet and find out its GHA for that hour from *The Nautical Almanac* and see which of the planets has roughly the same GHA.

The working out of planet sights is the same as for the sun, but for two exceptions:

1. The main correction of the sextant angle (Hs) is taken from the second or middle column of the table on the front page of the almanac. It is *always minus*. There are additional corrections to the main correction, in the right-hand column of the tables, the application of which will be easily understood upon inspection.
2. Besides the "d" correction at the bottom of the daily pages in the almanac, there is also a "v" correction. The "v" value is obtained in the yellow pages of the almanac in the same space as the "d" value and it is applied to the GHA. It is added or subtracted according to the sign at the foot of the column.

The same increment tables are used as for the sun throughout.

THE MOON   Because the moon changes her form so much, because her light is reflected to us from the sun, and because her course through the heavens is so erratic (or so it seems over a short period of time), the working out of a moon sight is more complicated than that of a sun or planet sight, but not much more so. The main difference between the moon and the other heavenly bodies is that the declination changes very rapidly, so the difference between the declinations as given for certain times in the almanac must be interpolated. Another difference is that an extra correction must be applied to the observed altitude. This is called the parallax-in-altitude (HP).

The corrections for the observed altitude sextant angle (Hs) of the moon are on the last two pages of *The Nautical Almanac*.

1. Use the dip. corrections table exactly the same as the one for the sun.
2. Having applied the dip. correction to the Hs, mark down the *dip.-corrected Hs*.
3. Go to the moon's main corrections table in the upper half of the

two back pages, with the single degrees and minutes of your dip.-corrected Hs and find them there; right below them you will find your proper full first correction, always in minutes. Write it down and remember which column it came from.

4. Now go to the white daily page of the almanac for the date and extract from the line for the GMT in hours for the sight, the GHA, the "v" correction, the declination, and the HP values from the "Moon" column. Write them down.

5. Go to the back cover of the almanac for the HP correction table, which is on the lower half of the two back pages. In each of the HP columns there is given a value for "L" and for "U." This means lower limb or upper limb (or edge) of the moon having been "brought down" to the horizon when you took the sight. The upper limb is used only when it is impossible to use the lower, because of the moon's shape. When that happens, an extra thirty minutes must be substracted from the total observed altitude (Ho).

6. Assuming you have taken a lower limb sight, go to the first corrections table (on the upper half of the page) and there under HP find the nearest equivalent value to the HP you wrote down from the daily page. Add the sum of these two HP figures to the dip.-corrected Hs. You now have the moon's sextant altitude (Ho).

The rest of the moon sight is worked out exactly as for a planet, with the "v" correction added to the GHA and the "d" correction added or subtracted from the declination according to the sign given.

When you turn to the yellow pages of the almanac for the increments for the minutes and seconds of your sight, make sure you go to the "Moon" column.

Apart from the above slight differences, the moon sight is worked out in the same way as a sun sight or planet sight, with the azimuth and the intercept found in the same way.

THE STARS* The altitude corrections for star sights are the simplest of all, for they need no main corrections; only the dip. and index error. These are usually unchanged during a series of sights, and thus they are known beforehand.

The GHA calculations for stars are worked out from the First Point of Aries (♈). This is a completely arbitrary point in the sky.

---

* Excluding Polaris, using HO 249 Volume 3.

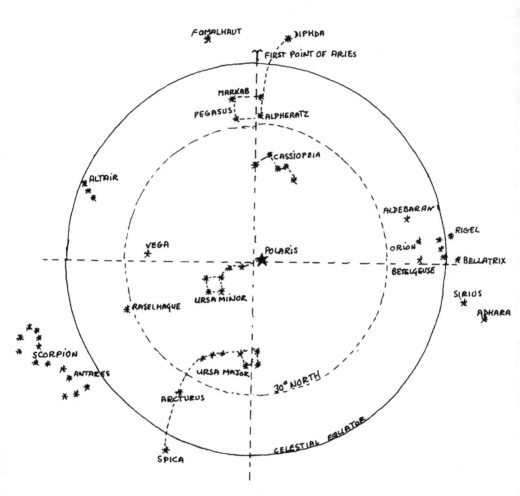

THE MAIN NAVIGATION STARS, NORTHERN HEMISPHERE

Tristan Jones
NYC 1982.

Figure 28

There are very good reasons for that particular point being chosen as the basis of star sights, but this is not the place to go into them. The First Point of Aries is indicated like this: ♈. Therefore, you will, when entering *The Nautical Almanac*, look for the GHA of Aries (♈).

Since the stars are fixed in relation to each other and to ♈, the distance, or angle, between the Gp of a star and the Gp of Aries is known as the sidereal hour angle (SHA). To find the GHA of a star* you must first find th eGHA of ♈ and then add onto it the SHA of the star. If the sum of these two angles comes to more than 360 degrees, the extra is subtracted from 360 to give the GHA. (*)

On the daily pages of the almanac, left-hand side, there is a list of fifty-seven different stars, with their declinations and SHA printed alongside each one.

Once the GHA of a star has been found, the calculations proceed exactly the same as for the sun.

Using HO 249 volume 3, follow this list to find a star suitable for navigation.

1. Before you begin shooting stars, obtain the GHA of Aries, for the time you intend to start shooting, from *The Nautical Almanac*. Then obtain the LHA of ♈ by adding or subtracting the assumed longitude.
2. Go to the HO 249 volume 3 with the LHA Aries and assumed latitude. There you will find that the seven most suitable stars for sighting at that time and place are listed.
3. Set the altitude of each star on the sextant in turn and look in the direction given in HO 249 volume 3 for azimuth (Z) and take your sights.
4. Adjust the resulting fix on the chart by referring to Table 4 in HO 249, "Corrections for Precession and Nutation," which are obtained by entering with LHA ♈, Latitude, and Year.

To calculate latitude by Polaris, only *The Nautical Almanac* is used. If the Pole Star were directly over the pole you could just get its angle above the horizon and that would be your latitude. *But Polaris isn't due north, so we must calculate where it is.* The easiest way to find it is to set your sextant scale at approximately your latitude plus one degree, look north, and you should pick up Polaris. Or follow a line through the front paws of Ursa Major—the Big Bear or Dipper—and there it is. Shoot Polaris and mark the time.

1. Apply corrections for dip. and index error, just as in any other sight.
2. Obtain the main correction from the "Stars and Planet" column on front cover of the almanac. Both dip. and main are minus corrections.

* See footnote, page 105.

3. Polaris, being almost directly over the pole, has no sidereal hour angle or declination. However, entering the daily white pages you need to find the LHA of Aries (♈) for the GMT of your sight (as for a normal star sight).

4. From the GHA (♈), subtract (in west longitude) or add (in east longitude) your D.R. position. This is LHA (♈).

5. With the LHA (♈) and the Ho, enter the Polaris tables on the last three pages of *The Nautical Almanac*. Here you find the additional correction to apply the Ho, to give you your exact latitude. Simple and accurate!

GREAT CIRCLE NAVIGATION   The shortest distance between two points on a globe appears as a straight line. When that line is transferred onto a flat chart it appears as a curve. In the Northern Hemisphere it appears as a line trending in its center toward the North Pole, in the Southern Hemisphere toward the South Pole. The farther north or south the great circle line is drawn, the more pronounced will be the curve toward the pole.

The problem in navigation is to shape the course along a great circle. In small craft this is done by following a series of straight courses on the chart, changing them periodically so that they conform as nearly as possible to a continuous curve.

One way to do this is to obtain a set of great circle course charts and to draw on them a series of straight lines following a great circle track. With powered vessels this can be drawn up before the voyage is started, but in small sailing craft, which may wander off preset courses through stress of weather, the courses must be continually redrawn. This can be a chore.

The easy way is to follow the checklist below (using HO 249 Sight Tables only).

1. Obtain a fix. Work out your sights and mark your position.
2. Call your latitude the Latitude in HO 249.
3. Call the latitude of your destination the declination in Ho 249.
4. Subtract your latitude from the latitude (dec.) of your destination (or vice versa, according to which is the smaller). Call the differences the LHA in HO 249.
5. Enter the HO 249 tables at the page for the latitude, the declination, and the LHA you have obtained.
6. Extract the calculated altitude (Hc) from HO 249 and subtract from 90 degrees.

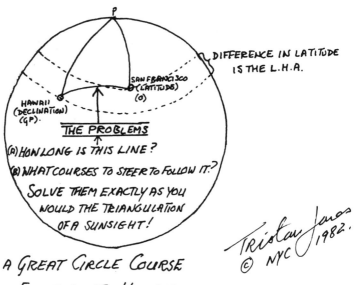

CALCULATING A GREAT CIRCLE COURSE
EXAMPLE: SAN FRANCISCO TO HAWAII

Figure 29

7. Convert this into minutes (i.e., nautical miles). Do this by multi-plying the degrees by 60 and adding on the odd minutes.
8. Apply the "d" correction according to the sign.

The result is the number of miles to your destination.

9. Extract the azimuth (Z) from HO 249 and apply to 180 or 360 (see rules). This will give you the course to follow on a great circle track to your destination. The sum will give you a true course, to which deviation and variation must be applied to give you a steering course to your destination along a great circle track.

Rules for applying Z to find the great circle course (GC course):

If you are in the Northern Hemisphere,
    going east, Z = GC course.
If you are in the Northern Hemisphere,
    going west, 360 minus Z = GC course.
If you are in the Southern Hemisphere,
    going east, 180 plus Z = GC course.
If you are in the Southern Hemisphere,
    going west, 180 minus Z = GC course.

This method does not need any special charts. The changes of course to follow a great circle track to your destination can be made anytime once you have a fix. Adhering as closely as possible to a great circle course on a transoceanic passage can save many miles of sailing. After some practice, the whole calculation can be made in a matter of a minute or so.

Emergency Gear, Tools, and Spares

A ROUND-THE-WORLDER should be prepared and equipped to make all replacements and repairs by and with his own resources, since for much of his passage he may be in nonadvanced areas where repair facilities, equipment, and personnel are not readily available.

In the case of boats equipped with mechanical or electrical gear, before sailing you should gather as much printed and verbal information as you can about the equipment onboard and file it methodically. I usually have a small filing card box with hints about gear that is not found in the makers' instruction books.

ALTERNATIVES TO ELECTRICITY   Wherever equipment relies on the engine's electricity to run it, an alternative "Armstrong," "handraulic," item should be shipped in case of electrical failure. (That is, the item should be hand-workable.)

This applies especially to the pumps, both bilge and fresh water. Apart from carrying a complete set of spares for all pumps on board, for the bilge pumps fit at least two hand-operated and also carry one spare.

It is necessary to carry alternatives to the lighting, especially the navigation lights. Recently very powerful flashing strobe lights have been developed with battery power for an average of one hundred hours. These can be hoisted to the masthead or the burgee halyard. However, do not trust electricity, even autonomous battery-operated equipment. Carry a kerosene-run dioptic lens light, which casts a beam five miles or more in normal conditions.

If you carry a depthfinder, make sure you also have a sounding lead, in case of power failure.

If the radio receiver runs off the main battery system, then an alternative receiver, run on its own autonomous dry cells, should be carried. This is in case of power failure when the signals, essential in the course of normal navigation to gain the longitude, are required.

This receiver should be capable of transoceanic reception. The only alternatives are either to have a reasonably accurate chronometer or to get the time by lunar distances—a complicated matter. So have a good independent radio receiver.

2 hand-operated bilge pumps	Independent radio receiver
1 hand-operated freshwater pump	Wind vane self-steerer plus
Kerosene-run dioptic lens light	spare vane
Sounding lead	2 fire extinguishers

DIESEL ENGINE SPARES   In diesel engines I have sailed with, the most common failures have been in the cooling system. So the first things I would make sure were available are a few spare cooling pump impellors, and an alternative method of getting suction to the cooling pump in case of a blockage of the cooling-water seacock. This can be done by running a flexible hose over the side. It would probably need priming from the outboard end to obtain suction.

The next most common failure is in the fuel system. Here you should have the tools to be able to bleed the system in case water gets into the fuel line, or even, as is commonly the case, air. The wrenches necessary for this are usually designed to slip out of your greasy hands into the bilge under the engine, so either carry a powerful magnet on the end of a rod for retrieving the wrenches, or even better, a spare set of wrenches and a magnet.

You should carry a spare fuel injector for each one fitted on the engine. These should be carefully preserved in grease in their original maker's wrappings. Also carry a set of spare injector lines.

If you are heading for the wild coasts of the world (which means about two-thirds of it), you should carry spare sets of valves and rods, main bearings and piston rings, and also a set of filters and gaskets. Don't forget the gasket cement.

Cooling pump impellor(s)	Rods
Wrenches	Main bearings
Magnet(s)	Piston rings
Fuel injector(s)	Filters
Injector lines	Gaskets
Valves	Gasket cement

GASOLINE ENGINE SPARES   For the gasoline engine (if you are brave enough to cross the ocean with one), you will require tappet wrenches, special wrenches to deal with the ignition points and carburetor, feeler gauges, and a valve grinder and paste.

Again, as for the diesel engine, you should carry a complete set of gaskets, valves and rods, piston rings and main bearings, and, if you can, a spare carburetor. Water pump spares are a must as are spare bolts. For the ignition system: enough spark plugs for three years' normal running, spare points, distributor cap and rotor high-tension leads, condenser and coil.

There are several efficient sprays available to protect the ignition system from damp.

Again, don't forget the gasket cement. Also, stern tube stuffing and grease.

Tappet wrenches	Gaskets
Wrenches for ignition points and carburetor	Valves
	Rods
Feeler gauges	Piston rings
Valve grinder and paste	Main bearings
Water pump spares	Carburetor
Belts	Rotor high tension leads
Spark plugs	Condenser
Spare points	Coil
Distributor cap	Gasket cement
Propeller	Stern tube stuffing
O/B propeller pins	Grease

AUXILIARY GENERATOR   Get the maker's recommendations on spares. Of course, the maker will generally tend to overestimate the reliability of his equipment under sea conditions. So if you have any doubts about any other parts that might fail, get the advice of a good independent artisan who has dealt with the gear, preferably on board a sailing vessel.

DAMAGE-CONTROL SPARES   In a fiberglass boat you will need to carry spare mat, cloth, resin, and epoxy—enough to deal with quite hefty damage to the hull. There should be enough marine ply boarding carried to cover all windows in the coachroof or sides, in case of damage. At least one wooden bung for each hull fitting should be stowed on board, also a number of hardwood wedges of various sizes, and a half dozen balks of timber suitable for shoring up the hull in case of serious damage.

Mat	Marine ply boarding
Cloth	Wooden bungs
Resin	Hardwood wedges
Epoxy	6 balks of timber

WHEEL STEERING   In boats equipped with wheel steering, I carry a spare steering cable and enough U-bolts to set it up in an emergency, when there probably would not be enough time to do a tidier job by splicing the wire up. In any case, there should be provision for tiller steering in case the wheel system gives out.

It's a good idea to have spare winch and reefing handles, since these sometimes are lost over the side.

Screws	Rigging screws
Nuts	Shackles
Bolts	Blocks
Nails	Winch handle(s)
Cotter pins	Reefing handle(s)
Thimbles	

ELECTRICAL TOOLS   If you must have them, they should be chosen bearing in mind that the current varies in different parts of the world. It also means carrying inverters or converters to step the ship's power up or down. I would advise against it because it means more bulky, vulnerable electrical gear; and if there are any fusspots on board, the boat generally deteriorates into a sort of do-it-yourself workshop, with all kinds of completely unnecessary additions, alterations, and general messing about going on. Anyone who has sat at anchor in a pleasant tropical bay and has heard the incessant whining and banging going on from vessels with electrical tools on board that are too easy to use will know what I mean.

For the electrical system you will need a set of small screwdrivers, soldering gear—preferably not electrical—wire cutters, and a meter for testing for current. Also spare fuses and spare wires.

The remainder of the mechanical tools carried should be capable of dealing with any other engineering jobs on board, such as a big wrench to bear down on the stern gland. A set of files are a necessity, half a dozen of each type—round, flat and rattail. One of the most used tools in a small vessel is a vise grip. One large and one small pipe wrench. A painter's blowtorch also is most useful, preferably the butane-gas-run kind, unless a gasoline engine is fitted and there is already a supply of that highly dangerous fuel on board. Personally, I think that crossing the ocean with more than a gallon of gasoline stowed is a bit like playing Russian roulette with five bullets in the cylinder.

Make sure that you can get good lighting into the engine space. This doesn't generally exist, so have a good wire-protected wandering lead and a fair supply of rubber flashlights. There's nothing worse than bouncing around in a cramped engine space in semidarkness, trying to fiddle around with the fuel system.

The hull itself requires a good think-out in the way of tools. Of course, if the boat is of wood construction, she is going to need more attention than if she is fiberglass or cement, and if she is steel she is going to need different tools. But regardless of the construction, I would certainly carry the tools I would need if she were wood, for most emergency repairs at sea are carried out with wood anyway, since it is the easiest material to work with in rough conditions.

OTHER TOOLS *Hammers* are important; in descending size I would carry a fourteen-pound sledge, very handy for chopping up the wire rigging in case of demasting; a seven-pound sledge; a carpenter's claw hammer; a ball peen hammer; and a small squared-off chisel hammer for little jobs, like tacking up wire staples.

One of the handiest and most used pieces of tool gear in any vessel is the *vise*. I would have a large one, say, six inches across the top of the jaws, and a small one, say, three inches. They should both be capable of being rigged up in the cockpit or somewhere down below. The latter especially where arctic or rainy tropical conditions are to be met.

A riveting tool comes in the form of a sort of gun affair, with long bronze rivets up to an inch and a half long. This is useful indeed for emergency repairs to the mast fittings, or even popping a wooden tingle over a stove-in ship side or deck. It can be operated with one hand and doesn't need anyone on the other side of the surface being riveted.

"Angel hair" is a kind of quick-cutting device for steel wire shrouds. It is wire covered with industrial diamond chips, and looks like a flexible small rattail file. It was invented during World War II and used successfully by imprisoned Allied agents to escape from barred cells. It can cut through a five-sixteenth steel wire in about

three minutes. It is used where it would be too rough and dangerous to use an axe or a sledge and chisel for chopping up the rigging in case of serious dismasting. It is about as efficient as wire cutters, but is much less bulky and so far much easier to stow. It can also be fitted with rings at each end so it can be rigged onto an extendable hacksaw.

A good hefty mallet; two hacksaws; a crosscut and a keyhole saw, both well greased, with spare blades.

Various sizes of chisels; brace and bits in various sizes up to about one and a half inches, also adjustable countersinkers for wood screws. Two small hand drills with three sets of all sizes of drill bits up to one inch.

Screwdrivers, all types, up to a monster about eighteen inches long and a good inch along the blade edge.

Rasps, flat, round and oval, two of the smaller sizes.

A whetstone and, if you're rich, a hand-driven grindstone.

A folding rule or a tape measure, in inches and metric.

A small level and a setsquare; a supply of chalk; a small plane, well greased, and, if the money will run to it, a large one also.

A good heavy tree-felling axe, well preserved in grease and paper —this for emergency chopping jobs, and perhaps, for the single-hander, self-defense in place of using the Very pistol.

If you have copper piping systems on board, such as the fresh-water or butane gas systems, then you will need tube cutters, flaring tools, and pipe wrenches. My advice is to have a good, thick plastic hose system at least for the fresh water; then it's simply a matter of pipe grips and a screwdriver, for temporary repairs until you reach port.

A very useful item is plenty of electrical tape. It serves an amazing number of purposes on board a sailing vessel.

There is a kit on sale for repairing braided lines. This is a fairly complicated job, but well worth mastering, since braided line is practically unobtainable in many parts of the world.

RIGGING TOOLS   For the rigging you will have to decide what tools are needed. Again, it's a case of "different ships, different longsplices." Certainly you need spare wire enough to make up the longest stay on board, also spare Norseman wire-swages. A marlinspike or two and a serving mallet, also at least two good resharpenable seaman's clasp knives or lanyards.

RIGGING KNIFE

LANYARD

Figure 30

DO NOT CARRY AN OPEN-BLADED KNIFE HABITUALLY;

it may look IMPRESSIVE, but it is NOT SEAMANLIKE.

SAILMAKER'S PALM AND RIGGER'S FID

Figure 31

SAIL TOOLS For the sails you will need at least one full set of sail repair gear, two palms, all sizes of needles up to a big three-inch long one. Take a good number of the smaller sizes, since they break often. Preserve them in a jar of petroleum jelly. A good amount of sailcloth and thread.

It's a good idea to carry a punch and block for making cringles in sails and awning or other canvas, together with the brass grommets.

Another good idea is to have a hand- or foot-driven sewing machine. This takes up some space, but is well worth it, even for the shoestring sailor, because he can often earn precious currency repairing the sails of other voyagers who have neither the machine nor the inclination toward tedious hand stitching. I know of one Danish couple who, while sitting in Las Palmas harbor, almost entirely financed an Atlantic crossing by repairing sails and running up curtains and cushion covers for other boats.

Screwdrivers
Soldering gear
Wire cutters
Meter for testing electrical
    current
Fuses
Wires
Keyhole saw
Chisels
Brace and bits
Counter sinkers
2 hand drills
Rasps
Whetstone or hand-driven
    grindstone
"Angel hair" wirecutting device
Mallet
2 hacksaws
Crosscut
Tape measure
Level
Set-square
Chalk
Plane
Axe
Tube cutters
Flaring tools
Plastic hose

Large wrench
Set of files
Vise grip
2 pipe wrenches
Blowtorch
Wandering lead
Rubber flashlights
14-pound sledge
7-pound sledge
Carpenter's claw hammer
Ball peen hammer
Chisel hammer
Wiring staples
2 vises
Riveting tool
Electrical tape
Kit for repairing braided lines
Rigging wire
Norseman wire-swages
Marlinspike
Clasp knives
Sail repair gear
2 palms
Needles
Sailcloth and thread
Punch and block
Brass grommets
Sewing machine

All in all, the single-hander should avoid fancy gadgets and over-sophisticated gear, which, efficient as it may be for short-distance voyaging in advanced areas, and helpful as it may be when racing on Long Island Sound or San Francisco Bay, may turn out to be difficult to maintain or inaccessible out in the ocean.

When it comes to gear, let simplicity be your watchword.

ARMS AND SELF-DEFENSE For protection against pirates, say off Columbia or in eastern waters, I recommend carrying a few sticks of dynamite. Do not carry arms. In many countries this can lead to interminable legal problems and even life imprisonment. Also, if you have a gun you might tend to drift into situations you would other-wise avoid. A stick of dynamite, lit, thrown into the wheelhouse of an aggressor craft, can work wonders of discouragement on the vile practice of piracy.

Anchors and Ground Tackle

IT's no good having a hefty anchor and a sound anchor chain and a good, strong anchor line if the holding bitts on board your vessel are weak. Therefore, the first thing to ensure is that the holding arrangements on deck are sturdy enough to enable the ground tackle to hold the vessel in a strong blow.

Anchors, like most other things concerned with small craft, have their own paradoxes. The best all-around anchor is the classic Fisherman or Herreshoff anchor. This is about as perfectly proportioned for the job as any fine-tuned instrument. The one great snag of the Fisherman-type anchor is that when the boat swings, with the wind or with the tide, the anchor rope or chain (known to mariners as the cable) can wrap around the fluke which is exposed and drag the anchor out of the sea bed. The Fisherman-type anchor holds well in most bottoms and it is the best anchor for rock or reef, but if there's a possibility of the boat swinging, you should set two anchors out to prevent fouling.

The next-best anchor for all-around usage and especially for the long-distance voyager who can expect to anchor in all types of bottoms is the CQR (Secure). This is my favorite when it comes to a working anchor. With a CQR you can swing on tide or wind with only one anchor set, and there will be no fouling because the CQR has no protuberances.

However, the CQR has three disadvantages: first, although it holds well in sand, shell, or gravel and is excellent in mud, it is not as good as the Fisherman for penetrating weed to get down to the bottom; second, the CQR is not the best anchor on a rocky bottom and I always set out a Fisherman storm anchor to back it up in these circumstances; and third, the CQR must be used with plenty of good-sized chain to hold the stock down and so allow the anchor to dig into hard sand bottoms.

The genuine CQR, which is drop-forged, has a lead-filled cavity in its bill, to assist in penetration. This works very well; so well that

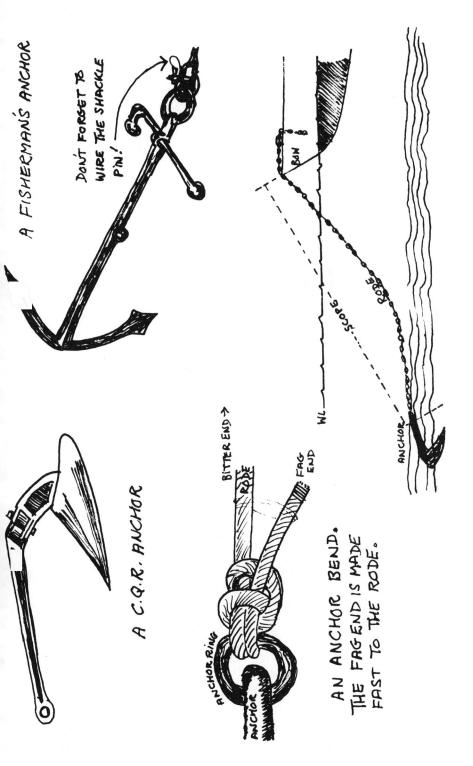

A FISHERMAN'S ANCHOR

DON'T FORGET TO WIRE THE SHACKLE PIN!

A C.Q.R. ANCHOR

BITTER END →

RODE

FAG END

ANCHOR RING

ANCHOR

AN ANCHOR BEND.
THE FAG END IS MADE
FAST TO THE RODE.

BOW

SCOPE

RODE

WL

ANCHOR

THE SCOPE IS THE DISTANCE FROM THE BOW TO THE ANCHOR.

Figure 32

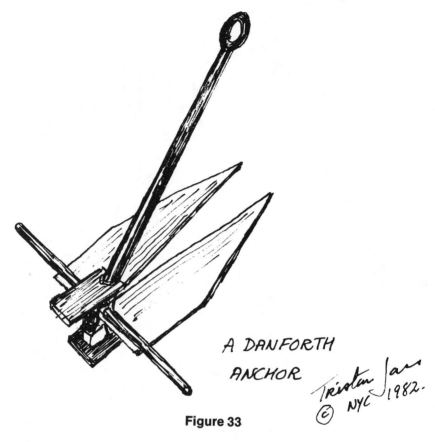

A DANFORTH
ANCHOR   Tristan Jan
© NYC 1982.

Figure 33

very often it is quite a heavy job to extract the anchor from sand
or mud.

The lightweight, stockless anchors, such as the Danforth, are in
my opinion suitable only for short-term anchorages in safe havens.
This is not only because they can foul easily but also because of their
comparatively weak construction. On a straight-pull situation in sand
or firm mud, the Danforth holds as well or even better than the Fisherman. But in soft mud it may dredge or drag along the surface of the
mud instead of digging down deeper. This is because of the Danforth's
light weight and flat-shaped palms. If the Danforth is dug into firm
mud and has to reset 180 degrees owing to the vessel's shifting with
the wind or tide, a lump of mud will often stay jammed between the
flukes and the shank, so the flukes will not hinge over and reset into
new ground. This is not the only way the Danforth may foul; often it
is brought up backward with the chain or rope wrapped around the
rectangular hinge plates.

Therefore, if you use Danforths you should use two anchors, if there's any chance of the vessel swinging with changing winds or tide.

Danforths sold today, like many cheaper anchors, are a welded fabrication. In fact, sometimes they are only spot-welded. I have seen many Danforths and other stockless-type anchors being repaired and rewelded in various parts of the world. The Danforth's straight-pull holding power is simply too great for its construction. The Danforth Company has acknowledged this by producing an anchor in mild steel, and a more expensive high-tensile model. High-tensile refers only to the type of steel used in the construction of the anchor, not to its method of construction. Fabricated, spot-welded anchors are, size for size, much weaker than drop-forged anchors.

ANCHOR CABLE   Chain is more reliable than rope; the weight of chain acts as a shock absorber, so no force is exerted on the shank of the anchor until all the chain is taut and lifted. Because of its weight, chain lies on the sea bottom and is less likely to foul your anchor. Also, if chain rubs against something sharp it won't chafe through and so part, allowing your vessel to drift.

However, chain has its drawbacks. It's heavy and expensive, and in most instances you need an anchor winch to handle it. Chain gets dirty and rusty. Chain must be stored carefully each time you use it so it doesn't jam in the chain locker when you next anchor. But none of these disadvantages affects the holding power of the ground tackle.

Nylon rope definitely has its uses. The second "lunch" bower anchor rode should be of thirty feet (9.1 m) of nylon with thirty feet (9.1 m) of bbb chain. (English chain of equivalent strength is short-link Lloyd's-tested.) Do not use proof coil or long-link chain. Proof coil is cheaper, but only every twentieth link is tested. When you need a second anchor set, it is much easier to row out in the dinghy with the nylon-chain rode than with an all-chain. Nylon rarely picks up mud, and when it does it washes off on the way up. Nylon is extremely strong because of its elasticity and in a groundswell will not jerk the anchor out of the bottom or violently jerk in its chock, as chain does. Also (and this is a great advantage), with nylon you can use a sheet winch as an anchor winch.

Designers and boat builders recommend lightweight stockless anchors and nylon rodes, but the reason for this is that they are a lot cheaper than chain and drop-forged anchors. Lightweight stockless anchors and nylon lines have become standard on racing boats, which rarely lie at anchor. But for serious cruising you will be spending much more time at anchor in all kinds of conditions, so the weight and cost of chains becomes secondary to complete dependability.

Laying your *ground tackle* carefully is, of course, important to prevent your vessel from dragging. If you drop the chain on top of your anchor, the chances are it will foul and drag. Spot your anchor where you want it, then pay out full scope. Only secure the bower rode when you have paid out full scope, then set the main anchor.

A tripline with a buoy is a very handy recovery gadget, especially where there is a rocky bottom or the bottom is foul. Unfortunately, triplines have a bad habit of fouling the anchor and causing dragging. You must always be careful to throw the tripline and buoy well away from the anchor before letting go.

Polypropylene line makes a good tripline. It tends to float away from the anchor with less chance of it fouling the flukes. If a motor boat accidentally cuts the tripline you could probably recover it at low tide. If the tripline is too short it can cause trouble, especially if the tripline buoy is of large size, as it may hold the anchor above the surface of the sea bottom, preventing it from digging in.

ESTIMATING THE SCOPE   For proper scope, especially in shallow anchorages, you must take into account the height of your bow (fairlead above water) and add it to the depth indicated by your depthfinder or your lead line. The lead line is accurate, cheaper, and often more reliable than a depthfinder for measuring the exact depth of water before you calculate your scope. If the lead is charged with tallow, soft beeswax, or even peanut butter, it can bring up a sample of the bottom and help you to site the best anchor to set out to avoid dragging.

Check the depth contours on your chart carefully before you go to anchor. Once the anchor is down and set, stay topsides to take bearings on the shore to make sure that the anchor is digging in properly. If you cannot see the shore and take bearings because of fog, or because perhaps you are in a wide river mouth, or it is nighttime, watch for the boat turning beam-on to the wind. If there is no tidal current, your anchor is probably dragging. In this case it would be wise to veer more anchor rode. Another way to tell if the boat is dragging is to watch the anchor rode under tension. If the rode rises slowly in the gusts, then lowers itself slowly as the tension eases, the anchor is biting. But if the rode is bobbing in a jerky fashion when it takes the strain, this is probably a sign that the anchor is thumping and slipping along the bottom, and the vessel is dragging.

A very good way of dealing with the problem of dragging at night is to rig a drift lead with the sounding lead line. Lower it amidships to the bottom, leave a bit of slack to allow for the boat swinging, then make it fast. If the lead line tautens, the boat has dragged. Don't be in so much of a rush to get under way as to forget to recover the lead line.

The rule, when anchoring in unaccustomed waters, is to pay out a scope of chain eight to ten times longer than the depth of water around the hull plus the height of the bow roller above sea level.

The anchor rode should be marked to measure its length. If it is chain, this is done by painting a link white every six feet along the length; if the rode is line, then short lengths of plastic tape are passed through the lay of the rope every six feet, with the measurement mark written on them in paint or indelible ink.

To guard against losing the anchor and its rode, the bitter, or inboard end of the rode should always be secured on board.

GETTING UNDERWAY First make sure the anchor rode is not fouling the boat. Then make sure there are no obstacles to leeward or downstream. If there are, plan to avoid them. Under sail, the main should be hoisted before the anchor is weighed and the headsails hanked onto their stays, ready to hoist. As the anchor is hauled up, it should be jerked up and down to rid it of grass or mud. As the boat drifts to leeward, get the anchor on board and loosely secured. Hoist the headsails. Make your way out to the offing, clear of other vessels and other hazards, then ease off the headsail sheets while coming up into the wind, go forward, secure the anchor properly, wash down any mud on the foredeck, then rehaul the headsails and carry on out into the offing.

Securing the anchor on board is important. Having an anchor washed or fall over the side whilst you are heeled over making five or six knots and taking its full scope of rode along with it can be, to say the least, an embarrassing predicament. A loose anchor, especially the larger, heavier type, sliding over the deck as the boat heels can result in severe injuries.

ANCHOR SIGNALS A vessel anchored is supposed to display a black ball forward during the day. At night (and I always do this) a white thirty-two-point light, visible for at least two miles, must be shown. It is best to rig this forward on the forestay where it can best be seen.

CAUTIONS   Guard against chafe on lines. Plastic hose can be split and tied over the rope in the chafing section, such as where it passes over fairleads or chocks, or where it chafes against the dolphin striker. The old-fashioned way was to wrap strips of canvas around the rope where it was likely to chafe. Nylon line below a half inch in diameter is very susceptible to damage from the ultraviolet rays of the sun, and it pays to make efforts to shade it. The fuzzing on the outside of nylon line through wear and tear is not serious; in fact it is a good thing, acting as a sort of "hedgehog" effect against further wear.

Anchor lines and cable should be inspected closely at regular intervals of one year, for signs of abrasion, wear, and damage.

The pin of the shackle that secures the line or chain to the head of the anchor must always be wired to prevent the pin from coming loose.

Again, the fastenings on deck, to which the anchor rode will be made fast, must be stout enough to sustain the sometimes very heavy shocks that will be imposed on them when the boat is at anchor in heavy weather. Remember that the anchor of a thirty-footer has to take a horizontal load of fourteen hundred pounds, and so do the bitt and cleats to which it is secured. Frequently bitts and cleats have been torn out of the decks of boats at anchor in heavy weather. You cannot, when surveying your ground-tackle-holding and mooring arrangements, have a jaundiced enough eye or be too pessimistic. Only the best will do.

Heavy Weather
and Other Hazards

The Risks

COLLISIONS   Given a properly equipped vessel and a good, reasonably healthy crew (even if it's a solo voyage), the main danger at sea these days, without any doubt, is collision. This falls into three main categories: first, with another vessel; second, with an animal such as a whale; and third, with an inanimate object, such as a derelict craft, a tree trunk, or even flotsam such as an oil barrel.

In the case of other vessels, collision can be guarded against to a great extent in several ways. First of all get off the shipping lanes as soon as possible and stay off them as much as you are able. You can obtain information on shipping routes from the applicable navy charts from the pilot book for areas where fleets of fishing craft might be encountered. Even in the middle of the ocean, it is surprising how the big ships stick to their lanes. Nowadays, if you sight one on a recognized route you will very likely sight another before too long. Sail away from them, at an angle, unless for some reason you want a vessel to sight you and perhaps report your position. Once this has been done, get away from the shipping lane. Be well clear of it by nightfall. Remember the old sailor's saying "If it's in sight, it's too near, unless it's your destination."

Secondly have a good, efficient radar reflector. If you don't know for certain that it gives off a strong reflection, ask someone with a radar set to give you a report. In harbor, ask a steamer, or even a ferry, or even one of those posh yachts that sport a set. My way is to approach the owner and express curiosity over the set, admiration, even. Then, when good relations are established, ask him to get a range on you when you pass his vessel. Once you have done this you will trust the radar reflector, and if you don't, change it.

When I sleep at sea I do so in two spells, given the usual circumstances of steady winds and running under self-steering gear. One spell is in the afternoon, for four hours, and one from dawn onward for about three hours. Both these periods are daylight hours. At night

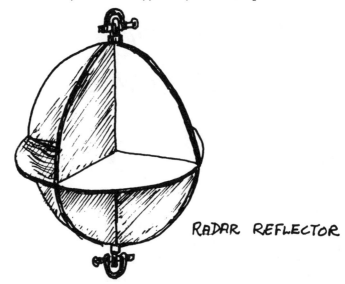

RADAR REFLECTOR

Figure 34

in good weather I am out in the cockpit, often with the radio receiver playing music where I can get good reception. In bad weather I am in the cabin, but taking a look around the horizon through the dog-house windows every few minutes. I always have an oil-burning dioptic light hanging from the backstays spreader, where it is not obscured by the sails from any direction for more than a few seconds at a time. Its range is five miles in good visibility, and it burns half a teacupful of kerosene a night, a small price to pay for the comfort it gives.

Whilst on the subject of sleep, it does not seem to be the same thing at sea, alone, as it is ashore. Onboard underway I sleep in a state of semiconsciousness and the slightest change in the way of the boat will wake me immediately. I do not suffer from this seeming failure to lose complete consciousness, and in fact I think I wake up more refreshed after my three- or four-hour sea sleep than I do after sleeping eight hours ashore, but maybe shoreside air pollution has something to do with this. I have woken many a time with the feeling that there is a human presence close; I have looked and listened, to find nothing; but sometime later, sure enough, way out on the horizon, the tiny, shining tops of a ship's mast will appear. This is an uncanny experience, but nevertheless most useful. I expect that human nature being much the same in many respects, other people have and can develop this sense.

The strange thing is that I seem to sleep much more soundly, even if it is for shorter periods, when alone, than when in a crewed vessel; I think that an instinctive distrust of other people's alertness is an inherent factor in human nature, at least when it comes to trusting a nightwatch. This happens even with my most trusted mates, and it seems to be more physical than mental. It's my body that distrusts, not my reason.

A good strobe light is probably the best type of night light, if you have the power to run it, but make sure it can be taken down in case of a heavy blow, when it might get damaged or blown away (the power of a seventy-knot wind at fifty feet above sea level has to be witnessed to be appreciated).

The sure trait of an inexperienced helmsman is the failure to look all around him continually—astern as well as ahead.

If you have an engine in the boat and you are anywhere near a shipping lane or a fishing ground, it should be ready to start, so that if you are on a collision course under sail and the other vessel has not seen you, you can hand the sails as you clear off out of the way under power. If you are becalmed, with a big tanker coming straight for you, don't hesitate—start the engine and clear off. Do not depend on any rules about right of way. If the other vessel is at all bigger than you, always navigate as if she has the right of way and is being steered by a lunatic.

In the matter of lights, the *legal* obligation for a boat "not under command" is to show two red lights, one above the other. But here there is the snag that red lights do not have the visibility of white. So, if you insist on being "legal," show the red lights, but I would still have a bright white light up fairly high. I personally think that a single bright light is better because it is so unusual that it makes the ship's officers very wary and they will make sure to avoid the object. They will be concerned because they may tend to think it signals a derelict, which could cause them severe damage.

The daytime legal signal for a boat not under command is two black balls, one over the other. But for a tanker to see these, even through high-power binoculars, at any distance, they would need to be enormous. Better a big, efficient radar reflector.

I think that the legal rules should be changed, to one bright white flasher (say two flashes every four seconds) at night, and the ensign worn up high on the mainmast during the day. This would be a simple, inexpensive solution to this grave problem, and if I was American I would let my congressman know what I thought.

Strobe lights are legal if they are used only in imminent danger of collision, not for continual use. This should be changed—they should be allowed.

Alternatively, a "D" flag of the International Code might be adopted as the signal for a single-hander's vessel, worn at the mainmast head. This is the signal for a vessel disabled, but if the position of the flag were promulgated and adhered to firmly by all yachtsmen, this would be very soon recognized the world over by all mariners, as a sign that there is only one person in the yacht.

Another risk to yachts, especially off the regular shipping lanes, is caused by vessels that, sighting them, approach too close, usually out of curiosity, to see whether the yacht is in distress. The main culprits in my experience are Greek and Indian ships. I know that their actions are the result of good intentions, but the road to hell is paved with the same. If a ship appears to alter course to approach you, the best thing to do is to make yourself plainly seen to the watchers on her bridge, and to unmistakably *ignore* them, for example by studiously turning your back to them. If they persist in approaching, then make the hand signal for "Okay"; this is understood the world over. I know it is hard to do this when perhaps you won't have seen another human in weeks, but for your safety it is necessary. Bear in mind that if a cargo ship of thirty thousand tons deadweight comes within twenty yards of your vessels, the suction from her screws is likely to drag your boat very fast under her stern. There will be, in short order, chaos, and you'll be lucky not to lose the boat. Never attempt to go alongside a large vessel in any kind of sea unless in extremis or unless the conditions are flat calm and she is hove-to with her propellers stopped. (Incidentally, the best ships for replying to a hail are British, American, and Soviet.)

Chay Blythe, in his circumnavigation in *British Steel*, used explosives to attract the attention of ships that might not have seen him. Chay was a soldier, a commando. I don't know the details of his method; maybe there was a safety factor built in, to prevent accidental combustion. If there was, then this would be for me.

With regard to collision with whales: Having survived three of these (one barely), I have some ideas on the subject. First of all, I would try not to sail in areas where whales are known to breed, unless this is unavoidable. The bulls are at their most aggressive when mating season comes around, and naturally enough do not like the appearance of what might seem to be a competitor. If I was in an area where whales breed, I would try to fix up some device to make a noise. If there were sufficient batteries I would play the radio loud when not watching out on deck. If not, I would hang up, say, a hammer to strike the frying pan every time the boat moved. Whales are said to have keen hearing and high intelligence, so the chances are that the old bull would figure out my boat was not a randy young bull or a big shark, and he would in all probability ignore me. I think red antifouling, which might seem to be blood, might attract the whale. Black, green, or white seems better.

It would be interesting to collect all the accounts of whale attacks and find out what the weather was like at the time. I have a hunch that the majority take place during fairly calm conditions, when the boat is quiet. I think it is the lack of noise that might lead them to believe that the craft is another whale or big fish. Of course, when a whale is sleeping on the surface at night, it is almost impossible to see it, and I think here that noise would wake it up and shift it. It might be that the brains can investigate this and come up with a sort of noisemaker that would send out an ultrasonic sound. What about the echo sounders; could they be modified to include a "ping" like sonar? Whales can detect noise over great distances, and this would give them good warning. There would have to be a light fitted to the gadget, to check if it was working.

If there is an engine on board I would start it, even idling, if I thought there was a school of whales around. That noise would send them off, I am fairly sure.

In the South Pacific and the Indian Ocean, great white sharks are sometimes big enough to damage a small craft in a collision.

With flotsam we have a difficult problem. It occurs all over the oceans. A floating ship's cargo-hatch board, for example, which has washed over the side in bad weather, can be anything up to forty feet long and weigh, sodden, a good four or five tons. Even a full oil drum can cause quite considerable damage if collided with whilst running free at seven knots. A good lookout is the answer, especially in shipping lanes.

We can try to stay, if possible, out of areas where natural flotsam is known to occur. This is true in places such as off some of the coasts of Africa, Asia, and South America, where mighty rivers sweep huge trees (some up to *two hundred* feet long, and as much as fifty feet in girth) way out to sea. This happens especially in high rainfall areas, such as off the coast of western Colombia, off the mouths of the Amazon and the Congo, around New Guinea, and many other places. If the land around the river is civilized, then there is less risk, for the scavengers will get the flotsam on its way out to sea, but in sparsely populated areas it is a very real hazard. In the daytime, whilst off river mouths, keep a good lookout. At night, stand offshore and hope that you will not have to use the damage-control gear you stowed on board before sailing, and the location of each piece of which you know by heart. In my experience, disaster strikes mainly at those who are unprepared for it.

Try not to sail single-handed across an ocean in a boat with an inside liner (or ceiling, to give it its proper name). The ship's side should be immediately accessible at any time. Lord knows how many small craft have foundered because the crew could not get at the side to bung up a hole. I cannot fathom why ceilings are fitted, apart from appearance, except maybe for insulation in extreme weather. But this should be done with simply removable panels. That goes for the deck head, too. As far as appearance goes, what could be nicer to look at than well-joined timber and fastenings? Inside a fiberglass boat stick some vinyl over the sides if you can't stand the sight of what appears to be a sheet of glued hairy string. In a metal boat, spray it with cork and paint it, but make sure you can get at what is the only thing between you and four thousand fathoms of salt water. In case of holing, if a ceiling is in the way, hack it away with an axe.

Incidentally, one of my objections to multihulls is their speed, which can multiply the risk of damage through a collision appreciably. Their lightness of construction is also a telling point against them.

Any ocean voyager should have at least one watertight bulkhead forward.

In fiberglass boats, the same remarks as made for wooden vessels apply, except that nails probably would not hold the patch. A better idea would be self-tapping screws. Get several of those in, then drill right through the patch and the hull, and fix the patch with drop-head bolts, on which large washers and nuts can be fixed inboard. This saves going over the side. The Simpson Gear would, of course, work well on any type of hull. With a steel vessel, I think that without the Simpson gear, drop-head bolts or a collision mat would be the only way of stopping a hole single-handed, unless welding gear could be used when conditions improved.

GROUNDING The next most common cause of vessels foundering is grounding. "If you can see it, it's too near, unless it is the destination." Here again, this applies to the shore, and a thousand times more so to a lee shore. Sea room, sea room, and more sea room should be your watchword. You can't have enough of it. This applies much, much more if you are alone. Some of the most experienced ocean voyagers in the world have lost vessels on a lee shore by grounding. I myself almost lost *Sea Dart* that way, off the coast of Uruguay, and if I'd had any chance in the raging sea at the time, would probably have abandoned her if I could swim. The finest boat-salvaging hand in existence must be a nonswimmer in a sea like that. If any of your friends are at all nervous about sailing, always advise them to make sure the skipper is a nonswimmer. Then they are much more sure of getting back in one piece.

If by misfortune you find your vessel being driven onshore, get the anchor over; get two anchors over if it is possible to claw your way off. If the worst happens, and she does touch, try to save her. In some conditions this would be beyond human capabilities or appear to be, but it's surprising how superhuman you can become when you are really driven. If the shore is sandy, it might even be best to let her drive onshore. She will pound, but if she is well constructed it will surprise anyone to see what a punishment a sound hull can take. When the weather abates there may be a chance to haul her off with the help of a bigger vessel. Or drag her farther up the beach, to make her sound again. With a really powerful winch on board, you might even be able to kedge her off yourself, as my friend Marcel Bardieaux did from a reef near New Caledonia, and I did off Montevideo in *Sea Dart*. As long as the boat is not in bits, never say die. While she's afloat, even if leaking, try to remember another sailor's saying: "If she'll float for twenty-four hours, she'll float you into haven."

Going aground seems to be about the best method ever thought up of rousing a person sleeping heavily, because nine times out of ten it happens when the navigator is so tired that it affects his judgment. If you are forced to navigate near a shore, perhaps to avoid the strength of a contrary current, and have to stay awake for long hours, perhaps days, then, as soon as you suspect that fatigue is affecting your ability to make logical decisions, stand off. Get out, and when you are well offshore, with no risk of drifting onto the coast, *sleep*, even if it is only for an hour or two. Sleep and eat. It doesn't matter if you have to give up twenty miles to the current. Losing a thousand miles is better than losing the boat. During my thirty-three-hundred-mile beat against wind and current off the west coast of South America, in the Humboldt, I was forced, every three days or so, when my eyes could hardly stay open, to head offshore, even with the risk of being swept out into the Pacific Ocean and not being able to beat back inshore again. I was forced to make for the offing and to give way to the current. I would rather have tackled the three-thousand-mile voyage to the Tuamotos on short water and food rations than risk putting *Sea Dart* ashore.

HEAVY WEATHER   Surprisingly enough, heavy weather is said by the insurance companies to be the cause of less loss of life than any of the other hazards mentioned.

A true voyager is never "caught out" in bad weather. He may "encounter" it, or "meet it" or "come across it," but never is he "caught out." The reason is that he is prepared for it. It is for this that the boat was constructed so soundly, that he was so choosy about what gear went into fitting her out, that he studied and learned as much as he could digest about it. He doesn't get "caught out." He should "catch" the weather "out." He gets caught out in harbor only if he is foolish enough to buy bad materials from unscrupulous yacht chandlers or boatyards.

When the wind rises into such a howling fury, and with it the sea, that it is risky even to keep the spitfire and the trysail up, consider lying ahull, or running under bare poles. The decision will depend on a number of factors. Is there sea room to run? Are you physically capable of handling the wheel or tiller in such weather, even under bare poles? What is the advantage of running before the wind?

I would say, nine times out of ten, unless off a lee-shore, *heave-to!* Under trysail or bare poles in a one-masted rig, under a reefed mizzen in a two-master. Don't stream anything out of the boat, let her drift. Given that everything is secured down, she should lie either beam-onto the seas, or, if a mizzen is used, have the sea on one bow. Once that is achieved, as violent as the motion may be, then it's time to secure yourself down. This does two things. It gets you out of the way of possible accidents, broken ribs and so forth, and it gives you time to think. Not to worry, to think. When the weather has reached this stage, what you think about is your own concern, because you will know that you have done all you can do, and now it's up to the boat and whatever or whomever else you believe in. The most comforting thought is that nothing lasts forever and every storm passes.

I am against sea anchors; in fact, in many circumstances I think they are downright dangerous. Anyone who has seen one in action in a real snorter of a storm will know that the tremendous shocks imparted to the deck fittings on the foredeck could be enough to pull the deck out of the hull. It appeared to me, on board the Dutch ketch *Slot Van Kappel* in a force twelve plus off Patagonia in '55, that the effect was about the same as dropping the boat from a height of fifty feet, with lines thirty feet in length bent on her deck fittings. I am against streaming anything over the bows, the sides, or the stern whilst hove-to ahull or otherwise. The vessel must become an entity of the kinetic motion generated by the wind and sea. She must *give way*. The only time I would stream anything in very heavy weather is if I was running before it under bare poles and the seas became too slow for the boat. By that I mean if her progress was driving her from one sea onto the one in front of it. Then I would stream a very long line over the stern; probably fifty fathoms of one-inch dacron, though this depends on how much I wanted to slow down. The more line out, the more braking power. This line would be a bight from one quarter out in a long loop to the other quarter. But unless this was necessary I would not do it; it is, I think, much more preferable to heave-to. If the seas threaten to curl over and break on board, even in a one-master I would try to rig some kind of trysail or to bring her bows up into the wind, even if this was only slightly. In that posture she will present less profile to the seas and probably make less drift.

Before the wind reached its height of force, all unshippable gear would be brought down below from aloft, and the boom would have been lowered when the trysail was rigged. The aim is to resist the wind and sea as little as possible. Nature damages the slender, bending reed much less than the rigid, solid oak.

With regard to lying ahull: Before you take off for Rapa Nui or wherever, try to get out in a stiff wind and sea and heave the boat to with all sail handed. See how she behaves. Don't panic if she rolls madly; in the ultimate storms the seas are much longer. Get used to the motion down below as well as topsides. I have seen inshore sailors in an absolute state of bewilderment when the engine has stopped on Long Island Sound. It's as if they see safety only in forward movement. There is often nothing more pleasant than stopping the boat dead in the water and just drifting around, with headsail backed and rudder lashed to windward, or under bare poles. You can rarely feel closer to the sea. This is not only a relief in Long Island Sound on a calm Sunday afternoon; it is also a relief in a southerly buster off to the south of Cape Aghulas. Instead of fighting nature you are going *with* her, and she becomes much kinder, once you get accustomed to the movement. And yet when you go below as the boat is ahull, you will be astonished at the comparative peace and quiet inside the hull. If your vessel is well chosen and cared for, you will be comforted indeed by the strength of everything that went into her, from the designer's integrity to the six coats of paint on the toe rail. Then your perspective of values will begin to harden, and you'll realize just how important those six coats of paint are, and how much more important are the unseen keel bolts. And when you come back ashore, your view of the world will be somehow different. And you will know what peace of mind really means.

FOG   In a number of parts of the world fog is endemic, not only in cold-weather areas, but also in tropical latitudes. Fog is, in fact, a very low cloud. It is a concentration of minute water droplets often so small that they cannot be seen, yet so dense that they obscure visibility to varying degrees. There are four types of fog.

Radiation fog occurs when the air directly above the surface of the earth is colder than the air above it. With clear skies, the sunshine heats the earth, which at night loses this heat by radiation to outer space. There must be a calm or very light breeze. This brings, if there is a flat calm, a low fog, often no higher than a man's head; but if there is a breeze, turbulence is caused, which sends the fog much higher. This type of fog is found in temperate zones and arctic latitudes. As soon as a moderate wind pipes up, it disperses. Radiation fog forms only at night, usually near lakes, rivers, and other places where the land is low. Given clear skies, it will start to clear from the bottom up. Over the sea it is slower to clear, as seawater does not cool nearly as rapidly as does the land. This is the type of fog found in places like the west coast of South America, the Mozambique Channel, the Adriatic, the western Mediterranean, and around the British Isles in summertime. It is, of course, also found on the coasts of the United States and Canada, chiefly, during the late summer and autumn.

Advection fog is similar to what sometimes happens when a troublemaking rowdy is thrown out of a bar. It means "transported by horizontal motion." Advection fog is caused by winds carrying warm, moist air over a colder surface. The air is cooled, as it passes, below its dew point by conduction and also by radiating its heat to the colder surface. For advection fog to form, the air at a height of one hundred feet or thereabouts must be warmer than the air at eye level, and the temperature of the sea must become progressively colder in the direction toward which the wind is blowing. Advection fog can form at any time, day or night, summer or winter, in any part of the world, even way out at sea, as it does often over the Grand Banks of Newfoundland when a southerly wind is blowing, against the cold Labrador Current. It is also found off Peru, when the wind shifts to southeast, from the land, and blows over the cold Humboldt Current and the Sea of Japan.

Advection fog also forms often on the coast of California and Oregon, where warm, moist winds from mid-Pacific blow inshore over cold coastal currents. This also happens on the east coast of the United States, when warm southerly winds blow across the Gulf Stream and meet the colder water of the remnants of the Labrador Current, as it moves southward.

On big rivers, such as the Mississippi, the Ohio, the Amazon, and the Plate, *steam fog*, which is a type of advection fog, forms very often. This is caused by colder air blowing over water that is much warmer. Because the water is much warmer than the air, it causes the air to rise, just as it does above a steaming kettle.

The last kind of fog is *precipitation fog*. This is, in fact, a form of rain. In British waters it is known as "Scotch mist." This term is used by sailors to describe anything that obviously exists, but which is strenuously denied by the powers that be. It is formed by rain falling from the higher, warmer air above, into colder air near the surface and partly evaporating, thus leaving tiny droplets suspended in the cold layer. This Scotch mist is, as the name indicates, prevalent in the northern waters of the British Isles, and it also occurs in winter all over northern Europe, southern Africa, and southern South America.

Away from the land—and by that I mean, say, a hundred miles out and more—the frequency of fog drops considerably. Out in the ocean, in the low latitudes around the Equator, it is practically nil, especially in the Trade Wind zones. Here then is another reason for keeping clear of the coasts. But if your cruising area demands that you navigate in fog zones, you must be prepared.

The type of foghorn carried around the United States, the aerosol type, is almost useless to the long-distance voyager. For one thing, he won't be able to obtain replacement cans easily, and if he carries spare cans over a period of years, they are liable to corrode and explode. So take along a good, hefty, hand-operated horn or siren. You may even consider adapting the horn fitted on the aerosol-type siren to the air nozzle on the dinghy inflation pump. In this way the horn can be operated with one foot, leaving the hands free.

The bell demanded by U.S. Coast Guard regulations is useless in a fog, though it makes a fine ornament down in the cabin or bent on the mizzen mast and is handy for calling "happy hour" or mealtimes.

To sound the siren continuously whilst sitting in a fog in unfrequented areas is an exercise in futility, apart from being very tiring, so the thing to do is to listen carefully for any engine noises. In a thick fog the direction from which a noise is coming is very difficult to perceive. The way I do it is to listen through a hollow tube. This can be a length of piping or even a rolled-up chart, or the round cardboard cases in which charts are delivered. You hold the tube up to your ear and slowly turn around. You will find that, after some practice, you can distinguish a certain difference in the sound when the tube is at one particular angle. This difference varies with different listeners and so is impossible to describe, but the direction from which the sound is different is the direction of the source of the noise. This goes also for the sound of breakers on a shore.

In a fog, soundings should be taken at frequent intervals, especially if the boat is in waters affected by currents or tides. If the soundings are seen to be diminishing, the boat should be anchored. I usually put the anchoring depth at ten fathoms, but this depends on many factors.

If you are anywhere near the entrance to a port or haven, light a strong lamp (a dioptic lens storm lantern or, better, a strobe light), and sound the siren continuously, at least ten seconds every minute. The radar reflector is a tremendous comfort in this situation.

If you have an engine in remote areas, do not run it in a fog, unless you are absolutely sure you know where the shore is and are running under power into the offing. It is much better to maintain absolute silence in order to hear any other craft or the sound of the sea breaking on the shore or on any outlying rocks.

In fog-prone areas, always check the charts for magnetic anomalies in the area. If any are shown, do not trust your compass until you can see where you are.

In the much frequented parts of the world, fog is our second-greatest hazard, next to collision with other craft. In the remote parts of the world, near the coasts, it is the greatest. It can be the most frightening phenomenon; the way to beat it is to keep your head, use your ears, and be prepared.

The best companion in a foggy area is, perhaps, a dog, for he can hear noises long before you, and has a much better idea of their direction in low visibility. Labrador dogs are ideal for this.

DISMASTING   The modern ocean and offshore sailing boat has either a deep keel or a drop keel. In both cases the possibilities of a capsize or a knockdown are greatly reduced. In deep-keel boats I have only had the spreaders in the sea half a dozen times, and on these occasions the weather conditions were exceptional.

The main risk to the masts, in a modern, deep-keeled yacht, with the masts stepped in the keel, is material failure. Nine times out of ten this, when it does happen, occurs in the masthead fittings. Usually on the tangs to which the backstays are rigged. This is because ocean voyages are usually made mostly running free before the wind; therefore, most of the strain is on the backstays, and in the course of an ocean crossing the sea transmits millions of shocks up through the stern, up the backstays, to the tangs on the mastcap.

In a passage made going to windward, the shocks go up the forestays to the mastcap. In time this is bound to tell, and the stainless steel of the masthead fitting may develop hairline fractures, impossible to detect with the naked eye in many cases. Therefore, I would advise anyone contemplating an ocean passage to have the masthead fitting either renewed or X-rayed. This is especially important in any boat that has previously put in plenty of sea time.

In most cases, in a modern-type Bermuda-rigged vessel, what happens is that everything is fine until all of a sudden there's a twang and the backstay collapses on deck. If there are two backstays, then the risk of the mast snapping at the spreaders and falling forward is greatly diminished. If there are not, then the mainsail should be handed fast, and the topping lift set up as a jury backstay, as taut as possible. For this reason, before setting off on an ocean crossing, make sure the topping lift is a good, hefty line, new.

The same goes for a boat going to windward. The topping lift can be taken forward, fast, and set up on one of the forward cleats.

The main halyard could be set up as a stay also. This is usually of wire rope. Once this is done, the topping lift can then be used to hoist the main again, but only as far up as the spreaders. To hoist it any farther, especially in a blow, is asking for trouble.

If the worst happens and the mast does collapse at the spreaders, then in most cases it will fall forward and to leeward. The mainsail will rend itself apart, more likely than not, and it will seem as if all hell is let loose.

Keep your head and capture the masthead.

You can do this by grabbing the topping lift and hauling it in, hard. Try to get the masthead down on deck, if possible, and lash it to the pulpit or anywhere else handy. If you cannot get it on deck, lash it alongside the hull as securely as you can. Then, when the

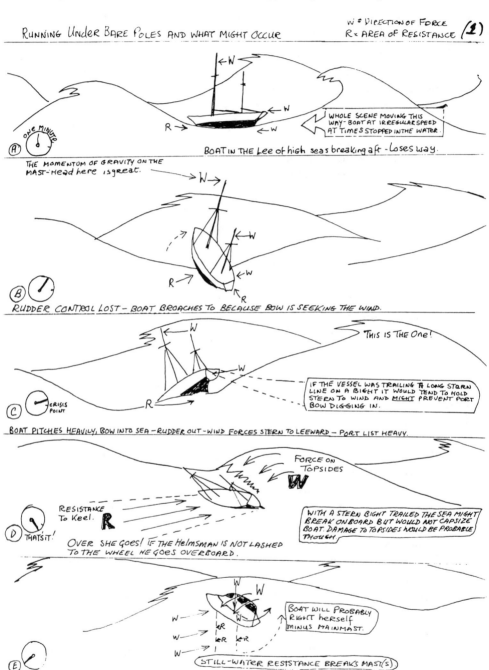

RUNNING UNDER BARE POLES AND WHAT MIGHT OCCUR

W = DIRECTION OF FORCE
R = AREA OF RESISTANCE **(1)**

(A) ONE MINUTE

WHOLE SCENE MOVING THIS WAY - BOAT AT IRREGULAR SPEED AT TIMES STOPPED IN THE WATER

BOAT IN THE LEE of high seas breaking aft - Loses way.

THE MOMENTUM OF GRAVITY ON THE MAST-HEAD here is great.

(B)

RUDDER CONTROL LOST - BOAT BROACHES TO BECAUSE BOW IS SEEKING THE WIND.

THIS IS THE ONE!

IF THE VESSEL WAS TRAILING A LONG STERN LINE ON A BIGHT IT WOULD TEND TO HOLD STERN TO WIND AND *MIGHT* PREVENT PORT BOW DIGGING IN.

(C) CRISIS POINT

BOAT PITCHES HEAVILY, BOW INTO SEA - RUDDER OUT - WIND FORCES STERN TO LEEWARD - PORT LIST HEAVY.

FORCE ON TOPSIDES **W**

RESISTANCE To Keel. **R**

WITH A STERN BIGHT TRAILED THE SEA MIGHT BREAK ONBOARD BUT WOULD NOT CAPSIZE BOAT. DAMAGE TO TOPSIDES WOULD BE PROBABLE THOUGH.

(D) THAT'S IT!

OVER SHE GOES! IF THE HELMSMAN IS NOT LASHED TO THE WHEEL HE GOES OVERBOARD.

BOAT WILL PROBABLY RIGHT herself MINUS MAINMAST.

(E)

STILL-WATER RESISTANCE BREAKS MAST(S)

Figure 35

HOVE TO UNDER MIZZEN, BARE POLES OR TRYSAIL — SAME SEA CONDITIONS.

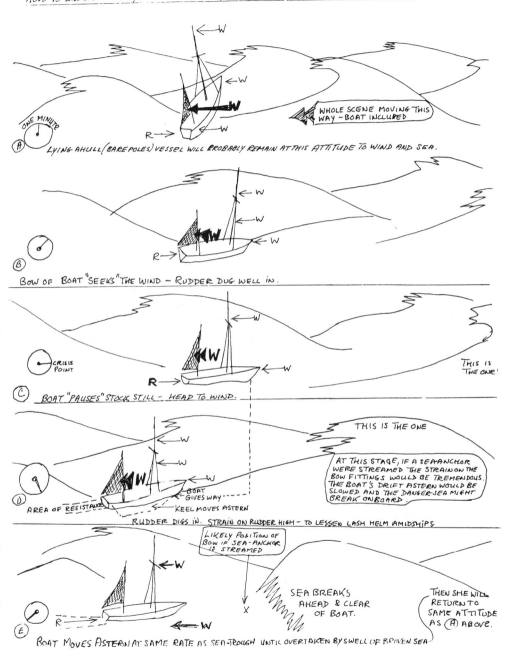

(A) ONE MINUTE

WHOLE SCENE MOVING THIS WAY — BOAT INCLUDED

LYING AHULL (BARE POLES) VESSEL WILL PROBABLY REMAIN AT THIS ATTITUDE TO WIND AND SEA.

(B) BOW OF BOAT "SEEKS" THE WIND — RUDDER DUG WELL IN.

(C) CRISIS POINT

BOAT "PAUSES" STOCK STILL — HEAD TO WIND.

THIS IS THE ONE!

(D) AREA OF RESISTANCE

BOAT GIVES WAY

KEEL MOVES ASTERN

RUDDER DIGS IN. STRAIN ON RUDDER HIGH — TO LESSEN LASH HELM AMIDSHIPS.

THIS IS THE ONE

AT THIS STAGE, IF A SEA ANCHOR WERE STREAMED THE STRAIN ON THE BOW FITTINGS WOULD BE TREMENDOUS. THE BOAT'S DRIFT ASTERN WOULD BE SLOWED AND THE DANGER SEA MIGHT BREAK ONBOARD.

(E)

LIKELY POSITION OF BOW IF SEA-ANCHOR IS STREAMED

SEA BREAKS AHEAD & CLEAR OF BOAT.

THEN SHE WILL RETURN TO SAME ATTITUDE AS (A) ABOVE.

BOAT MOVES ASTERN AT SAME RATE AS SEA-TROUGH UNTIL OVERTAKEN BY SWELL OF BROKEN SEA.

Figure 36

weather subsides, you can shin up to the spreaders with a hacksaw and cut the mast at the break, so the upper half can be got down and lashed on deck.

If the upper mast snaps off at the spreaders, the best thing to do is to cut it loose and either get it on board or get rid of it. The ideal thing to do is to "capture" the masthead and release and secure the stays from it, also the halyards. These will be needed for setting up the mast stump, forward and aft, for a jury rig.

In these days, with the extensive use of turnbuckles, it may not be necessary to cut the wires, but in a very furious storm it will not be easy to fiddle around with pliers and levers. It may be necessary to cut the wires, and for this reason a very sharp ax, well preserved in grease and paper, should be kept on board. Also a seven-pound hammer and three or four cold chisels, with a metal block for placing under the wires. All these tools should have lanyards, so they can be tied to whoever is using them. Keep a good supply of hacksaw blades, too, well greased and kept sacred for dire emergencies.

If possible, try to keep down low when working in bad weather. Always wear a lifeline, and do as much as you can sitting down.

If you carry a storm trysail, this can be rigged on the stump of the mast, as a jury main, to steady the boat. One of the jibs can be hanked onto the forestay, when it has been seized onto the mast stump. In this way, slowly, you will be able to make way, running off the wind, to the nearest shipping lane or haven.

If you are dismasted offshore, not intending an ocean passage, and cannot contact the coast guard, the best thing is to heave-to and patiently wait for a vessel to come into sight—that is, if your engine is out of order, of course. If it's not, head in, but in any case make a signal to the first craft you come across.

I firmly believe that the next great advance in small-vessel safety is going to be some safe and sure system of getting rid of the top hamper, and by that I mean masts and rigging, because if this could be done we could lie hove-to forever, with much less hazard. The vessel would present a low profile and be snug. The Arab dhows have this great advantage. Once the lateen boom is down they present only a short, stubby mast to the elements. No stays, no shrouds, no rigging to resist the wind. Just imagine what a blessing it would be if, after returning to the mooring you could press a button, or wind a handle, and all that ridiculous (in harbor) web of spars and wire disappeared to deck level!

A New Mast

Constructing a Hollow Wooden Mast

Before setting off on long-distance voyaging, it is worthwhile to consider taking along with you the materials and tools to build a replacement mast in case you lose the first.

It would be even better if all the parts could be made up accurately before you commence the voyage. Each piece would need to be marked. If this was done, a replacement mast could be constructed when needed very quickly, in no more time than would be required to assemble the precut pieces and glue them together. In a typical thirty-foot sloop, for example, Bermuda-rigged, with a thirty-six-foot-long mast keel-stepped, each side of the mast would consist of three preformed, prescarfed pieces, each about fourteen feet long (allowing for extra lengths for scarfs). These could be carried on the cabin deckhead under the side decks, even if it meant passing them through a bulkhead in order to fit them in, all twelve pieces. In a new wooden hull construction these pieces might even be incorporated in the wooden cabin sole.

It would be very difficult to construct a hollow wooden mast from uncut pieces on board a dismasted vessel, though I have no doubt that some of the skillful carpentry wizards I have known could do it, despite the boat's movement. In a crewed vessel it would be much more of a possibility.

Erecting such a mast at sea in, say, a thirty-foot sloop, alone, would be a difficult task indeed, but I am sure that in a crewed boat, if, in the absence of a mizzen mast, some sort of sampson post could be rigged up aft capable of supporting the weight of the new mast, it would be worth a try, if all the moves were carefully thought out before the task was attempted, and given calm weather conditions. In any case, if there was a need to build even a short jury stub mast, these instructions could be helpful to the builder.

In a yawl or a ketch, which could use the mizzen-mast as a

sampson post, the erection of a full-size mast might be easier, but not much more so.

For all that, if our hardy, handy mariner finds himself dismasted on a well-wooded shore, the following information might be of use to him when he sets about replacing his mast.

To keep the job as simple as possible, I have made use of outside-the-mast halyards, rove through external blocks. This makes for a simple masthead arrangement. For vessels over thirty feet LOA, the main halyard block should be double-sheaved, and a single-sheave block on the head of the mainsail. This avoids having to fit a main halyard winch. Galvanized and hardwood fittings with mild steel or bronze fastenings can be used on a wooden mast. There is no fear of galvanic corrosion, as there would be with an alloy mast, where stainless steel fittings must be used.

MATERIALS FOR A GLUED HOLLOW MAST   Wood is compartively easy to work and requires only simple tools. Almost any kind of wood will do, though the best are, in order of preference, spruce, Douglas fir, pitchpine, mahogany, hemlock, ash, cedar, and teak. Spruce is the lightest for a given strength (twenty-six pounds per cubic foot). The box-section mast shown in *Figure 37* is the natural choice for a jury-rig. It has very simple butt joints that are easy to fit perfectly. The flat port and starboard sides of this mast will make a natural base for all the hardware. The hollow interior space is rectangular, so it's easy to fit in the necessary solid blocks in high-load areas. Obtain rift or edge-sawn timber for the box-section mast. This will ensure that it planes easily when you are rounding off the spar. The timber you order should have about 14 percent moisture content and should be stowed in a fairly dry place. Choose timber to stagger the scarfs so that none will be side by side on the completed mast. Have the timber planed to accurate thickness, according to your mast plans.

Make sure you get enough timber to make the scarfs and blocks.

Resorcinal glue is the best proved for the job, although it demands a minimum drying temperature of twenty-one degrees Celcius for full strength. Waterproof resorcinal glue is one part powder and one part liquid and so needs mixing, but it is more certain to do the job than the newer products.

TOOLS REQUIRED TO MAKE A HOLLOW WOODEN MAST   Many of the necessary tools will be on board anyway: six clamps as in *Figure 41B* or six G-clamps; jack plane; claw hammer; ordinary ripping and crosscut saw; 25-mm wood chisel; square; old paintbrush for glue; pen-knife; brace and bits; plywood straight-edge one meter long; 6×30-mm (¼×1¼ inches) pine batten, five to six meters long (this can be stowed on deck, along toe-rail); putty knife. The timber listed in the chapter on emergency gear can be used to make temporary supports for the construction.

METHOD OF CONSTRUCTION   For further clarity I have identified the surfaces of the box-mast as they appear with the mast erected, i.e., port (P), starboard (S), forward (F), and after (A). I have called the P and S surfaces "sides" and the F and A surfaces "faces."

The thinner P and S side pieces of the mast are the first to be prepared (see *Figures 37D, E*). They must be scarfed and glued together to form the length of the mast (a simple scarfing jig, *Figure 37C*). The identical aligning cleats should be fixed on both sides of the plywood straight-edge to make this. The same jig can be used to transfer the exact scarfing angle to all the edges of all the timber. The jig illustrated is designed to give a 12-inch-long (300 mm) scarf on 1-inch-thick (25 mm) timber. This gives a safe minimum scarfing ratio for the spar.

Use the scarfing jig to guide your penknife whilst you cut a mark carefully from the squared edge to the end of the timber and mark each edge of both places. The line you have inscribed is your exact jointing line. Now lay the two boards you are scarfing end to end, "inside" up, *Figure 37D*. Check that the waste wood is being removed from the correct side of each board. Now make saw cuts an inch apart through the "waste" material to within 1/16 inch of the line you have scribed with your penknife. Chisel off the waste wood, using the saw cuts as guides, then plane the remaining waste wood to the scribe-lines, checking across the scarf with the straight-edge under the sole of your plane. Set the plane-blade shallowly and keep the joint fair and true as you work slowly down to the scribe-line (*Figure 37C*).

Now test your scarf for fit. One finishing nail driven in from the inside of the timber will help in aligning and gluing. The joint should be tight and straight along the scribe-line. If it isn't, remove the aligning nail and slightly hollow the scarf 1/54 inch across its face. Re-clamp and check the fit until the point is true and tight.

Now glue up the scarf. Replace the aligning nail, apply both surfaces of the scarfs with plenty of glue, and clamp both surfaces together and adjust them so they are straight along the edges. Scrape

Box-Mast Diagrams

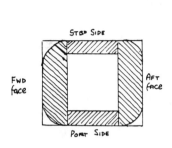

STB^D SIDE

FWD face

AFT face

PORT SIDE

A. *Cross-section of Box-Mast*

(*The shaded area shows finished section.*)

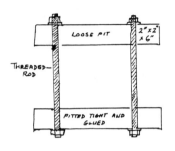

LOOSE FIT

2"×2" ×6"

THREADED-ROD

FITTED TIGHT AND GLUED

B. *Home-made clamp — Cross section.*

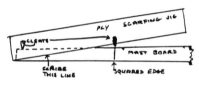

PLY   SCARFING JIG

CLEATS

MAST BOARD

SCRIBE THIS LINE

SQUARED EDGE

C. *Home-made Scarfing Jig*

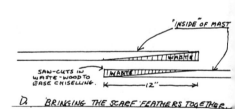

"INSIDE" OF MAST

SAW-CUTS IN WASTE-WOOD TO EASE CHISELLING.

|←————12"————→|

D.   *Bringing the scarf feathers together.*

G. Assembly.

MASTHEAD.   AFT. FACE.

①   SIDES P & S WITH BLOCKING GLUED ON.

FORWD FACE

AFTER FACE COMPLETE

②   INSERT ALUMINUM FOIL NOW.

FORWARD FACE

③

FIX MASTHEAD CAP.

FORWARD FACE COMPLETE.

④

Figure 37

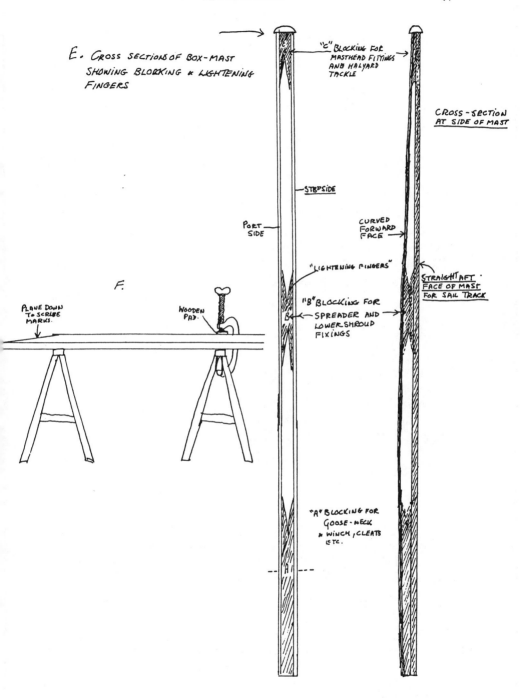

E. CROSS SECTIONS OF BOX-MAST SHOWING BLOCKING & LIGHTENING FINGERS

"C" BLOCKING FOR MASTHEAD FITTINGS AND HALYARD TACKLE

CROSS-SECTION AT SIDE OF MAST

STEPSIDE

PORT SIDE

CURVED FORWARD FACE

"LIGHTENING FINGERS"

"B" BLOCKING FOR SPREADER AND LOWER SHROUD FIXINGS

STRAIGHT AFT FACE OF MAST FOR SAIL TRACK

B

F.

PLANE DOWN TO SCRIBE MARKS.

WOODEN PAD.

"A" BLOCKING FOR GOOSE-NECK & WINCH, CLEATS ETC.

A

off the excess glue with a putty knife. When the glue is dry, plane both sides of the scarf so the result is two continuous flat P and S mast sides. The two (forward and after) faces are then built up the same way.

Our box-section mast will have the after, or sail-track face, straight (*Figure 37E*). The forward or leading side of the mast will be tapered toward the masthead. The taper could expose some of the defects in the timber, so now is the time to decide which is to be the forward or the after face of the mast, and which is to be up. Clamp the after and forward full-length faces together inside to inside and plane the two sail-track edges and flush (*Figure 37E*). The resulting straight after-face will be the baseline for measuring the gradual taper of the mast. Unclamp the full-length F and A faces and turn the inside up. At the top of one side measure from the straight (after) sail-track face, the width of the side at the masthead, minus the thickness of the fore and aft faces. Carry on down the mast sides, measuring and marking the width of the mast sides at the appropriate spacing. Lightly nail the long batten to the marks on the inside of the timber. The batten should bend in a smooth curve. If not, adjust the nails until a smooth curve is obtained. Now pencil a mark along the batten and saw off the waste wood. Keep the saw square. If it is impossible to do this, cut the waste wood off on the waste side of the pencil line and square it off later.

Using the shaped side as a pattern, pencil-mark and cut the other side. Once this has been done, the two full-length sides can be clamped together insides facing in, and the fore and aft edges of both sides can be squared off at the same time. The two mast sides will now have a fair curve on the forward edges and be square straight on the after edges.

Blocking is used to take the compression strain at the butt (foot) and the masthead, to take the strain of through-bolts, and to provide extra bearing surfaces for the fasteners at the shroud fittings. Internal blocking enables this type of mast to be glued up in easy stages. This is important to the lone sailor who has only two hands and a limited number of clamps.

POSITIONING THE INTERNAL SOLID BLOCKING   To show this I will use as an example a keel-stepped masthead sloop-rig with one set of spreaders (*Figure 37E*). This type of construction works as well for any Bermuda-rigged mast, however.

Shape block A to fit between the P and S sides, giving it the correct dimensions and taper. The fore and aft dimensions of block A should be left about 1/16 inch (1.5 mm) larger than the sides. It will be planed down later.

The lightening fingers are now cut into the top of block A. These four fingers should be about 18 inches (450 mm) long in the average forty-foot spar, to spread the bending load over a large area. Completely solid blocking would not spread the load and would cause hard spots in the mast, tending to weaken it under strain.

After cutting out the wedges that form the fingers you must now figure out how and where to install drain holes. In a short block, vertical drain holes can be easily drilled through the length of the block, but the longer butt (mast-foot) (A) block will have to be glued together in two pieces with a groove cut in each to make a drain hole when they are brought together.

Clamp block A between the two P and S mast sides. Clamp the tapered fingers to the sides using G-clamps, or slide the cut-out wedges back in place and clamp with your homemade spar clamps. If all looks fair, take it apart and glue it, then reclamp it together.

Now fit blocks B and C, one at a time or both together, using the same steps as for block A.

With all the blocks now glued into place between the port and starboard sides, you are ready to plane the fore and after edges of the P and S sides and the blocking in between.

The most difficult part of the mast construction is now completed. All that remains is to fit the top and bottom of the mastbox and the thicker forward and after faces. The reason that these two faces of the mast are thicker than the sides is because this allows for large-radius rounded-off forward corners to the mast and also gives extra depth for sail-track screws.

Check the forward and after faces across the grain with the straight-edge for dishing and hollowing. Get the two faces as flat as possible.

Lay on the first plank as in *Figure 37G(1)*. Center it using one clamp every 10 to 12 inches. Clamp the plank in place dry and check the fit of the jointing surfaces. Mark the mast taper on the first plank by running a pencil along the P and S side pieces next to the jointing edge. Unclamp. If there is now more than ¼ inch extra width, saw down just to the pencil mark, leaving about 1/16 inch to be planed off when the glue is dry.

If all checks out well, brush on glue and clamp up, using a flat block with wax paper under the clamp to hold the feather edge of the scarf tight. After the glue is set, carefully unclamp and lift the flat block from the feather edge of the scarf, chisel any glue off the scarfing surface, then clamp the next piece in place. Mark, cut to width, then glue in place.

Turn the now three-sided box-mast over as in *Figure 37G(3)*, but before you put the last face on put into the hollow mast a filling of crumpled household aluminum foil. This will, when the mast is completed and erected, give you a great long, very efficient flat-sided radar reflector.

Now the F and A faces as shown in *Figure 37G* can be glued on. The box-section mast will look ready to be rounded off. But don't do this until you have marked out the locations of all the hardware on the mast: spreaders, winches, cleats, etc.

Once this has been done you can round off the leading corners of the mast and complete the job.

The best plan for a long-distance vessel is to apply several coats of varnish, and then, having rough-rubbed the final dry coat, apply two or three thin coats of white or light gray gloss paint.

MATERIALS AND TOOLS LIST

Mast port side pieces	Square
Mast starboard side pieces	Paintbrush
Mast after face pieces	1-m ply straight-edge
Mast forward face pieces	$\frac{1}{4} \times 1\frac{1}{4}$-inch pine batten
Timber for blocks	5 to 6 m long
Glue	Putty knife
6 G-clamps	Aluminum foil
Wax paper	Sail track
Jack plane	Double blocks (2)
Claw hammer	Single blocks (3)
Penknife	4 $\frac{1}{2}$-inch diameter ring bolts
Saw	(mild steel)
25-mm wood chisel	6 foot $\frac{1}{4}$-inch screwed rod
Pencil	with nuts

Staying Alive

THE first virtue required of a budding single-hander is patience. Patience to master thoroughly all the aspects of seamanship; not just how to sail his boat in all conditions of weather and environment, but how to keep each and every one of the hundreds of essential bits of gear, tackle, tools and equipment, spares and rigs, in good order—"Ship-shape and Bristol fashion," as the saying goes.

One thing the visitor to a single-hander's vessel must not do is to pick something up, say, a book off the library shelf, or perhaps a knife or spike hanging in its bulkhead stowage, without first asking. Nothing is more infuriating to the solo sailor, after being alone for several weeks, taking religious care that everything is in its place, than to have things moving by a means outside the skipper's control. It's not only the fear of losing material possessions; it's that everything must be controlled.

PATIENCE, FORESIGHT, AND SELF-DISCIPLINE By foresight I mean the ability always to have alternatives to any course of action that is under way, and to be able to put them in order of preference. As Napoleon said, "A good army always covers its line of retreat." No one has to be Merlin, or sit gazing into a crystal ball, but the single-hander should have enough experience (which can only be truly gained by sailing in other craft with experienced sailors) to know the possible consequences of a set of circumstances and to be ready to put any one of a set of alternatives afoot. He should always be ready to turn around 180 degrees, if necessary.

Consider my own example, which whilst it is perhaps an exaggeration of the usual problem-alternative process, is nevertheless a good object lesson.

I had sailed almost across the Indian Ocean from Madagascar, on my way to the Straits of Malacca, the China Sea, and the Pacific Ocean, intent on reaching the coast of Peru, in order to haul across

151

the Andes to Lake Titicaca. In the Seychelles, having received news from Peru (my foresight and caution had caused me to contact yachtsmen in that far-off country whilst I was yet in Israel) that my vessel could not be hauled up from the Pacific coast, I thereupon made a 180-degree turn and sailed for the Amazon, half a world away, around the Cape of Good Hope. And again, having reached halfway up the Amazon and finding it impossible to go on because of the strong current and other insurmountable factors, I turned around yet again and sought other alternatives.

A single-hander should never put himself on a course, in any activity, that leaves him no alternatives. For instance, he never puts himself, if he can possibly avoid it, anywhere near a coast, just in case it turns into a lee shore. If there is more than one possible haven, on a coast, he will always shape his course for the one farthest to windward; he then has the option of running down onto any one of the other havens. If he enters a crowded roadstead he will anchor or heave-to well out, clear of the other vessels, and either row in by dinghy or await assistance to enter, rather than risk damaging his own or other craft. There is no shame in this; it is simply good seamanship. There is no such thing as macho at sea. The only thing that matters is the well-being of first your own vessel, then other vessels.

The concept of solo sailing across the oceans is pregnant with boldness, adventure, and audacity. But that's only the concept, the strategy of the voyage, if you like. In the everyday activity, in the tactics, the watchword is, and indeed must be, *wariness*. Every move must be thought out before it is made, every possible consequence examined, every alternative plotted. There's an old sailor's saying, "If it looks bad, it usually is."

Now, being wary and pessimistic does not mean that you must be miserable. The joy comes in finding, as you will about 65 percent of the time, that you have indeed chosen the right alternative. If you can get that percentage up to 75, then you can consider yourself a true solo sailor; up to 85, you will be a paragon.

Solo sailing in coastal waters or on inland waters is much more of a strain, is significantly more nerve-wracking, than being alone way out in the ocean. It is for this reason that the single-hander should always get out and away from the shore, regardless of his eventual course. When approaching a destination after a longish, or indeed any single-handed passage, the rule is to stay well out until you are at right angles to the destination; then, if there are no obstacles to the approach, always make the approach at right angles to the destination, and, if possible, a little to windward of it. That way you will be more likely to avoid any uncharted obstacles (which are always a hazard, especially in the out-of-the-way parts of the world), and you will keep a commanding wind.

Approaching a destination at night, heave-to, just in range of the lights (or, if there are none, even farther out), and make your approach at dawn. On approaching coral from the *west*, try to make the approach in the afternoon; from the *east*, in the morning, when the sun will be shining behind your back, delineating the underwater hazards. This is especially so where there are no markers or lights.

If the entry to an unmarked or unlit haven seems to be too dangerous, do not hesitate to put about into the offing. If the land is inhabited, someone will have seen you (another reason for the daylight approach) and will perhaps come out to guide you in; if it is not, press on to a safer destination if you can.

In this respect, except perhaps for various parts of Central America, northern South America, the Middle East, and Indonesia, there is generally nothing to fear from local inhabitants. The average inhabitant is a pretty pleasant, honest guy and will help and welcome you.

On coastal passages or in inland waters, a constant lookout must always be kept, for other craft, for tides and currents, for outlying hazards, for fishing nets and a hundred other obstacles that might bring at the least embarrassment, at the most complete disaster.

My own passages down the west coast of South America, or in the confined waters of the Red Sea and Gulf of Aden, were a thousand times more tiresome and wearying than any ocean crossing I have made, especially as these coastal passages were made directly against the prevailing winds and currents.

On coastal passages or on inland waters, the helm should not be left to look after itself, nor the constant lookout neglected for more than a few minutes at a time. Don't forget that if you are making five knots and a steamer or fishing boat is making eighteen, your combined, converging speed is twenty-three knots—that's around thirty miles an hour. In moderate visibility this means that a steamer that was below your horizon when you went below can collide with your vessel in around twenty minutes, and if it's a big tanker or grain ship the chances are that her helmsman will not even see you.

If you are single-handing to windward along the coast, you must sleep in snatches during the day whilst you are on the offshore tack. Your alarm clock must be tested each time you set it. Several craft have been lost because of the failure of an alarm. A fail-safe arrangement I had was a pipe wrench hanging over my bunk on a thin sail-maker's thread that chafed on a lamp bracket over my feet. The thread would wear through, because of the violent movement of the boat, in roughly twenty-five minutes and the pipe wrench would fall on my feet. A bit painful, but effective.

A dog is very handy in this respect, for he can be trained to wake you up if he sees anything. The way you do this is to get out in the offing and feed him only when there are other craft around or when you come into sight of the shore. He very soon gets the idea. But of course animals need food, so I, in a very small vessel, adopted the sore feet routine.

Another idea is to have two or more alarm clocks; then if one fails, the other will wake you.

As regards sleep, in my experience, I found that a total of four hours in twenty-four was sufficient, regardless of how long the naps were. The longest I have stayed awake was five days, but I was much younger then and doubt if I could do it now; indeed, I see no reason why I should, because the reason for not being able to sleep is anxiety, and reason shows that no hazard exists for more than a brief spell at a time. Even in the worst situations I now manage to drop off for a few minutes. That few minutes can work wonders. My advice to any-one shipwrecked, for example, is to try to sleep as soon as it is safely possible to do so, if it's only for a few seconds. Sleep is probably the animal answer to anxiety, which is dangerous, for it brings on fear, despair, and even death. Once you are accustomed to your vessel and the way she behaves, you can sleep soundly even in heavy weather. In a yawl I simply hand everything but the mizzen and let her lie-to. In a sloop or cutter I dowse all sail and let her drift, almost beam-on to weather, with the helm lashed down. It's a bit bouncy, but it allows me to get a nap.

If I am on a lee shore, I make my way out into the offing a good distance, maybe seven miles or more, before I take a nap. The boat usually makes about a knot and a half leeway, so that gives me a margin of around four hours in which to sleep one hour.

Out on the ocean, I still sleep during the day, with the boat self-steering. The reason is that if there are any ships around, there is a much better chance that the lookout will see me, especially as I always rig a radar reflector. Also, the less I perspire, the less fresh water I need to drink. Anyway, I prefer to be up and around at night, for often out in the wide ocean even the starlight is bright enough to be able to read by. My ocean routine is to wake around 4:00 P.M., make a meal before sunset (enough for two helpings), make star sights at dusk, then settle down to odd chores (sail repairs, check, etc.). If I can get radio reception, I listen to that for a while. Star sights at dawn. Doze from dawn to 8:00 A.M. Second meal. Cleanup below, on deck, and self (rub over with damp freshwater flannel), odd jobs until noon. Noon sights, then turn in.

If becalmed, I sometimes go over the side after dowsing the sails and flounder around on the end of a securely tied line. When I'm back on board I sponge off again in a little fresh water to avoid salt-water sores. In the clear water of the ocean I also take the opportunity to check the bottom, and even to scrub off the waterline, which soon gets pretty foul. The risk of attacks by sharks is minimal. They are cowardly creatures, except maybe the great white, and he generally sticks to coral reefs, where he is assured of a plentiful food supply. But if I did see one, I would soon be back on board, just in case.

NAVIGATION LIGHTS   The International Marine Conference's (IMCO) new Regulations for the Prevention of Collisions at Sea, which affect all craft except on inland waters, came into force in July 1977. There are many changes in the requirements of all lights for most types of vessels.

The calculations of candlepower (measured in candela) required to obtain visibility at various ranges in various conditions is obtained from the following formula. If this baffles you as much as it did me at first, skip it, but environmentalists will find it both edifying and alarming.

Now: I   equals $0.686 \times T \times D^2 \times K - D$

Where I   equals candela required

D   equals distance in nautical miles

K   equals *atmospheric transmissivity*

T   equals threshold factor. $(2 \times 10 - 7)$ (Don't let this boggle you, just accept it, just like we accept the statue of Liberty —it's there!)

In this formula, K is the most important factor. It expresses the difference between clean air, with no dust, no fog, no smog, no humidity, and dirty air. Absolutely clean air is expressed at 1.0. And any other condition down to thick fog is expressed as a fraction of this. A clear dark night was called 0.9K in former years, but (and this is indeed a sign of the times) it was recently found in European waters that a visibility of 0.9K, "a clear dark night," existed on less than 5 *percent* of days! This was because of the increase in air pollution over the past two decades. This tells more than all the student screaming about pollution on earth.

Now the situation is such that IMCO has agreed on a "clear dark night" being 0.8K. In two decades, near the continents, the harum-scarum chase-ass of so-called advanced society has deprived us of 10 percent of our visibility!

Even more telling is the fact that the lighthouse authorities in most European and American countries are now using 0.74K as the figure for "a clear dark night." That's *more than a quarter of our visibility*, since 1912, *gone!*

Table 1 shows candlepower required for navigation lights at various ranges, by the IMCO (1977 rules).

Table 1 VISIBILITY AND CANDLEPOWER

D	K 0.9	K 0.8	K 0.74
0.5	0.181	0.192	0.199
1	0.762	0.858	0.927
2	3.387	4.288	5.011
3	8.469	12.059	15.236
4	16.729	26.796	36.603
5	29.043	52.337	77.286
6	46.469	94.207	150.396
7	70.278	160.284	276.629
8	101.991	261.688	488.259
9	143.42	413.998	835.071
10	196.742	638.887	1399.178

The visibility ranges in nautical miles required by the new rules are shown in *Table 2*.

Table 2

LOA	Light	Power boat	Sail boat
Over 12 meters but less than 20 meters	Masthead	3	3*
	Side	2	2
	Stern	2	2
Less than 12 meters	Masthead	2	2*
	Side	1	1
	Stern	2	2

* When under power

So we see that with a modern "clear dark night" as defined by IMCO at 0.8, to be seen at five miles' range we need 52.5 candle-power. At ten miles' range, 639 candela. Given the restrictions of space and electrical power available in a small sailing craft, say, of less than forty feet, I would aim for a visibility of six miles at visibility of 0.8K. This means 94.25 candela for the masthead light, and a visibility of three miles for the red and green lights on each side and the white light astern. The power of these lights would, therefore, be twelve and a bit candela.

Bear in mind that for the masthead light I have recommended double the visibility distance (D) that IMCO asks for, but kept in step with them for the steaming lights.

The approximate candlepower of a good-quality dioptic lens kerosene lantern I guess at around 5.0 candela. This is the size with a three-quarter-inch wick. On clear nights, at anchor, it could be seen from just under four miles away, but I had to look carefully for it whilst at three and a half miles away. It was remarkable (this word used in the original, the navigator's way, which means that if your head is pointed in that direction, with your eyes open, and given that your eyesight is normal, you can see it easily). At three miles it was bright and clear. I know, because at one time my old dioptic light, which, incidentally, I bought for less than a dollar one Sunday morning in London's Petticoat Lane, was the *only* navigational light on the whole of Lake Titicaca, which is full of hazards and about as big as Chesapeake Bay! It was used to mark a tiny harbor, with a twelve-foot-wide entrance, encumbered for miles out with reed beds, when I would be sailing in at night with a wind of around forty knots blowing onshore! On Taquila Island, one of the most beautiful spots on God's earth. For remote open waters I would use a one-inch wick dioptic kerosene lantern.

Keeping the Vessel Afloat

Defend the vessel and she'll look after you.

It is often far safer to be in a damaged yacht, in open waters, even if she is partly flooded, than in any life raft in existence today. The chances of survival and of being sighted and rescued are far higher in the larger craft, if she can be kept afloat and does not have to be abandoned, even if she is seriously damaged below the waterline. To my mind, a skipper who allows the crew to abandon ship before it is really necessary, before all hope of keeping the yacht afloat is gone, is

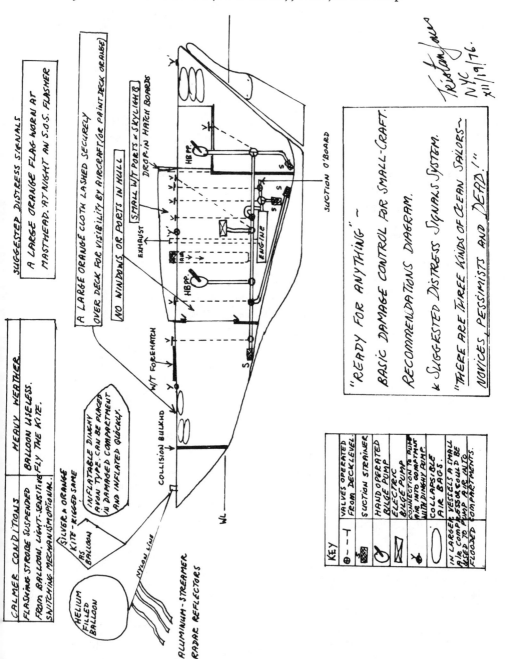

Figure 38

guilty of nothing less than intended, as actual, manslaughter. In recent years this situation has occurred time after time; it's about time it ceased, or at least diminished.

We must think up methods of keeping the boat afloat even though the hull has been badly damaged by, for example, collision with an iceberg or other inanimate flotsam, or, as very nearly happened to me in mid–Indian Ocean, with an uncharted reef, or even with sea monsters such as whales or great white sharks, or swordfish.

The cost of making a vessel ready in terms of watertight integrity before she sails is far, far less than the cost of search and rescue by aircraft or other vessels, or of losing the boat by her foundering.

The first provision for readiness might be two watertight bulkheads in every vessel that may be expected to make an ocean crossing. This would make a three-watertight-compartment hull. Lloyds, in their requirements for ocean racing, ask for a third, collision bulkhead forward, ahead of the anchor and chain stowage, and of course they are right. At the forward end of the cabin there should be a bulkhead, with a watertight self-closing door, up to deck-head level.

At the after end of the cabin there should be a watertight bulkhead up to companionway hatch or coaming level. Close attention should be paid to the watertight integrity of any pipes or electric leads that pierce these bulkheads. The recommended test for watertightness of all compartments down below is low air pressure pumped into three pounds per square inch.

Both the main watertight bulkheads, at the forward and after ends of the main cabin, should be double-skinned and filled with close-cell polyurethane foam. This will provide extra strength and buoyancy.

Wherever there are empty spaces that might fill up with water if the boat were damaged, these should be filled with closed cell syntatic foam. These will resist waterlogging for up to two months. Ping-Pong balls sealed in plastic bags could serve also.

In my thirty-footer, if she is to be fiberglass, I would ask for double-skin hull from the waterline to the keel. This would be filled with foam.

INFLATABLE BAGS These should be carried in case of very heavy damage. They should be cylindrical in shape and are inflated in the same way as a rubber dinghy. There should be enough of these to give positive buoyancy to the hull. Collapsed and stowed, they take up very small space compared to the comfort provided by their presence.

The design of hatches in small craft leaves, generally, much to be desired, especially forehatches. The number of boats that have foundered as a result of being flooded through a broken-off forehatch approaches stellar proportions. The forehatch must be strong enough to resist the weight of a two-hundred-pound mass dropping straight onto it from the masthead. It must be secured all around, in a similar fashion to a spider-locked door. Ideally, it should be large enough for use as an escape hatch, oval, with the small radius facing forward and aft, thus giving less resistance to head seas. Ideally, the forehatch would be surrounded by a low, strong, breakwater.

If the after end of the boat is flooded, provision must be made for running the engine (if fitted) underwater. The air intake and the exhaust should be led to above deck level for this purpose. The engine water suction intake should be fitted with a remotely-controlled on-deck bypass valve, so that suction can be taken from the bilge. This is termed the salvage suction.

At least one bilge pump, preferably the one of largest capacity, must be operable from deck. All filling and air vents to tanks, fuel, and fresh water, must be led to a point *above* deck level. In heavy-weather or hazardous areas, the main engine batteries must be sealed off with polythene.

DAMAGE-CONTROL GEAR   Apprentice seaman shouts to grizzled bosun: "There's water coming thru the 'ole, boats!" Bosun mutters: "Well, wot d'ye expect, bloody *champagne?*"

In case you collide with another ship, a whale, or flotsam, you should be prepared to deal with any but the most serious hull damage. The ideal hull would be built of rubber, or perhaps newspaper impregnated with rubber solution; then objects would just bounce off. But that, perhaps, is in the future. As it is, we have wood, fiberglass, metal, or concrete. I know very little about the effect of heavy impacts on concrete, so I will not discuss it. With wood, repairs are comparatively easy. It is a matter of having some fairly large (according to the space available) sheets of marine ply on board, some shoring timbers at least the length of the vessel's beam, and a riveting tool or one of those very strong stapling machines. If your money won't run to that, then have a good supply of galvanized nails longer than the hull thickness and a hefty hammer. If the damage can be tackled from outboard, so much the better, but if not, it will be a case of getting the patch on from inboard. If the holed area is extensive, don't attempt to put the patch on right away; try to stuff a blanket or even a sail into the hole first, to reduce the inrush of sea water, then shore the patch onto the hole with the timbers, and rivet it or nail it. Once the nails are through they must be bent over, either inboard or outboard, on the other side of the hull. If you have to go over the side to do this, don't forget, in the rush, to wear a safety harness and lifeline. In arctic areas carry a wetsuit, but wear woolies under it.

There is a quite effective ready-made damage-control hole bunger on the market. It is shaped something like a square umbrella, and the action is much the same. The unopened umbrella is poked through the hole from inboard, then opened, and the flat, square canvas hood opens up, covering the hole. It is then kept in place by a kind of submarine hatch-bolt inside the hull, and also by water pressure outside. I have seen one of these, though not in use. I think they must be very effective and would recommend that they be carried on a trans-oceanic voyage. They are made by Simpson, in England (trust an Englishman to come up with an *umbrella*) and, as we might expect, they are known as Simpson Gear.

The old-fashioned type of collision mat, with its long lines to be passed around the hull outboard, its guys and weights, while it can be made up cheaply, is unwieldy on small, single-handed craft, though it can be a potential godsend on the larger, with a crew.

COLLISION MATS   When a yacht is extensively damaged below the waterline, it can be almost impossible to deal with repairs from inside the boat. Except in the case of a small through-hull breach, the chances of forcing an umbrella-type hole stopper, or a sail, or a blanket into the hole are minimal. The force of the water would likely be far too great for any but the strongest man. Therefore, we must think about tackling the job from outside in the quickest, easiest manner. We do not want to go over the side, especially if single-handed and a non-swimmer. I used the following method, known as the Jonah line.

A collision mat is carried according to the size of vessel. It should be made of heavy canvas, triangular, about four feet on each side for a thirty-footer. Lines and clips are secured to each corner and the mat is kept on deck, in a weatherproof stowage, yet easily accessible. Three people are going to block the hole in *less than one minute*, a single-hander in two minutes.

At sea, a bottom-line messenger is permanently rigged (see *Figure 42*), led from about the foot of the rigging screws above water, around the bow through a hollow weight (which is releasable from the cockpit), and so to the rigging screws on the opposite side. The

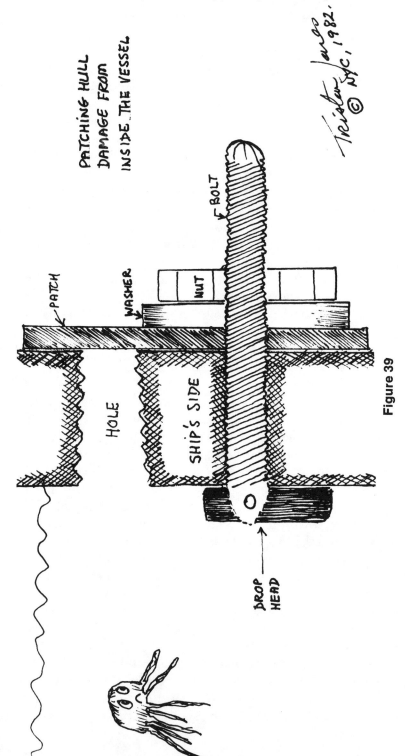

PATCHING HULL DAMAGE FROM INSIDE THE VESSEL

Tristan Jones © NYC, 1982.

PATCH

WASHER

NUT

BOLT

HOLE

SHIP'S SIDE

DROP → HEAD

Figure 39

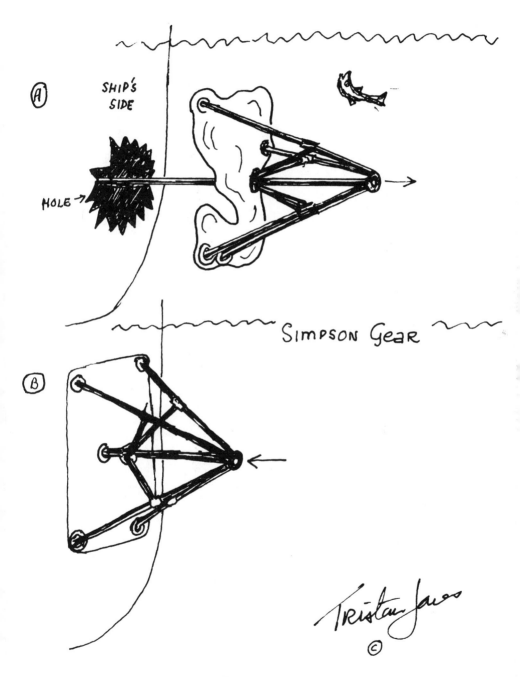

SHIP'S SIDE

(A)

HOLE

SIMPSON GEAR

(B)

Figure 40

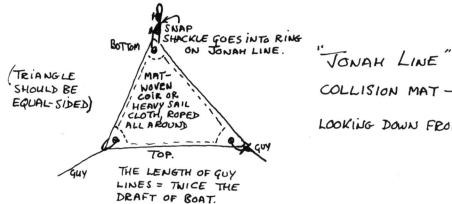

SNAP SHACKLE GOES INTO RING ON JONAH LINE.

BOTTOM

(TRIANGLE SHOULD BE EQUAL-SIDED)

MAT— WOVEN COIR OR HEAVY SAIL CLOTH, ROPED ALL AROUND

GUY

TOP.

GUY

THE LENGTH OF GUY LINES = TWICE THE DRAFT OF BOAT.

"JONAH LINE"

COLLISION MAT —

LOOKING DOWN FROM DECK

ANOTHER WAY TO REPAIR HULL DAMAGE

WEIGHT

LARGE VESSELS ONLY →

BOOM

DAMAGE

WEIGHT

IN CALM CONDITIONS THE BOAT CAN BE HEELED OVER. KEEP STEERAGE-WAY ON WITH A SMALL HEADSAIL UNTIL HOLE IS PATCHED.

© Tristan Jas NYC. VI/24/82.

Figure 41

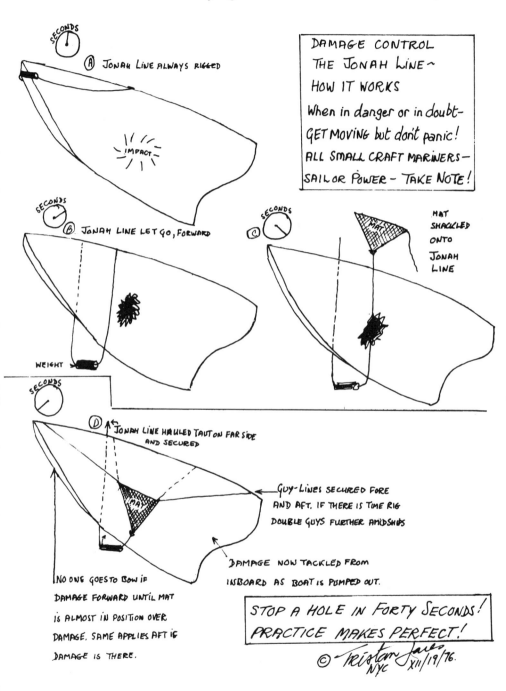

Figure 42

line used should be hefty enough to use as a securing line to a towing hawser, in case that should be needed.

The in-use routine is as follows: Secure one corner of the mat to the messenger. Release the messenger. When the mat is in position over the damage, haul the messenger up the undamaged side, keeping the two other corners of the mat taut with the fore and aft guys. Secure all in place taut and tackle the damage from inside of the hull. This will be much easier now that the flow of water has been staunched.

Lastly, practice with the system before you leave harbor. Iron out all the potential problems.

YACHT TENDERS AND LIFE RAFTS   The question often arises as to whether or not the dinghy or tender should be carried on board or towed astern. This depends on a number of factors: the type and size of dinghy, the size of the mothercraft, the area being sailed, and the weather to be expected.

In large craft (over, say, forty feet LOA) on transoceanic passages, the dinghy can probably be stowed on deck if it is the rigid type, or down below, deflated, if it is an inflatable. In small craft, under thirty feet, it is practically impossible to stow the tender on deck because of its size and the extra windage created, especially going to windward. Therefore, the best type of dinghy for the small craft is the inflatable. The inflatable tender, for the same reasons, has many advantages for the larger craft also.

Another advantage of the inflatable is that in small craft, if an outboard engine is carried as the auxiliary unit it can also be fitted on the dinghy for longish harbor trips. But the greatest attraction of the inflatable, to a pessimist (and we should all be that), is that in extremis, if the boat is severely damaged and in danger of foundering, the rubber dinghy can be inflated inside the hull as an emergency flotation device.

Nowadays the reputable rubber dinghy manufacturers turn out very hard-wearing craft, although none of the American models have yet reached the standard of excellence demonstrated by the British (Avon) and the French (Zodiac). The average life expectancy of one of these yacht tenders, in the eight- or nine-foot-length range, given reasonable care, is around five years. If damaged they are comparatively easy to repair, and, unlike the wooden, fiberglass, or metal dinghies, they are almost noiseless when they are bobbing alongside the mother craft and cause no damage even if they collide with the yacht.

If the dinghy is towed astern because of lack of space to stow it on board it will to some extent affect the speed of the yacht, especially when going to windward. Running downwind, it should be towed on a fairly long line, but going to windward it should be hauled in until the bow of the dinghy is practically resting on the yacht's counter. In this way, only the stern of the dinghy will be dragging in the water. The dinghy should not be hauled up completely to the vessel's counter, as otherwise the wind will get underneath it and overturn it. Therefore, it follows that whenever a dinghy is being towed it should not have any loose gear, such as unsecured oars or lifejackets, in it.

If there is no through-hull log fitting in the craft, a counter-speed log is used. On this type of log there is a long line streamed out astern; this is where one of the snags of towing a dinghy occurs, for when running before a stern wind (as in most transoceanic passages), the dinghy is strung out on a longish line. It sways from side to side continually, and there is a risk that it will foul the log line. In this case the dinghy must be towed up close when running as well as when reaching. This will cause wear and tear on the dinghy bow, with the continual chafing, so some kind of rubbing guard should be rigged on the dinghy bow. A very good method is to secure, either by gluing or tying, part of an old car inner tube over the dinghy bow.

As shown in the chapter on self-steering gear, if a wind-vane steerer is fitted, or an automatic pilot, a lifesaver line should be towed astern in case anyone falls overboard. On the lifesaver line a separate lanyard is strung, which when pulled will trip the self-steering gear. Here, then, is another stern line for the dinghy to foul, and yet another reason for finding some method of stowing the dinghy on board.

The best way of stowing the tender on deck is to try to obtain one that will fit upside down on the coachroof fully inflated. If this cannot be done, half of the inflatable compartments of the dinghy should be deflated and the dinghy stowed on deck in this manner. Rubber boat manufacturers supply quick-inflation devices, and one of these can be fitted to the deflated section(s). In this matter the dinghy can be released from its stowage and fully inflated in a matter of a minute. This is important when navigating in shipping lanes or in areas where whales are known to congregate. In these areas, in a very small craft, where it is impossible to stow the dinghy on deck in any form, it should be towed astern, ready for use, regardless of the possibilities of fouling stern lines.

The dinghy oars should be secured down on deck, and there should be a spare pair carried below. At sea an abandon-ship kit, packed in a plastic container, should be carried not too far from the cockpit, secured to a two-gallon can of fresh water. The dinghy kit should contain waterproof matches, a flashlight with spare batteries, a small compass, a pencil and notepad, vitamin tablets, a small mirror, a dinghy repair kit, a set of small emergency flares and smoke signals, and a couple of fishing lines and several hooks. A small orange kite with a long line would also be handy as a signaling device to other vessels and aircraft.

Nonemergency gear for the dinghy should include a small grapnel anchor secured to a one-and-a-half-inch dacron line, ten fathoms long, a flashlight in working order, and, if an outboard engine is fitted, a set of engine tools in a sealed plastic container, an airpump, and a small dinghy repair kit.

In a small craft cruising in out-of-the-way areas, a dinghy is absolutely essential, because it is often impossible to go alongside for various reasons: lack of jetties, rats and other animals, thieves, or the overexuberance of enthusiastic visitors. Therefore, the dinghy is like the crutch to the cripple, and must be maintained and guarded well. In fishing harbors it is a good idea either to bribe someone trustworthy to guard the tender for you, or if this is impossible, to moor it out from the jetty. Then the oars and the anchor and other paraphernalia must be taken ashore with you and placed somewhere safe, such as a shop or café.

SAFETY HARNESS   The reputable types of safety harness are of stitched canvas webbing over nylon line. This is fitted with stainless steel snap-shackles; the whole rig has a breaking strain of two thousand pounds. However, it is no good wearing a safety harness and then fastening the snap-shackles to a fitting with a breaking strain of only two hundred pounds. The usual method of securing the harness to the boat is either on the guardrail or on the coachroof handholes. The former, on many production-type vessels, is dubious, as the guardrails and their stanchions are just not capable of holding a two-hundred-pound man, being swept away by two tons of seawater or not, whilst the latter in the case of the ordinary wooden hand holds, is often semi-suicide. The best method is to run a stainless steel rigging wire right along the length of the coachroof, making sure it is securely fastened to fittings strong enough to equal the breaking strain of the harness. The fixing and the length of the harness-securing wire will depend on the on-deck characteristics of the vessel, but it should be rigged in a way that enables whoever is wearing the harness to reach all parts of the topsides, from water level to a height of six feet above deck level, or as near to that as is possible.

It is too much to expect the ocean navigator, even the single-hander, to wear a safety harness at all times at sea, particularly in fine weather. In some crewed boats I have sailed in there has, in the past, been a sort of macho thing about leaving the harness off even when a storm was howling. This is foolishness. A skipper of a crewed boat should insist on harnesses being worn whenever there is only one person on watch, especially at night when the rest of the company are sleeping, and by everyone on deck whenever there is a wind harder, or a sea rougher, than the average. Single-handers have only themselves to worry about. On the other hand, there is no one nearby to worry about them; therefore, they should be even more careful to wear a harness, to keep down low on deck, to grab a good handhold, and to keep a good foothold all the time, in fair weather or foul.

CHECKLIST OF SAFETY ITEMS

Alarm clock
Radar reflector
Dinghy
Oars
Spare oars
Outboard motor
Tools for above
Dinghy anchor
10-fathom line
Quick inflater
Safety harness(es)
Harness cable
Lifejackets
Lights for above
Batteries for above
Bailer

Dinghy Emergency Kit

Plastic sheeting, tubing, funnel
    bags, solar still(s) and lashing
    lanyard
2-gallon fresh water container
1 radar reflector on pole

Flashlight
Spare flashlight batteries
Waterproof matches
Emergency position indicator
    radio beacon on 2182 Mhz
Small compass
Knife and sharpener
Pencil and notepad
Electrical tape
Small mirror
Dinghy repair kit
Fishing kit
Signaling system (radio)
2 reflector space blankets
Emergency flares
Whistle
Smoke signals
2 fishing lines and hooks
Gaff hook
Small kite and line
Plankton net
Sunglasses
Sewing kit, SS needles and
    nylon thread

Medical Kit

Antibiotics
Splints
Tape
Bandages
Painkillers
Skin ointment
Vitamin tablets (especially
    iron and vitamin C)

Food

Yeast tablets
Carbohydrates
Glucose

Candies
Vitamin biscuits
Honey
Condensed milk
Dried-frozen beef sticks

Miscellaneous

Masthead light
Side lights
Stern lights
Dioptic lens kerosene lamp
Inflatable bags
Jonah line with hollow weight
Collision mat, lines, and clips

Note: The emergency solar fresh-water still should *not* be towed astern of the dinghy, as generally recommended by the makers. If the weather is boisterous, the still will be jerked and the fresh-water-making process ruined. The still should be lashed *alongside* the dinghy. This makes its movement steadier and ensures a sufficient fresh-water supply.

A short, but important, note on nautical grammar: Because of the special relationship of mariners to their vessels, the ship or yacht is never referred to as "it." She is always "she" in the English language. By custom and usage immemorial, it is the only case of the use of a genitive personal pronoun applied to an inanimate entity (except in the U.K., where "she" can be correctly used when referring to a sovereign country). To refer to a ship or any other craft (except small, uninhabitable boats) as "it" is incorrect.

When speaking of vessel never, again by ancient custom, use "the" before her name. "Q.E.2 is departing" is correct. "*The* Q.E.2" is not.

Ensigns and flags, burgees and pennants (the correct spelling is pendants) are *worn* aboard any vessel. They are *not* "flown."

Destinations, landfalls, ports, havens, and so on are *fetched*; "arrived at" is not strictly correct, although it may be used. Sailors do not "leave" a ship (unless permanently)—they "go off" her.

Table 3

Letter	Morse	Phonetic	International Code (Single-Letter Signals)	To Help Your Memory— Key Phrase
A	•–	Alpha	I have a diver down—keep clear.	Away!
B	–•••	Bravo	I am taking in explosives.	Bang!
C	–•–•	Charlie	Yes.	Si!
D	–••	Delta	I am maneuvering with difficulty.	Danger
E	•	Echo	I am altering my course to starboard.	Screech
F	••–•	Foxtrot	I am disabled—communicate with me.	Floundering
G	––•	Golf	Require a pilot.	Guide me
H	••••	Hotel	I have pilot on board.	Have guide
I	••	India	Altering my course to port.	In-port
J	•––––	Juliett	I am on fire and have explosives on board.	In a jam
K	–•–	Kilo	I wish to communicate with you.	Kom here
L	•–••	Lima	You should stop your vessel instantly.	Lie Down
M	––	Mike	My vessel is stopped.	Mud
N	–•	November	No.	No
O	–––	Oscar	Man overboard.	Overboard
P	•––•	Papa	I am about to proceed out of port.	Pilot
Q	––•–	Quebec	My vessel is healthy. I require pratique.	Prati–Q
R	•–•	Romeo		
S	•••	Sierra	I am going astern.	Stern
T	–	Tango	Keep clear of me.	I'm a terror
U	••–	Uniform	You are running into danger.	You!
V	•••–	Victor	I require assistance.	Vish
W	•––	Whisky	I require medical assistance.	Want
X	–••–	X-Ray	Stop carrying out your intentions —watch for my signals.	Xed
Y	–•––	Yankee	I am dragging my anchor.	Yelp
Z	––••	Zulu	I require a tug.	Zeecure

Table 4 INTERNATIONAL CODE: TWO-LETTER GROUP
SIGNALS FOR EMERGENCIES AND INFORMATION

Letters		*Signals*
AE	•— •	I must abandon ship.
CI	—•—• ••	Can I help you?
CN	—•—• —•	I cannot help you.
JI	•——— ••	Are you aground?
JL	•——— •—••	You are in danger of going aground.
JW	•——— •——	My ship is leaking.
KN	—•— —•	I cannot tow you.
LN	•—•• —•	The light at ——— is not working.
LO	•—•• ———	I am not in position (used by light-ship).
LR	•—•• •—•	The entrance is not dangerous.
LS	•—•• •••	The entrance is dangerous.
MF	—— ••—•	Your course to reach me is . . .
MG	—— ——•	You should steer . . .
NF	—• ••—•	You are running into danger.
NG	—• ——•	You are in danger.
PD	•——• •—••	Your navigation lights are out.
PT	•——• —	What is the state of tide?
QX	——•— —••—	Can I anchor?
RY	•—• —•——	Slow down passing me.
UF	••— ••—•	Follow pilot boat.
UO	••— ———	Do not enter . . .
UT	••— —	Where are you bound for?
YK	—•—— —•—	I cannot answer you.
ZM	——•• ——	Speak (or send) more slowly.
ZP	——•• •——•	My last signal is canceled. I will remake it.
ZQ	——•• ——•—	Your last signal is garbled. Please repeat.

Fiberglass in Plain English

As a retort to one or two critics who say that I am "anachronistic" and "born too late," and without using too much technical jargon, I make these observations on modern fiberglass hull building and repairing practices in Britain and the United States. However, I am also writing for people who have at least an elementary knowledge of the makeup of fiberglass.

The advantages of fiberglass over other constructions when it comes to maintenance of the hull are too well known to be dealt with here. I will, therefore, deal with basics of hull construction and of hull repairs, and I will leave it to you to draw your own conclusions as to the relative advantages of fiberglass over other construction materials.

Materials

Fiberglass is known in the boat building trade as glass-reinforced plastic or GRP. GRP and concrete and similar constructions are different from steel or wood in that these materials are mixed and the structure is fabricated at the boat building site, usually by semi-skilled labor. Therefore they cannot be subject to good internal inspection before using. The content of the structure, the nature of the resin, the resin/glass ratio, the type of glass, the type of accelerator, the structure of the gel coat, pigments, and a precise definition of the lay-up plan are obscured by the necessarily fast curing process. Wood and metal, of course, can be examined before using and after erection can be given inspection, but this is not possible without elaborate analysis in the case of fiberglass.

Therefore, quality in fiberglass hulls can only be assured by rigid control of purity and adequate quality control in the laying-out shop. Polyester resins, the usual boat building materials, are sensitive to shock temperatures and liable to considerable degradation of properties by contaminants, dust, carbon, etc. This particular aspect can be monitored only by on-site quality control.

THE GEL COAT   If the gel coat is faulty, or too thin, we can expect a lack of impact resistance, and flaking, surface crazing, and cracking. Since the main body of the GRP is not pigmented, the gel coat produces the hull color, but it is also perfectly practical to produce a hull without a pigmented gel coat.

These days a gel coat may be considered as an 0.015-inch-thick coat of a selected polyester resin formulated to provide flexibility and impact resistance. A thixotrophic (a "vertical fixer") additive is necessary to prevent drainage of the gel coat on vertical surfaces. Very often a thin glass cloth or tissue is incorporated at the back of the gel coat to improve impact resistance and decrease a tendency to surface cracking.

RESIN   The group of resins from which boat building materials are selected can be considered as an assembly of long chainlike molecules or polymers, not all of which are used for synthetic resins. Many members of the group form the basis of other substances such as polypropylene, dacron, nylon, etc. They are all derived from the hydrocarbon chains based on oil.

Long-chain molecules are common in nature. Cellulose is the link molecule for the oldest known form of plastic wood. Other examples of natural polymers are spider webs, silk, and human hair. (There's nothing new under the sun.)

Polymer molecules are like a long row of atoms shaped something like a strip of Velcro, which will join freely to a similar strip and so form a bond. Molecules are said to be unsaturated because they are a bit like Casanova; they have atoms in them that have a desire for linkage with another atom, and given the chance (that is if they are close to another suitable interface molecule) will lock together and cure into a solid. In boat building polyesters, the interface molecule is liquid styrene and a boat building resin consists of a 60/40 percent solution of a polyester in styrene. No styrene, no cure, is the rule, and it is for this reason that sometimes large surfaces are covered with plastic sheeting to prevent too much loss of styrene inhibiting a cure. At the same time the covering preserves the surface in a condition to accept a further layer of cloth and resin.

The change from a solution of polyester resin in styrene into a rubberlike solid needs time and temperature, but the gel time is greatly reduced and the resin is cured to a hard, tough material by introducing a catalyst. This promotes the curing by providing chemicals essential to the reaction. Catalysts are usually organic peroxides and hence exceedingly dangerous. They should be kept securely away from children. Other than that, a catalyst is a substance that speeds up or slows down a chemical process. The catalyst itself does not change while this is going on. It is a bit like a pushy salesman—his potential customers may turn hot or cold, but his purpose remains.

The curing process, even with a catalyst, can be lengthy and incomplete without the application of heat and ultra-violet light, so an *accelerator* is added to reduce the gel time from days to hours and achieve a full cure. These are usually various compounds of tin, vanadium, zirconium, cobalt, and others. The change from liquid to solid generates heat, so the process is exothermic, and the heat generated is essential to accelerate it and complete the cure. Much of the trouble with gel coats arises because of their thin layer, which does not provide adequate exotherm, and extra accelerator is used to insure the cure. The result is that the gel coat treads a tightrope; on one side not enough accelerator; on the other too much, which may attack the pigment and cause discoloration of the outer surface.

The polyester group of resins is not the only possible plastic boat building material; there are others, such as the *epoxides*, which are much more expensive, have greater flexibility and greater heat resistance when heat-cured, and are very useful for tough gel coats and other surfaces that suffer considerable distortion, such as fishing rods. The great advantages of epoxides is their tolerance to cold damp conditions, and for that reason they are much more useful for repair jobs in the open. Unfortunately, epoxides are not compatible with polyesters, so you cannot use epoxides for gel coats over polyester laminate. The polyesters will not stick to the slightly greasy epoxides, which contain chemicals that inhibit polyester cure and reduce polyester strength.

One of the troubles with the polyesters is that they have a linkage point for another molecule to which substances like carbon readily latch, thus destroying the bond. Hence the need for cleanliness in laying-up shops.

Now that there is a polyester resin that is acceptable to the Classification Society, builders can proceed to use less of various additives such as pigments and fillers (the latter by sheer bulk reduce the cost of the mix). In the best-quality work the use of fillers is discouraged, although pigments up to a maximum of 4 percent are acceptable. In some cases there is little difference between an additive and a contaminant, and it is important that unsuitable additives do not take up the linkage molecules mentioned above and destroy the bond; in particular, the use of carbon as a pigment must be avoided.

All polyester resins are unstable. They have a limited shelf life, especially in the presence of sunlight, but an unpigmented polyester resin usually has a longer shelf life than one that has been pigmented, a sure indication that the linkage positions have been interfered with by pigments, although careful selection of chemically inert pigments can avoid this problem.

Fillers, by increasing bulk, reduce the cost of the mix and thus can be regarded as cheapeners, but by careful selection it is sometimes possible to improve abrasive resistance by their use.

Thus, we can see that the boat building resins are complex molecular assemblies, usually of polyester consisting of a polymer dissolved in styrene, which is essential for satisfactory curing. The mix consists of 60 percent resin and 40 percent styrene, of which 20 percent evaporates and 20 percent remains for linkage purposes. To assist the resin on vertical surfaces, a thixotropic agent is added. A catalyst cures the resin into a hard solid, assisted by the accelerator, which speeds the process.

GLASS   The fabrication and use of glass has been known for over a thousand years, and glass filaments, as used in boat construction, have been made and used since the early thirties. Nowadays the filaments are mainly made of TE glass, which is a low-alkaline borosilicate and is a mixture of silicone, aluminum, iron, calcium, manganese, barium, and sodium oxides. The filaments are some half-thousandths of an inch in diameter and in their early drawn state have a tensile strength of half a million pounds per square inch, which is ten times as strong as mild steel. Several filaments make a strand, and fifty or sixty strands combine to make a roving. But, unfortunately, glass is not a stable substance and deteriorates in time because of the presence of free radicals in the surface film. A free radical is not a liberated soap-box orator; it is a molecular pair waiting to capture another molecule from the air. Once this is achieved, the strength of the glass rapidly decreases.

To prevent this deterioration, the drawn filaments are immediately sprayed with either silane or chrome protector and coupling agent. It is also the custom to treat the glass to aid resin wetting; this is either carried out at the time the glass is drawn, in the case of woven rovings, or weaving size is removed by heat and another finish or binding agent is applied if the glass is in the form of a woven cloth.

Glass is a difficult material to resin-wet, it has an affinity for water, not resin, with the result that wetting out with resin is a difficult task.

There are differing ideas on how the resin grips the glass. Since polyester resin can contract up to 7 percent in bulk on curing, or 21 percent linearly, some people maintain that the grip is pure friction. The school of chemical bond theory points out that a wise choice of silane will strengthen the bond by at least one-third. The counter argument is that silane/chrome is more effective in preventing air attack and that the grip is still by friction. Still, glass will, with some reluctance, form a satisfactory interface with resin, but how it does so is a mystery.

The most commonly used reinforcement material is chopped strand mat, made of short lengths (two inches) of glass strands in a random mat, weighing one ounce, one and a half ounces, or two ounces per square foot.

The alternative reinforcement to augment strength is woven roving, which can be said to be a very coarse cloth, the warp and weft of which consist of bundles of untwisted glass strands, some fifty to sixty to a bundle, and the warp is considered as straight and continuous while the wefts pass over two or three warps, then under one warp, continuing its progress.

For really high-quality work such as nose cones for aircraft, GRP using fine woven glass cloth is utilized. The resulting laminate has high glass content and correspondingly good strength properties.

GRP is a versatile material, and naturally there are other possibilities. One worth mentioning is unidirectional woven roving, which is really a bundle of strands that can be used to augment strength in one direction only. These strands are held together by light wefts.

On their own, these glass cloths are highly flexible materials, and when encapsulated in resin they exhibit markedly different qualities according to which direction they are tested. When neighboring layers are separated, the bond is entirely dependent upon the strength of the resin, whilst along the warps of woven fiberglass it exhibits a very considerable tensile strength.

LAY-UP   The first necessity is care in cleanliness and measuring. The resin is decanted, the catalyst is added, the accelerator is tossed in, and we have the makings of a glass-reinforced plastic laminate that can then be rolled out into the glass fiber cloth. A table of properties we may expect once the material is cured is given at the end of this chapter. There is also a table giving the properties and costs that may be expected in the eighties, prices for glass resin, and various competitive or associated materials.

Resin in the cured state is a hard, brittle material, so it is important to incorporate as much glass as possible in order to obtain the best possible tensile strength, bending stiffness and impact resistance. Polyester chopped strand mat lay-ups rarely have more than 30 percent glass, while a woven roving will have at least 50 percent glass. Hence the woven roving's superior properties.

As seen in *Table 5*, all fiberglass materials here are light in weight, very strong in tension, but highly elastic and very bendy substances

Table 5 RELIABLE PRODUCTION FIGURES

Material	Ultimate Tensile Strength (lb/in²)	Ultimate Compressive Strength (lb/in²)	Youngs Modulus a Measure of Stiffness in Bending (lb/in²)	Specific Gravity	Glass Content (%)
Polyester (chopped strand, mat)	15,000	20,000	1×10^6	1.6	30
Polyester (woven roving)	30,000	25,000	2×10^6	1.7	50
Polyester (unidirectional roving)	50,000	40,000	4.0×10^6	1.8	50–60
Polyester (woven cloth)	60,000	60,000	3.5×10^6	1.9	70
Polyester resin	9,000	25,000	0.5×10^6	1.3	Nil
Epoxide resin	8,000	20,000	0.35×10^6	1.3	Nil
Mild steel	67,000	67,000	30×10^6	7.8	Nil
Aluminum alloy	30,000	12,000	10×10^6	2.7	Nil
Titanium	130,000	—	16×10^6	4.6	Nil
Mahogany	8,400	4,000	0.7×10^6	0.6	Nil
Glass filament	500,000	—	11×10^6	2.6	100
Carbon filament	320,000	—	45×10^6	1.8	Nil
Boron filament	400,000	—	60×10^6	2.7	Nil
Kevlar—an organic fiber by DuPont, basically an aromatic polyamide	525,000	—	19×10^6	1.44	Nil

with most marked property differences depending on direction of tests.

The boat builder usually aims for thickness and bulk, not tensile strength, throughout the hull. The exceptions are in the positions of

Table 6   CROSS-SECTION TO GIVE SAME

Material	Elongation	Bending	Ultimate Strength
Steel	1.0	1.0	1.0
Polyester unidirectional rovings, 70% glass	5.2	1.7	0.6
Polyester woven roving, 50% glass	13.0	2.5	1.7
Polyester chopped strand mat, 30% glass	30.0	3.1	2.6
Sheet aluminum	2.3	1.3	2.0
Basic Material Cost to Give Same			
Steel	1.0	1.0	1.0
Polyester unidirectional rovings, 70% glass	4.7	1.6	0.8
Polyester woven roving, 50% glass	10.5	2.3	2.3
Polyester chopped strand mat, 30% glass	20.6	2.2	3.2
Sheet aluminum	5.1	2.6	4.5
Weight to Give Same			
Steel	1.0	1.0	1.0
Polyester unidirectional rovings, 70% glass	1.2	0.4	0.2
Polyester woven roving, 50% glass	2.7	0.6	0.6
Polyester chopped strand mat, 30% glass	5.7	0.6	0.9
Sheet aluminum	0.8	0.4	0.7

pure tension such as shroud plates, backstay ram seats, etc., and similar positions.

When designing for equivalent compressive stiffness there is very little to choose between chopped strand mat and woven rovings, but the woven rovings offer double the tensile strength and bending resistance. Also with woven rovings there is a marked increase in fire resistance. This latter property is, of course, tremendously interesting to all of us.

Chopped strand mat fiberglass will readily burn, but woven roving fiberglass provides a fire curtain effect and so is largely resistant to fire, at least in the short term.

When it comes to cost there are other factors involved in choosing between fiberglass and other materials. Steel and aluminum structures are expensive, but whilst the initial mold cost for fiberglass structures is high, the unit cost falls sharply with quantity of output. The more the cheaper. With wood, costs are high and there is a high wastage rate. In advanced countries this makes wood now more expensive than fiberglass per ton worked into position. High-class timber and skilled labor are in very short supply, so for craft up to about seventy feet there is no reasonable alternative to fiberglass moldings, unless of course we choose ultimate performance regardless of cost for a one-off boat, when aluminum becames attractive, except for the fire hazard.

The difference in price between woven roving and chopped strand mat lay-up is still considerable. However, since the cost of labor to lay-up chopped strand mat is usually reckoned to be twice the material cost, as against two and a half to three times for woven roving, the price differential in the mold can be much more, depending on the mold size, which is a powerful reason to stick to chopped strand mat, with its considerable added advantage of being equally strong in all directions. Compare the cost of various complexities of construction using the best mixture of practices; I have attempted this in *Table* 7. There is an obvious need for a well-thought-out lay-up plan that will exploit to the full various advantages presented by the various glass reinforcements, to say nothing of considerable shopping around for materials.

OTHER POSSIBLE REINFORCING MATERIALS   There are some other, more exotic fibers besides glass that can be used to reinforce resin. These are carbon filaments, boron filaments, and the DuPont aromatic polyamide (aramid), which goes under the trade name of Kevlar. How-

Table 7 COSTS AT AUGUST 1977 PRICES

Material	£ per Ton*
Type E glass	
Unidirectional roving	1,400
Woven roving	1,400
Chopped strand mat	1,350
Polyester resin	550
Epoxide resin	1,500
Mahogany	600
Marine ply	2,000
Steel plate	200
Aluminum plate	1,300
Lead	400
Laminates laid up in the mold:	
A very simple structure with mixture of woven roving and CSM with little in way of internal structure	1,300
With rather more floors and stringers	2,200
A complex boat form with numerous floors, stringers, internal stiffening, bulkheads, etc.	3,500

* These prices in pounds sterling may be converted into dollars at the current rate. For 1982 prices for the U.S., add 15 percent.

ever, all these materials are in the nature of expensive, esoteric exotica. These uncommon materials have considerable advantages over glass when incorporated in a resin because they are either appreciably lighter or have better resistance to bending than the ordinary fiberglass laminates.

Carbon fibers have been around for over twenty years, but their use is still restricted to various specialized areas where high strength is at a premium and tortional bending stiffness of the utmost importance. The cost of carbon fiber is a major obstacle, and although the tensile strength is extremely high, the fibers are weak in shear and can be easily broken during the weaving process.

Although the potential advantages of carbon fibers are obvious, the cost and the necessity to check the compatability of the resin with the carbon (you will recall that carbon is one of the most dangerous contaminants of the polyester-type resin) have restricted the use of carbon fibers to the odd fishing rod, parts of racing car bodies, trimming on aircraft wings, helicopter blade leading engines, missile fins, and the like, although at least one of the yachts in the last Whitbread Round-the-World Race had a carbon fiber mast.

At the bottom of the strength table is a brief mention of the fairly new DuPont aromatic polyamide (aramid), with quite remarkable properties. In its filament form it is stronger than glass, and has roughly twice the bending resistance than glass and half the weight. The result is that DuPont feels that Kevlar can outperform glass-fiber-reinforced plastic, or indeed carbon-reinforced plastic. The cost is high, about ten times as expensive as glass, but somewhat better than carbon fiber. In appearance this material is smooth woven cloth rather like fiber glass but with a golden yellowish tint. If its properties are realized in practice and no important snags develop as experience is gained in its usage, then clearly it is a sort of happy medium, as far as cost is concerned, between glass and the more expensive carbon/boron filaments. In most cases, designers do not aim for ultimate tensile strength but for resistance to bending and impact. In these latter fields the carbon/boron filaments have a very considerable advantage.

There have occasionally been suggestions that it might be advantageous to fabricate mixtures of glass and one or another of the exotica which could be used with profit in the high-stress areas of plastic-reinforced structure.

But a mixture of high-tensile-strength, low-elongation materials, with a greater volume of medium-strength, high-elongation materials must inevitably lead to the stiffer materials snatching an undue share of the load and the more elastic materials taking little or no interest in what's going on.

Imagine an aluminum mast whose shrouds consist of a mixture of dacron rope and stainless steel wire. No matter how tight the dacron was made, it would not contribute a great deal to the support of the mast because the stainless steel would snatch almost all of the load. However, such a simple analogy begins to fail when the two materials are bonded into a low elongation or brittle resin. Therefore, another method, which is a bit more pragmatic and divorces itself from such theoretical considerations, is to make up mixtures of high-strength fiber and glass fiber into various types of laminates, and then to proceed from an analysis of the test results, to correlate these results with the cost of the mixture, and try to optimize the best strength/cost ratio. Utilizing this type of approach, carbon glass polyester resins do seem to offer considerable advantages in fatigue life and bonding strength, but at such a cost as to strictly limit usage to high-stress areas.

Repairs to Fiberglass

Sooner or later every fiberglass hull comes to grief in one way or another. There may be a big scratch sustained when coming alongside, damaging the gel coat and exposing the fibers. Or continual bumping against a buoy may abrade the gel coat, to say nothing of physical crushing and other damages caused by impact.

To commence the repair process it is necessary to cut away the damaged areas, working a long scarf exposing the fibers in an effort to key a patch or repair onto the damaged area.

Such a repair must be supported by a temporary mold at least on the inside, and the joint between the old and the new structure is not a bond of the type which was on when the boat was laid up in the mold, but is much more in the nature of a resin glue. Therefore there is a potential weakness across the joint that can only be satisfactorily resolved by a reinforcing lay-up on the inside, which is again complicated by the fact that the main part of the hull is no longer "green" and so is reluctant to take the linking action I mentioned earlier. The inside of the hull is therefore disc-abraded or shot-blasted to obtain a suitable surface for bonding.

However, such repairs can be carried out quickly and satisfactorily, but of course they do not have a gel coat on the outside that is in any way comparable with the original finish. We are, in effect, building the boat inside out, so that when the lay-up is completed we place on a scrim cloth, which would be the backing to the gel coat, and then apply the gel coat in its pigmented form by brush.

However much work has been done on the underlying layers of the fiberglass repair, to make it smooth and compatible with the original hull, laying on the gel coat by brush must inevitably produce a less satisfactory finish than that on the neighboring parts of the hull, and so the only solution is an extensive process of rubbing down with wet-and-dry followed by polishing. A satisfactory repair is usually possible.

An alternative and perhaps better method, if it is possible, when extensive hull repairs are needed, is to lay up a mat over the identical area of a similar boat, using the resulting molding to act as a female mold for a part hull to scarf over the damage. Excellent and rapid repairs are possible using this method, and strict control of pigments by resin manufacturers make excellent matching a really practical proposition.

Manufacturers occasionally find boats in which the gel coat is unsatisfactory when the hull is removed from the mold. In such cases they have two possible solutions: They can either rub down the hull and apply another gel coat by brush, accepting the poor finish that would result and secure a good finish by abrasion and polishing, or they can paint the hull.

Painting of fiberglass hulls can be a tricky process because the fiberglass tries hard to retain some of the parting agent, and paint will not stick to parting agents. Occasionally wax is applied to the mold, and this enables the mold to be easily removed from the hull; but more commonly the parting agent is polyvinyl alcohol. This latter material does not contaminate the gel coat as much as a wax parting agent, and as a result it is possible to remove the polyvinyl alcohol with a washdown using a strong detergent.

When a cured example of polyester resin is examined, it will be found that the whole of the styrene cross linkages are not taken up, and as a result, even in an old hull, there are available some styrene points not otherwise engaged. Therefore, if we could devise a molecular bond that would link onto these available locations, we would come a long way toward applying an almost perfect surface. Some paint firms claim to be able to do just that.

The process starts with the application to the washed and in some cases wet-and-dry-sanded hull of an isocyanate-based wash primer, which is claimed to latch onto the unbonded molecules of the gel coat, thus forming a good basis for the subsequent application of a polyurethane, which being of the same general family as polyester is said to make an excellent surface bond. What is more important, the polyurethane is harder than the original gel coat and thus resists abrasion even better than the original hull.

After the wash primer has gone off, two casts of two-pack polyurethane are sprayed on and then cut back with an abrasive polishing medium, followed by a final burnish, which results in a hull almost indistinguishable from the original gel coat.

Hulls that have suffered from gel coat wrinkling or have definitely used wax as a parting agent, or alternatively had deep scours and abrasive gashes caused by careless handling of the ship, must be given a cut back to a fair surface using wet-and-dry before attempting the polyurethane treatment.

The chemistry of fiberglass is a complex subject. There is still controversy about the actual mechanics of the various processes. Therefore, your ordinary fiberglass cruiser does in many ways resemble a considerable chemical technological exercise. Treat the process with very considerable respect and care, and do not take it for granted unless you are looking for trouble.

REFINISHING Refinishing of a fiberglass repair takes time and effort. Obtaining a result similar to the original manufacturer's finish is not easy.

Epoxy paints, whilst easy to apply, will powder after a few years and dull. Polyester coatings are better. The big disadvantage of polyester finishes is the difficulty of application, as they cannot be applied in a perfectly smooth coating. They must be mechanically finished after application, that is, sanded, wet-dried, and polished. Here is the method:

The hull surface to be refinished should be sanded with fine sandpaper (about 0.150-grit). If this is done by hand, it should be with a vibrator-pad sander or with a soft disc sander, preferably employing a flexible swivel head. The type of sanders with firm rubber discs are unsuitable as they leave gouges in the surface, which are hard to disguise. Cracks or gouges, if present, should first be filled and finished off with suitable repair materials. When the final sanding is completed, the surface should be absolutely smooth and free of flaws. The sanded surface at this point should not be touched by hand or any other part of the body, as traces of skin oil remaining will cause the polyester surface coating when applied to "crawl."

When you have finished sanding the surface to be refinished, wipe it with acetone applied with a clean cloth. After the acetone has evaporated, rub down the surface again using a clean "tack" cloth, which you can probably obtain from a car body repair shop. This will remove all traces of dust on the surface.

All adjacent areas to the surface to be refinished should be masked off, and the masking tape should be pressed down very firmly to prevent any entry of the finish under the tape.

The polyester coating can be done by hand or spray; but generally the spray equipment needed is very expensive, and requires a highly skilled operator. For the amateur, brushing is the best way.

The brush used should be a good pure-bristle type with, preferably, tapered bristle ends. A brush that is too stiff or too soft will not do. A three- or four-inch-wide brush is generally suitable, but if there is considerable trim work, a narrow trim brush should also be used.

The application of polyester coating should not be done in direct sunlight. The best conditions are a shady place or a cloudy day. Make sure that no dust or flying insects, which both have an affinity for wet polyesters, are able to approach the finish. Polyester material is usually obtainable in small batches in the original hull manufacturer's colors from the builders. If it is not, the surfacing resin, white or clear, should be obtainable from a chandler's, along with pigment of the desired color.

The polyester material should be checked for pot life and thixotrophy (this means vertical stiffness and holding power). A surfacing additive should be mixed in with the polyester material, or, if not, it should be a non-air-inhibited resin containing a wax additive to accelerate the cure. The materials should be heavy enough to be flowed on with the brush in a heavy (10 mL) coating without crawling or slopping about. Regular gel coats are generally thixotrophic anyway, but if they are too thick they can be thinned by adding a small amount of styrene (a nonevaporate thinner for polyesters). If styrene is not at hand, add small amounts of lay-up resin to thin the polyester.

The polyester materials should be catalyzed so that the cure is as rapid as possible within the time allowance for the work. The amount mixed at any one time is generally about one quart, and this can be easily applied within twenty minutes of mixing.

The catalyst should be thoroughly stirred into the polyester material for a least one minute. The sides and the bottom of the can should be wiped with a stick to ensure that there is no uncatalyzed resin hiding there. It is best to pour the mixed polyester from the mixing can into another container, which is used for the actual application brushing. This is another way of making sure that no uncatalyzed polyester is hiding.

The polyester should be laid on in a heavy thickness using horizontal strokes, working from top to bottom. Try as hard as possible to avoid rebrushing, as this could displace the wax surface additive film. Overlapping with the paint brush should be done while the polyester is wet, as it does not lose solvents in the same way as paints.

Clean your brush in acetone after applying each quart of polyester and shake and dry out the brushes afterward to ensure that no acetone is left in the brushes, or on the metal brushholder.

Usually only one heavy coat is required. Sometimes, however, if there are opacity problems, it will be found necessary to apply two coats. In this case there should be a light sanding between applications.

Once the polyester coating is cured, it then will need to be block-sanded using fine sandpaper to remove all brush marks and any odd

or high spots. After this it should be wet-sanded with 400-grit sandpaper, then with 600-grit wet/dry sandpaper. Finally it should be
polished and waxed.

With luck, after you have sweated away at the above technique
the refinishing will be as good as the original factory-finish gel coat.

Outboard Motors

Most oceangoing yachts these days carry outboard motors of one size or another, and some of the smaller yachts use them as main-propulsion units. During the past two decades the efficiency and dependability of outboard motors have increased enormously. The same cannot be said of the average standard of maintenance.

Before you set out on a long-distance voyage, the outboard motor(s) should be, if possible, serviced by a qualified mechanic. If this is not possible, you will have to do it yourself. In any case it is a good idea to become thoroughly familiar with the outboard motor before making your departure, as in less advanced areas of the world it will be necessary for you to maintain the unit.

STARTING RIGHT   The checkup commences with water testing of the motor in order to burn out any winterizing oil or softened carbon deposit with the old spark plugs. The motor should not be run out of the water, as dry-running would damage the water pump. Once the in-water testing is completed, the old spark plugs should be removed. This will prevent accidental starting. Replacement spark plugs should be of the same type as specified in the outboard owner's manual.

IGNITION SYSTEM   This should be inspected for any damaged or worn wires and loose or corroded connections. If major problems are suspected, the best thing to do is to contact a qualified mechanic before interfering with the ignition system.

FUEL FILTFR   If the filter element is of the permanent type it should be cleaned with a neutral solvent and a clean brush. If the filter is replaceable, a new one should be installed. After the filter unit is reassembled, connect the fuel line to the gasoline tank and prime the filter by squeezing the primer bulb. Check for leaks in the re-assembled filter and also in the fuel system.

LOWER UNIT The outboard motor lower unit should be lubricated at this point. Stand the motor in an upright position and drain out the old oil from the lower unit into a pan. Check the color of the drained oil for water content. If it has taken on a caramel color, this shows water in the gear case. If traces of water are found, a thorough check of the lower unit must be made in order to find the crack or broken seal where the water has entered. If there has been an accident to the propeller during previous use of the motor, you may find that the lower unit also has been damaged. Damage can also occur if the unit has been stored in a cold place, where water has leaked into the gear case, frozen, and expanded. If there are any gear-case cracks or leaks, again a qualified mechanic should be asked to service the unit.

Replacement gear-case oil should follow the owner's manual recommendation. This is important.

Check the outboard motor for the capacity of the gear case and fill the unit until the lubricant reaches the oil-level hull. The oil-level plug should be installed before the lubricating tube is removed from the oil drain/fill hull. This will prevent any loss of lubricant. Any air still trapped inside the gear case will vent and escape once the motor is started or if it is stood in a vertical position for a number of hours. You must always make sure that the lower case lubricant is at the correct level.

Other parts of the motor will require lubrication; this also should be done with the proper oils as listed in the owner's manual. The throttle and gear linkage lubrication should be given special attention, but too much oil and grease will collect dirt and grime.

If the motor has a battery, check this with a hydrometer, clean the terminals and the cable connections, and coat the terminals with petroleum jelly.

PROPELLER The propeller should be inspected for any damage. A malfunctioning propeller can lead to severe effects on the motor's performance, such as slowing down or excessive vibration. An improperly pitched propeller or one that is too large or too small can overload or overspeed the unit. An outboard motor dealer can advise you on the correct propeller for your motor.

The exterior of the outboard should be cleaned, rinsed, and wiped dry.

An outboard motor should not be run with its cover removed under normal circumstances. The danger of injury caused by the moving parts is quite serious, especially for a single-hander at sea.

However, in small craft the outboard well is sometimes at the after end of the cockpit, and in very hot weather in the tropics, it is sometimes impossible to run the engine inside the well without removing the cover, because of oxygen starvation. In this case a metal net guard should be made up, which can be fitted over the well opening after the engine is in place.

ENGINE SECURITY   In many parts of the world any removable item left on deck stands the risk of being stolen. Chains and locks are available to secure the outboard engine topsides. However, even these will not prevent theft. Therefore, in most parts of the world the engine should be stored below deck. If this is done, any gasoline in the fuel system should be drained out before the engine is stowed below. Engrave the boat's name on the cylinder block of the motor.

GOING FOREIGN   Nowadays in most parts of the world, the most common makes of outboard motors (Evinrude, Johnson) are in use by local fishermen. This means that spares may be available. Nevertheless, you should make sure that sufficient spares are taken on board to be efficient for normal engine usage, and the makers should be asked for their advice on this. In any case, with regard to smaller models, below ten horsepower, a full set of spares should be stored on board, along with at least two spare propellers.

STORING THE OUTBOARD MOTOR   On the larger yachts with inboard engines, the likelihood of using the outboard motor during the transoceanic voyage is slim. In most of the ports of call en route, the yacht anchorages are close enough to the jetty for oars to be used in the dinghy, if the yacht cannot get alongside the dock. On smaller craft, the outboard is unlikely to be used at sea because of the amount of fuel consumed and the difficulty of storing this. Nine times out of ten the outboard motor is going to be stowed down below for the voyage. This should be done properly.

If the outboard motor has been used in salt water, this needs to be flushed out by running the motor in a freshwater tank. For the larger models of outboards that are too heavy to be put into a freshwater tank, this can be done by connecting up the cooling system with a hose according to the directions in the manufacturer's manual.

After the cooling system has been thoroughly flushed out with fresh water, the fuel shut-off valve and the air-vent screws should be shut and the motor allowed to run at idling speed until the fuel remaining in the system runs out and the motor stops by itself. Just before the motor stops, some rust-preventive should be squirted into the carburetor intake; this should be done slowly so that the engine does not stop too soon.

After the motor has stopped, remove the flushing plugs in the cooling system so as to allow all the remaining water to drain out completely, check your motor, and inspect the motor itself. Be sure that you haven't forgotten any plugs, since even a small drop of water trapped in a confined passage can cause serious damage if it is allowed to freeze there, although unless you are heading for cold climates this is improbable.

Next, drain the fuel tank of all gasoline, disconnect the fuel line at the carburetor, and empty this also. Remove each spark plug and introduce a few rops of lubricating oil into each spark plug hole. Then crank the motor over by hand a few times, after which a few more drops of oil should be added through each plug hole. Repeat the cranking operation again to make sure that the oil is evenly spread over the cylinder wall, then replace the spark plugs after cleaning and adjusting them.

All the moving parts on the exterior should then be lubricated with a waterproof grease: the throttle linkage, steering system, swivel pins, and tilt mechanism—all should be lubricated. The electric wiring and ignition system, as well as the outside of the plugs, should be sprayed with a penetrating oil, such as WD-40, CRC, or LPS. Then the motor should be wiped down with an oily rag and placed in a large plastic bag, such as the type used as garbage bags, which should be well sealed. Then the motor can be stowed and wedged firmly inside the hull.

If the motor has electric starting, disconnect the storage battery and make sure that it is stored in a reasonably dry, warm place inboard. The battery, during the voyage, should be charged periodically with a trickle charger.

COLD-CLIMATE STORAGE If the projected voyage is to a cold-climate area, it is a good idea to pour colored alcohol into the cooling system before running the engine. This will prevent freezing. Ethylene glycol antifreeze, which is a rust inhibitor, is ideal for this purpose.

Engine cranks but will not start, or starts hard:

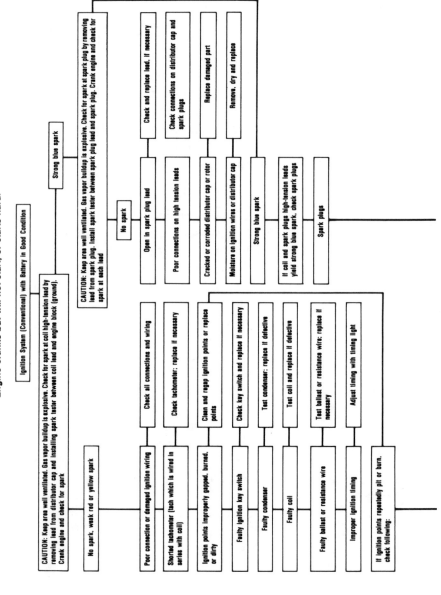

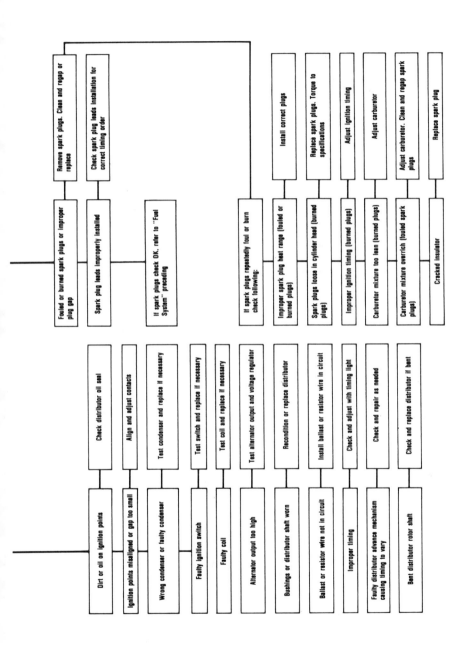

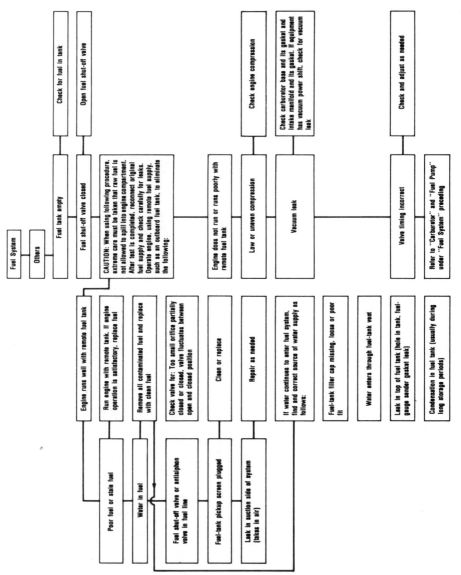

Engine cranks but will not start, or starts hard:

Fuel System
Others

Check for fuel in tank
Open fuel shut-off valve

Fuel tank empty
Fuel shut-off valve closed

CAUTION: When using following procedure, extreme care must be taken that raw fuel is not allowed to spill into engine compartment. After test is completed, reconnect original fuel supply and check carefully for leaks. Operate engine, using remote fuel supply, such as an outboard fuel tank, to eliminate the following:

Engine does not run or runs poorly with remote fuel tank

Low or uneven compression
Check engine compression

Vacuum leak
Check carburetor base and its gasket and intake manifold and its gasket. If equipment has vacuum power shift, check for vacuum leak

Valve timing incorrect
Check and adjust as needed

Refer to "Carburetor" and "Fuel Pump" under "Fuel System" preceding

Engine runs well with remote fuel tank

Run engine with remote tank. If engine operation is satisfactory, replace fuel

Remove all contaminated fuel and replace with clean fuel

Check valve for: Too small orifice partially closed or closed, valve fluctuates between open and closed position

Clean or replace

Repair as needed

If water continues to enter fuel system, find and correct source of water supply as follows:

Fuel-tank filler cap missing, loose or poor fit

Water enters through fuel-tank vent

Leak in top of fuel tank (hole in tank, fuel-gauge sender gasket leak)

Condensation in fuel tank (usually during long storage periods)

Poor fuel or stale fuel

Water in fuel

Fuel shut-off valve or antisiphon valve in fuel line

Fuel-tank pickup screen plugged

Leak in suction side of system (takes in air)

Engine cranks but will not start, or starts hard:

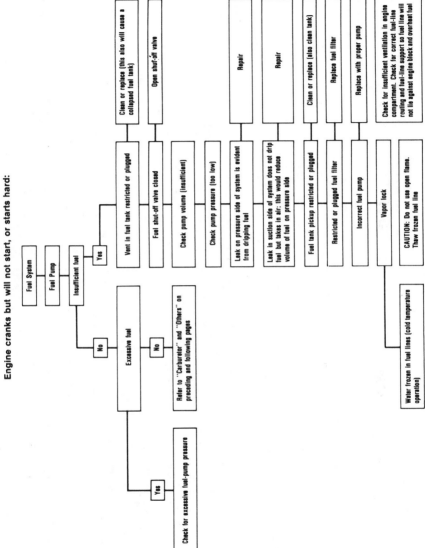

GASOLINE-ENGINE FAULTFINDING

Troubleshooting an engine that starts hard or won't start at all, as any professional mechanic will tell you, is a simple matter of following clues and eliminating possibilities until the fault is located.

Begin the process of elimination with spark condition; if the spark is strong and blue and the plugs seem in good shape, proceed with the fuel-system checks below; if the spark is weak, begin with the electrical-system checks. And have faith. There is nothing mystical about mechanical troubleshooting; gasoline engines are rational machines.

Engine cranks but will not start, or starts hard:

Fuel System → Carburetor

Carburetor floods — Yes → Needle and seat worn, damaged, or dirty → Clean or replace needle and seat

Float adjustment incorrect → Adjust float

Leaky Float → Replace float

Carburetor gaskets leaking (broken or brittle material; loose screws) → Tighten screws or replace gasket

Cracked carburetor body → Replace carburetor body

Automatic choke defective or out of adjustment (flooding on hot starting) → Replace or adjust choke

Excessive fuel-pump pressure → Refer to "Fuel Pump" on next page

Clogged flame arrester → Clean flame arrester

Carburetor floods — No

Insufficient fuel from carburetor — No → Refer to "Fuel Pump" and "Others" (following) of these "Fuel-System" charts

Insufficient fuel from carburetor — Yes

Carburetor dirty with restricted or plugged fuel passages → Clean and repair with necessary repair kit

Insufficient fuel supply to carburetor → Refer to "Fuel Pump" on next page

Carburetor filter plugged → Clean or replace

Small-Craft Cooking

As you will have restricted space in which to prepare and store food, a small stove, with perhaps only one or two burners, and no refrigerator, it is obvious that some thought must be given to meal storage and preparation while the boat is ocean voyaging. In harbor or at anchor things will be easier, as local supplies can be obtained to restock at frequent intervals. At sea, the only supplies available from outside the boat are fish, and you cannot depend on catching them. So supplies must be carried whilst passage-making, to cover the whole voyage, plus a margin of at least one-quarter extra, in case of breakdown or being becalmed.

I have made a list of food that provides satisfactory nutrition, yet which needs no refrigeration and can be prepared easily. My recipes are worked out so that wherever possible they can be cooked in one pan and will provide at least two meals for one person. In this way kerosene fuel, preparation and cooking time, and labor are saved. Eating out of the pan can be pleasant and saves washing up.

Shoreside practices, such as always cooking in fresh water, or peeling roots such as potatoes and carrots, should be avoided, as they waste both water and good, edible food. Water for boiling food should consist of one part seawater to two parts fresh water. For hot drinks it should, of course, be only fresh water. Salt should not be eaten with food; keep your salt intake capacity for what you'll get from the water.

Washing up utensils, plates, pans, etc., should, of course, be done in salt water. A good cleaning agent for obstinate pan stains is sand. Teeth can be cleaned with salt water.

Some of the recipes mention an oven. A pressure cooker with the pressure weight removed serves very well as a small oven. Bread, cakes, and biscuits will not brown, but they will be crusty and tasty.

Many canned foods, such as tomatoes, peas, beans, and corned beef, can be eaten without cooking. In the tropics it is no hardship to eat them cold, and it saves a lot of kerosene and keeps the cabin cooler.

Good-tasting, easily cooked fish that can be caught at sea vary from hammerhead shark—tough and stringy—to dorado (or dolphin-fish, as it is known in some parts of the world). If possible, you should have on board a book showing the species of fish and naming them as edible or poisonous. There are several of these on the market. Shark liver is nutritious, but very greasy.

In cold waters, cod, herring, and halibut are fairly common and are easily boiled, steamed, or fried.

Flying fish can be trapped on board in the tropics simply by hanging out a white night light. The flying fish jump at it and fall on deck, ready to make a tasty though bony, breakfast.

Stingrays' "wing" edges taste very much like sole or flounder, but you must be very careful landing the fish, making sure his tail sting doesn't get anywhere near you. The best thing is to try to lasso the tail while the fish is in the water, then haul his tail out of the way. If you're in company, someone can keep the tail pinned to the deck with a broom or dinghy oar, then cut off the tail end.

Turtles are fairly easy to catch, being slow swimmers. If you stun the animal, you can then keep him alive until you are ready to cut him up, by tying a line around his hind leg and towing him astern. I know this sounds cruel, but I've seen turtles kept like this for days, and they seemed happy enough. Turtle meat can be cooked just like beef; in fact, it tastes something like stewing beef, but it is, of course, salty, so don't add any salt to the meat, and stew it in fresh water.

Dolphins and porpoises can be eaten but they are very ill-tasting, being extremely oily and "raw-fishy." Besides, there's a moral objection to killing them, as far as I'm concerned. I don't know why this should be—we kill cows and sheep. But there's something about the porpoise-type mammals—it would be like killing a dog to eat him, at least that's the way I feel. In extremis, though, they can be killed quite readily with a harpoon, though you have to be quick.

Unless you are in danger of starvation it's just not worth trapping sea birds. Their meat is tough, stringy, and very salty, and there is usually not enough of it to make the effort worth the reward.

LOCAL FOOD   In many parts of the world locally produced food is far cheaper than imported products. This is especially so in the Third World countries and on ocean islands. Breadfruit and mangoes are staple foods on many islands, and coconut, avocado, and fish will give you all the proteins and minerals you need.

Breadfruit is simply sliced up and fried. Some people are allergic to certain tropical fruits, such as mangoes, so it would not be advisable to take to sea fruit you have not tried previously.

Pineapples, green melons, and cantaloupes keep for a few days in the tropics. Try to keep all fresh fruits out of direct sunlight to prevent overripening. In the case of unripened fruit, wrapping it in aluminum foil and placing it in the sun will accelerate the ripening process. If possible, store all fresh fruit separately; should that be impossible, check the fruit regularly for mold and fungus. Should you find a moldy fruit, toss it out and wash the remaining ones thoroughly, drying them well before re-storing them.

Green bananas and plantains can be taken to sea on the stalk—but be careful not to take too many at the same ripening stage; otherwise you'll find you have a hundred and fifty bananas all going ripe at the same time.

Any fruits, vegetables, or meat bought in local markets in Third World countries should be inspected closely for insects and mildew. The best thing is to wash it all in a solution of fresh water and permanganate of potash as soon as it's on board, then dry it out well. Rice, flour, sugar, and biscuits should be carefully sifted for bugs, and once sorted out should be kept in hermetically sealed containers.

The first encounter with a Third World local market can be a traumatic shock to anyone accustomed to Western standards of hygiene. However, don't let your initial disgust put you off. Clean the food off carefully and remember the money you are saving. Over a period of time you will build up a resistance both to the visual impact of the food being handled and also to any odd bugs that slip through your cleaning net.

The prices offered in local markets in any but the most advanced countries are not the prices you are expected to pay. They are the seller's starting point for bargaining. Depending on the locality, the asking price can be anything up to 50 percent more than the lowest price the shopkeeper is prepared to accept. But this is part of the fun of market shopping, so never be shy of beating the local prices down. The more you do this, the more you will be respected.

In Arab, Asian, and black African countries it often pays to "adopt" one of the street boys hanging around the market to accompany you on shopping forays. You will soon know by the shopkeeper's attitude toward him if he is trustworthy. This will cost you something in the area of 50 percent of the average minimum laborer's wage in that country. You will be surprised how low this is, and also how much money it will save you on the day's shopping. When you get to know the lad well, he can also be hired to guard the boat when there is no one on board. Here again, his fee should not be more than 50 percent of the minimum wage for every four hours on guard.

It is well worth your while, before commencing the voyage, to obtain from the local customs a list of duty-free ports around the world. Here, not only booze and tobacco goods, but also canned and dried foods can be bought without payment of duty and taxes. This makes a terrific difference to the money laid out—up to 50 percent and more. You won't be able to get the duty-free goods on board until just before you sail, and there will be an amount of paperwork to wade through, but the savings make this more than worthwhile.

AT-SEA FOOD AND BARTER STORES LIST   As a guide to fridgeless storing, I give here my rations list for a solo 80-day voyage.

	Amount	Comments
Fresh water	32 gallons (120 L)	
Kerosene	13 gallons (50 L)	This is more than enough, but it is best to stock good supplies.
Methylated spirits	2 ½ gallons (9 L)	(same as above)
Candles	50	Very useful for bartering.
Kent cigarettes	200 (?)	Ditto. For some reason I cannot fathom, these are valued above all others in out-of-the-way areas.
Old-fashioned, collarless shirts, linen or cotton, with tails fore and aft	(?)	Highly appreciated as gifts to headmen in remote villages, especially in Moslem areas. 1 shirt = 3 weeks' supply of fruit and fish.
Potatoes	44 lbs. (20-kg)	

	Amount	Comments
Onions	9 lbs. (4-kg)	These are the best-keeping root vegetable.
Apples	34	These must not have been refrigerated.
Lemons	12	Wrapped in foil
Eggs	7 dozen	Dipped in melted wax, stored in sawdust.
Butter	7 lbs. (3-kg)	In 4- or 6-oz. cans
Lard	7 lbs. (3-kg)	Or 5½ lbs. (2.5-kg) in biscuit tin, in which fried beef had been placed.
Cheese	3 lbs. (1.5-kg)	
Flour	9 lbs. (4-kg)	
Cake	6½ lbs. (3-kg)	
Rice	18 lbs. (8-kg)	
Oats	9 lbs. (4-kg)	
Cereal	4 packets	
Sugar	9 lbs. (4-kg)	
Coffee	½ lb. (226-grams)	Coffee drinkers exchange this amount with tea below.
Tea	9 lbs. (4-kg)	
Cocoa	9 lbs. (4-kg)	
Candy	6½ lbs. (3-kg)	
Pickled onions	3 lbs. (1.5-kg)	
Meat	30 12-oz. (340-gram) cans	
Fish	24 8-oz. (226-gram) cans	
Soup	20 10-oz. (283-gram) cans	
Evaporated milk	14 24-oz. (450-gram) cans	
Dried milk	4½ lbs. (2-kg)	
Vegetables	8 10-oz. (283-gram) cans	
Baked beans	12 6-oz. (170-gram) cans	
Nuts	44 lbs. (20-kg)	More than ample for eighty days, but also stocked for emergencies.

	Amount	Comments
Salt	3 lbs. (1.5-kg)	In case of going inland in remote areas: good for bartering.
Pepper	3 lbs. (1.5-kg)	
Curry powder	1½ lbs. (453-grams)	
Vitamin tablets	100 "all-around" type	
Bacon	7 lbs. (3-kg)	Buried in salt.
Biscuits	2 5-lb. (2.2-kg) tins	
Ham	1	Good medium-size, cured and hung.
Yeast	12 ozs. (226-grams)	
Baking powder	12 ozs. (226-grams)	
Dried fruit	10 lbs. (4.4-kg)	

The above fed one man for eighty days, effectively.

The cooking routine at sea is dealt with elsewhere in this book. All that remains now is to give you a few typical menus, using canned, dried, and pickled boat stores and fresh food caught at sea and bought in the local markets.

Cooking for yourself can be a chore. Take heart—all these menus are easy and quick to prepare, they are all cooked in one pan (except where stated) and they can all be used for at least two consecutive meals.

WHITE BREAD

¼ cup warm water*	2 tablespoons sugar
1 package yeast	2 teaspoons salt
1 cup milk	6 cups unsifted flour
1 tablespoon butter	1 cup lukewarm water

Place ¼ cup warm water in small bowl. Sprinkle yeast over the water, stirring till dissolved. Add melted butter, sugar, salt, and milk. Add 2 cups of flour to mixture. Add 1 cup of lukewarm water and remaining 4 cups of flour, and beat with spoon until smooth.

Grease the palms of your hands, then roll the mixture into a ball,

* In the tropics water should be warm enough to use directly from tank without pre-heating.

kneading and punching the dough until a smooth ball. Place back in bowl, cover, and place in a warm place until doubled. (Test by poking dough; if the dents remain, the dough has risen.)

Re-form ball and cut in half. Lightly grease pan and place dough inside, covering with a cloth until dough has risen to the top of the pan. Preheat pressure cooker, without lid, to 400 degrees. Place pan inside of pressure cooker with the pressure weight removed, and bake for 40 minutes. The bread will not brown. To test if the bread is done, remove the bread from the pan. Tap the center of the loaf. A hollow sound indicates bread is done. If not, return to pan and pressure cooker for additional 5–10 minutes.

While first loaf is baking, additional ingredients can be added to remaining dough, such as raisins, cheese, etc.

Makes two small loaves. Store in plastic or wax paper to preserve.

BAKING POWDER BISCUITS

2 cups sifted flour
3 teaspoons baking powder
½ teaspoon salt

¼ cup lard
¾ cup milk (reconstituted)

Combine flour, baking powder, and salt in bowl. Add lard, working it in with your fingers until mixture resembles coarse meal. Add milk a little at a time, stirring often. To ease handling of mixture, dust flour over your hands. Knead out on flat, lightly floured board. Flatten (or roll with drinking glass) out to ½-inch thickness. Cut dough into squares and place in pan, edges touching for soft biscuits, farther apart for a crustier biscuit.

Preheat pressure cooker to 450 degrees, leaving lid off. Bake for 15 minutes with lid on, pressure weight removed.

To store biscuits, place in plastic bag and draw out air. Or place in tin biscuit box.

Note: There are a number of inexpensive, plastic kitchen storage containers that allow you to "burp" them (draw out all air) after closing. These would seem ideal for baked storage.

Breakfasts

OATMEAL

1 ½ cups salt water   ½ cup dried fruit (optional)
9 heaping tablespoons oats   ¼ cup condensed milk
1 tablespoon sugar

Bring salt water to boil. Stir in oats, bring water back to boiling, then simmer for 5 minutes.

Remove from heat, stir in sugar, milk, and fruit.

A quick and easy breakfast, especially easy to clean up after.

BACON AND BEANS

¼ pound bacon   1 6-ounce can baked beans

Lightly brown bacon in skillet. Drain bacon drippings and add beans. Simmer for 5 minutes.

The bacon drippings can be eaten on bread, as a side dish.

CHEESE PANCAKE

½ cup flour   2 tablespoons evaporated milk
1 egg   ¼ pound grated or sliced cheese

Combine flour, egg and milk, beating well to blend. Pour into pre-heated skillet, lightly greased. Fry until solid and lightly browned on underside. Add cheese and fold pancake over. Continue frying until cheese is melted. Remove from heat and serve.

Precooked bacon, ham or canned meat can be added, as desired.

Main Meals

BEEF PIE

3 potatoes, peeled and diced
Lard, bacon fat, or butter
1 small onion, diced
1 cup bread, broken into crumbs

1 can beef
1 egg or egg powder
1 can peas
Seasoning (as desired)

Lightly brown potatoes and onion in lard, bacon fat, or butter. Remove from heat and allow to cool. Combine potatoes, onion, bread, beef, egg, and peas. Place in pan. Preheat pressure cooker with weight removed to 350 degrees. Place pan in cooker and bake for 30–35 minutes, or until top is firm. Remove and serve hot. Also delicious cold.

AVOCADO AND FISH SALAD

1 large, ripe avocado
1 can tomatoes (or 2 fresh
    tomatoes, if available)
1 tablespoon curry powder (or
    chili powder if available)

1 tablespoon pepper
1 8-ounce can of fish (or 1 ½
    cups of fresh, boiled fish)

Peel and slice avocado, mash with fork. Drain canned tomatoes and add to avocado. Add curry and pepper. Mix well and combine fish. Store in shade, in a cool place.

POACHED FISH

1 cup fresh water
1–2 pounds fresh fish
1 can string beans (or other
    vegetable)

Juice of one lemon
3 tablespoons melted butter

Bring water to boil. Simmer fish for about 15 minutes, until skin is firm and flesh is white or translucent. Drain and add string beans. Simmer additional 5 minutes, until beans are tender. Remove from heat and serve, garnished with lemon juice and melted butter.

CURRY

1 medium-size onion, minced
2 tablespoons butter
1 tablespoon curry powder
1 peeled apple, minced
1 can chicken or beef broth

2 tablespoons dried fruit
1 cup rice
8–12 ounces beef, fish, etc.
Pepper and salt to taste

Brown onion in butter. Add curry powder and apple. Cook until almost like a puree. Add broth and dried fruit. Cook until the mixture thickens. Remove from heat.

In a separate pot boil rice until done, add meat or fish and simmer 2–3 additional minutes. Stir in curry sauce. Season with salt and pepper to taste. Store in hay-box to keep hot.

ESCALLOPED POTATOES AND HAM

Slice raw potatoes. Place in a buttered pan, alternating layers of thinly sliced ham and potatoes. Each layer should be sprinkled with salt, pepper and one tablespoon of flour per layer. Add enough milk to cover completely. Bake in preheated pressure cooker (450 degrees) with weight removed until potatoes are tender and crust has formed on top.

CREAMED ONIONS AND BEEF

1 can cream of mushroom or
    celery soup
2 medium-size onions, sliced
1 can beef

Salt and pepper to taste
2 tablespoons milk
1 tablespoon butter

Bring soup to boil. Add sliced onion and simmer till tender. Season beef with salt and pepper to taste, and add to soup. Simmer for 5–10 minutes. Add milk and butter and beat before serving.

CORNED BEEF HASH WITH EGGS

Slice corned beef thickly. Fry in bacon drippings or lard until browned on both sides. Serve with fried egg atop each slice.

All of the above main-meal recipes have been chosen with the use of alternatives in mind. All of these recipes are delicious with canned or fresh fish, chicken, beef, ham, substituted for whatever each recipe calls for.

Two other recipes that come in handy, especially when beating into heavy weather, when you don't know when you'll have time to prepare your next meal, are lobscouse and burgoo.

Lobscouse is a very old method of cooking several meals at once in one pot. Thinly sliced potatoes go on the bottom, layered about two inches thick, then a root vegetable such as carrots or turnips is added, followed by cut cabbage and sliced onions, a one-inch layer, then on top of it all fish or meat cut into small chunks, just the flesh. Add enough water to just cover the food, plus a cube or two of beef bouillon. Bring to a boil and simmer for several hours, until the fish or meat falls to pieces and mixes with the rest. A pressure cooker three-quarters full will provide about four meals.

Burgoo is especially suited for cold-weather passages, as it can be stored topsides and eaten right out of the container. Prepare porridge and pour an inch layer in a container. Cover with a layer of bacon. Another layer of porridge, then add a layer of beef. Alternate layers of porridge, beef, fish, and bacon. Lace each layer of meat or fish with a few drops of whisky. In tropical regions a smaller amount is made. If the outer edges begin to turn moldy, they can be scraped away and the remaining burgoo can still be eaten.

Catching Fish

THE one great food and money saver at sea is fishing. However, no matter how much the area you are to cruise is supposed to abound with fish, no matter how sanguine your expectations of a good catch every day, in the hopes that fish will make up your rations, never understock your galley with food before sailing. Fish should be looked upon merely as a serendipitous supplementary. But if you carry the right tackle, or "rigs" as fishermen call them, and if you study the type of fish that inhabit the areas you will pass through and are prepared to make the effort to troll properly while underway, or to bottom-fish while at anchor, you stand a good chance of gaining good, tasty, nutritious food, which in time, as you gain experience, can amount to a good percentage of your food intake and save a lot of money.

The study of methods of sea fishing can do nothing but good, even if you are well-off enough to be able to afford to buy all the food for your voyage. First, there is nothing available ashore, not even in the finest *cordon bleu* restaurants, to compare with the taste and goodness of freshly caught fish straight out of the sea. Second, in otherwise seemingly eventless days and nights of ocean cruising, fishing affords the opportunity of an extra bit of anticipation, added achievement, the excitement of pulling in the catch. Obtaining food in any other way, with the exception perhaps of hunting, cannot be compared to catching your own, and the skill, the luck, the anticipation, the success—all are transmitted to the taste of the fish itself. Third, if worse ever comes to worst and you are shipwrecked, in a dinghy alone on the ocean, you will have the tackle, the skill, and the experience to catch fish; this will probably mean the difference between survival and death. Fish not only provide protein, but squeezed raw also provide fresh water.

There are two kinds of fishing for the sailing man under way. One is artificial luring and the other is bait luring. Good artificial lures are expensive, but it pays to have a couple on board in case of the absence of readily caught fresh bait, such as flying fish. The silverspoon-type artificial lure, about four inches long, with a triple-pointed hook on the end, is about the best for general use. But if for any reason artificial lures are not carried, or have been lost, bear in mind that in the deep-ocean areas, say, more than three hundred miles offshore, many fish will, in their comparative innocence of the ways of man, go for a small light-colored rag strip. This should be about six inches long and cut into more or less the shape of a small fish.

The hooks you need should be of good quality, made of an alloy of nickel and steel, which does not corrode in salt water. Other types available are stainless steel (which are expensive, but last forever) and tin- or cadmium-plated. These last are very popular but are more expensive than the alloy hooks, and after much use the plating wears off so that the hooks rust. But regardless of the type used, they should be stored in a watertight tin or plastic box and kept smeared with light grease.

There are many different styles of hook for bait fishing, but the best of all is the O'Shaughnessy. It is very strongly made from hefty material and, most of the ocean fish being slow-biting and heavy-mouthed, the O'Shaughnessy withstands the strains and hooks well and truly into the fish's mouth. The point of the O'Shaughnessy has an outward slant away from the shank of the hook, which allows the fish to chomp surely on the point.

You should buy hooks from about a half inch in length to the monster six-inch hook for shark fishing. The number of hooks carried will depend on several factors, such as the cost, the funds available, and the length of the voyage. As a general rule I would say three each of the smaller sizes up to two and a half inches in length for every two months of expected sea time, and one each of the bigger sizes. As your experience grows, so the rate of loss of hooks will diminish; but if you have started out with too many, bear in mind that in remote islands and coasts a good fishing tackle is worth a great deal as a bargaining commodity.

Sinkers are used to keep the bait at a selected level underwater. Always use the lightest sinker that will do the job, so as not to scare off the fish when they come in to bite. You should take a good selection of these. The handiest and simplest to use are the diamond-shaped casting sinkers. These are designed to avoid twisting the line, and the best are those with a swivel attachment at each end. Another good type for seawater fishing is the Pyramid sinker, but this is best when bottom-fishing at anchor. There are several different designs of these, for rough- and soft-bottom use, so the best buy is the type of sinker on which the securing eye can be secured on either the top or the bottom, according to the nature of the anchoring ground. The idea is to have the Pyramid sink sharp end first into a soft bottom, but to have its flat base rest on the hard bottom where the surface is rough.

Floats are the next item on the fishing-tackle list. These, of course, are used when fishing off the bottom at anchor. They come in a bewildering array of shapes and sizes. A very craftily made and productive float is the plopping-cork type. This is long and cone-shaped, hollowed out, with a line-holding device passing through the cone. The small end of the cone is weighted, and the bait is suspended below the float. When the line is jiggled, the float makes a slopping noise, like a fish feeding on the surface. This, and the bait, will bring in customers for the hook.

Leader wires come in three types: piano wire, which is used in lengths up to six feet for big fish, such as shark; braided wire; and braided wire covered with nylon. The nylon-covered wire is best for smaller fish, as the covering prevents the wire from kinking and also helps to disguise it from the fish. Several strengths of wire are available. I suggest one-hundred-pound strength for small and medium fish and a thousand pounds for the big trade.

The actual fishing line should be nylon monofil. You should carry several of these, of different strengths, up to five hundred pounds for the small to medium catches and to two thousand pounds for sharks.

Under way at sea it would not do to have three or four lines of different lengths streamed out astern of the boat. For one thing they would probably tangle up with the log line when the vessel swerved with the action of the sea. It is a good idea, instead, to stream the lines from a "spreader," which is towed astern abaft the log spinner, on one line. Then from the spreader three or four lines of differing lengths and strengths, according to the type of fish in the area, are streamed. The spreader can be made up from a lightweight aluminum or wood pole. But this is best used when the going is steady and no changes of course are expected. If the course is changed while the spreader is out, the easiest and quickest way to deal with not getting the lines fouled is to ease the spreader out as far as you can from the stern. It will then follow the boat around in a gentler curve. Of course, trolling is usually done at a fairly slow hull speed.

OPEN-WATER FISHING   The sheer numbers of species of ocean fish are incredible. Their variety is astonishing, from the huge monster white sharks, weighing several tons, to the trillions of tiny tiddlers. It would be impossible in anything short of a full-blown library to go into all the different species, so here we will deal with the more common and well-known ones: the tarpon, the bluefish, barracuda, groupers which are denizens of the continental shelves, swimming around anything up to five hundred miles out from the shores. Then, way out in the deep blue ocean waters is the home of the big sharks, the sailfish and marlin, mackerel and tunas, and the best eating of all—the dolphin. This is not the mammal dolphin (God forbid that you should ever be in such dire hunger as to eat one of those friendly intelligences!) but is a fish known in some parts of the world as the dorado. Also shoals of mullet are there for the taking. Out on the open ocean the easiest bait fish to come across is the flying fish. He will just jump on board if you have a light in the rigging at night. His silvery color is ideal for attracting big-game fish. His flesh is firm, so he stays on the hook, but if it looks as if there's any chance he might fall off, lash the dead fish on the hook with some strong cotton.

If your boat has any growth on the bottom, there will probably be a few mollusks of one kind or another leeching on. For more certain catching of a bait fish, such as a smallish mullet to catch a big dorado, for example, you can always heave-to and go over the side to scrape some of the mollusks off for use as bait. Mind you, mullet are very good eating in themselves, so cut a strip off and use that as bait for something else while you cook the mullet. A bird in the hand is worth two in the bush!

Pilchards also make excellent bait fish, as do mackerel, but if you're fishing for eating and not for sport, then these themselves fry up and steam very well.

One of the main problems, especially for a single-hander with no refrigerator, is that having caught a big twenty-pounder he has no way of storing it. The thing to do is to cook as much of it as will make four meals. Some of it can be fried up, some steamed, and the rest put into a lobscouse stew. The unused meat can be pickled in lemon juice to make "cerviche" or, shame though it is, must be thrown away. But cheer up, the seemingly wasted portion will soon be digested by other inhabitants of the deep and so return to the food chain. But if your food stocks are very low, it is well worthwhile drying out some of the excess and laying it down in salt, as described later.

FISHING CLOSE INSHORE OR WHILE AT ANCHOR   Inside protected bays and leads, behind the great coral reefs, and inside atoll anchorages are many prolific fishing grounds. There you will find channel bass, weakfish, bonefish, croakers, snappers, and whole schools of small-fry just waiting to be exactly that. Some sharks, such as the gray and the hammerhead, also come close inshore to make good sport as well as fair eating. Cod and pollock are denizens of inshore areas where the water is cold, while in warmer waters speckled trout, redfish, and striped bass swarm, especially over mud, while over rocky ground the sheepshead lies in wait for the crabs.

Also inshore are the mollusks: oysters, clams, scallops, conch, sea urchins, and, surprisingly, the squid, which is simply a mollusk that turned itself inside out during the process of evolution in the dim and distant past. Another food inshore is the crustacean, shrimp and crab. But if these are difficult to gather, at least there is the consolation that where they are, so are the predator fish: croakers, sheepsheads, drums.

Of course, if you are at anchor in protected water it is fairly easy to find bait by knocking the mollusks off the rocks, digging the worms out of the sand. If the area is particularly good in fishing, it is worthwhile considering staying there for a few days, catching a good number of fat, juicy fish, and salting them after drying them out in the sun. But if you do this, store the dried fish in the coolest place you have and make sure that their container is alsolutely airtight. The best way is to bury the fish in fine salt. Even if you never eat it yourself, it can be used as strip bait to catch other fish when you're under way.

In the tropics, small conches and shellfish for bait can be picked up on beaches, especially after a storm, or on the low flats when the tide has receded. They are tough little devils, but the easiest way to extract the meat from the shells is to boil them in water. Then their "foot" pokes out and can be pulled out. A good tug with a pair of pliers will do the trick.

Clams and mussels make pretty good eating of themselves and can be picked up from rocks on the shore. Also remember when in tropical areas such as East Africa or Central America, where there are mangrove trees growing right up to seawater, on the branches that droop into the water mussels and even a small type of oyster make their homes, and can be harvested straight from the dinghy. These mollusks make excellent bait for catching fish and even for eating direct.

The problem with baiting a line with mollusks is keeping the bait on the hook. The way to do that with bivalves (oysters, scallops, clams) is to put the point of the hook through the adductor muscles. These are the two tough, knobby muscles that attach the animal to its shell. With univalves, like whelks and conches, the hook should be pushed through the extremely tough "foot" muscle. That way there is less chance of the bait coming loose from the hook.

On most tropical coasts sea urchins grow on the sea bottom, even on otherwise featureless sandy stretches. These can be gathered, if you are extremely careful not to get one of the spines into your hand or foot. The best thing is to wear gloves and deck shoes. The green sea urchins are edible. The purple ones are poisonous and should absolutely be left alone. Sea urchins can be eaten raw and are full of protein and minerals. However, if you are at all squeamish about eating raw mollusks, just pick up a few of them and use them for bait to catch regular fish. If you do get a sea urchin spine in you, remember that it can be removed by burning a rag black, letting it cool off, then placing it over the place where the spine entered; the spine will then probably emerge from the skin.

In advanced countries, and indeed in many not so advanced, it is well to bear in mind that there are laws regulating the taking of many types of fish, mollusks, and crustaceans, but in remote areas this is hardly a problem.

Remember, in poverty-stricken areas do not fish for sport alone. If you can, share some of your catch with the locals. They will appreciate it greatly, and if trouble blows up, they will not forget your gift.

FISHING TACKLE LIST

Artificial lures
  Small
  Large
Hooks
  Small
  Medium
  Large
Sinkers
  Diamond-shaped
  Pyramid
Floats
  Solid
  "Plopping"

Leader wires
  Small, up to two feet, braided
  wire, nylon-covered
  Medium, up to four feet,
  braided wire, nylon-covered
  Large, piano wire, up to six feet
Fishing lines
  Small, up to 500-lb. strain
  Large, up to 2,000-lb. strain
Spreader
Cork-handled knife
  (unsinkable) with lanyard
Watertight container for hooks
Light grease for hooks

THE MOST COMMON TYPES OF EDIBLE SALTWATER FISH,
AND THE BEST BAIT TO USE

Fish	*Bait*
Albacore	Flying fish
Black Drum	Shrimp, squid, mollusk meat, crabs
Bluefish	Flying fish, artificial lure
Bonito	Small bait fish, strip baits, flying fish
Cobia (ling)	Flying fish
Codfish	Clams, squid, cut bait, live smelt, or other small fish
Dolphin (dorado)	Flying fish, other bait fishes, artificial lure
Great barracuda	Flying fish
Groupers (various)	Cut and strip baits, shrimp, crabs, bait fish
Halibut, flounder, and other flatfish	Marine worms, shrimp, cut bait, clams, crabs, small bait fish
King mackerel (kingfish)	Flying fish
Mackerels (various)	Shrimp, small crabs
Marlin (all species)	Flying fish, mullet, squid, cut strips
Pollock	Cut bait, clams, squid, small fish
Sailfish	Strip baits mullet, bonito, flying fish, artificial lure
Sharks	Whole fish, cut bait, artificial lure
Sheepshead	Fiddler crabs, shrimp
Spanish mackerel	Flying fish
Striped bass	Shrimp, crabs, mullet, flying fish, artificial lure
Swordfish	Mackerel, squid, flying fish, artificial lure
Tarpon	Crabs, pinfish
Tautog (blackfish)	Fiddler and green crabs, almost any available bait
Tuna	Herring
Weakfish (all species)	Crabs, sea worms, small fish

I give here a few seafood recipes I've used over the years. They are ideal for the single-hander, as they can be cooked in one pot, and

I have proportioned the meals to suit one man for two main meals. Crewed-vessel cooks can increase the proportions as needed.

SOLE MEUNIÈRE

2/3 pound sole or flounder
1 tablespoon flour
4 tablespoons butter

Minced onion (as desired)
Lemon juice

Dust fish with flour. Melt butter in large skillet. Place fish in butter and lightly brown on each side; baste. Lightly fry onion in butter until soft. Garnish fish with fried onion and lemon juice and serve.

POLLOCK CREOLE

1 pound pollock
Pepper, curry (garlic, thyme,
    basil—if available)
2 tablespoons butter

1 large onion, chopped
1 can tomatoes
1 cup fresh water
1 teaspoon sugar

Season fish with pepper, curry, etc. In large skillet melt butter. Add onion and cook until lightly browned. Strain tomatoes and add to skillet. Bring to a boil. Add fish and just enough water until mixture covers fish. Cook at low heat for 20 minutes, or until fish breaks easily with fork.

MUSSELS BORDELAISE

1 quart mussels
1 tablespoon butter
Juice of one lemon (if available)
1 whole egg

1 cup beef broth (canned or bouillon)
Salt and pepper

In large pot or skillet, bring salt water to a boil. Boil scrubbed mussels until shells open (they will open of themselves in cooking). Drain and remove mussels from shells. Combine butter, lemon juice and egg; beat until thickened. Heat broth and add butter, lemon and egg mixture. Add seasoning and simmer for 5 minutes.

SCALLOPED CRABS

1 cup crabmeat
1 ½ tablespoons minced onion
2 tablespoons butter
2 tablespoons flour
1 cup condensed milk

1 egg yolk
½ cup biscuit or bread crumbs
2 tablespoons grated cheese
Lemon

Precook crabmeat by boiling in salt water until meat is flaky. In a large skillet fry onion in butter until lightly browned. Stir in flour and milk; simmer. Turn off heat and beat in egg yolk. Add crabmeat. Over the top spread crumbs and cheese. Cover skillet and cook over low heat 25–35 minutes. Serve lightly browned with lemon.

BAKED CODFISH

1 pound codfish
2 tablespoons cooking oil
2 tablespoons raisins or other dried fruit
2 tablespoons grated cheese
1 cup biscuit or bread crumbs

1 small onion, minced
2 medium-size potatoes, sliced thin
1 tablespoon water
Pepper

Cut codfish into thin strips. In large skillet or pressure cooker with weight removed, heat 1 tablespoon cooking oil. Combine other ingredients and layer alternately with fish. Add water and remaining cooking oil. Cover and cook over low light until potatoes are tender (around 30 minutes).

SQUID WITH ONIONS

1 pound fresh squid
1 large onion, sliced
¼ cup cooking oil

½ cup water
Salt and pepper

Clean squid thoroughly in salt water, removing intestines, outer skin, eyes. Cut off head and tentacles. Cut squid into small rings. Brown onions in oil, add squid, water, and seasonings, and cook until tender over medium flame, stirring occasionally. Serve hot.

CONCHES

2 large conches (about 3 inches
   in diameter)
Chopped garlic or onion to taste
Juice of one lemon

¼ cup cooking oil
Salt and pepper
Oregano, parsley, etc. (if
   available)

Clean conches in warm water with vegetable- or toothbrush until all sand is removed. Bring water to a rapid boil and submerge conches. Lower flame and boil (tightly covered) for 1 hour or so, until meat protrudes from shell about halfway. Remove meat from shell, and remove hard outer cover. Combine remaining ingredients in pan and roll conches in the mixture. Cover and simmer over a low heat for 5 minutes. Serve hot.

Epilogue HOW TO ENSURE
JOYFUL DEPARTURES

If you can keep your head when all about you
　　Are losing theirs and blaming it on you;
If you can trust yourself when all men doubt you,
　　But make allowance for their doubting too;
If you can wait and not be tired by waiting,
　　Or being lied about, don't deal in lies,
Or, being hated, don't give way to hating,
　　And yet don't look too good, nor talk too wise;

If you can dream—and not make dreams your master;
　　If you can think—and not make thoughts your aim;
If you can meet with triumph and disaster
　　And treat those two imposters just the same;
If you can bear to hear the truth you've spoken
　　Twisted by knaves to make a trap for fools,
Or watch the things you gave your life to, broken,
　　And stoop and build 'em up with worn-out tools;

If you can make one heap of all your winnings
　　And risk it on one turn of pitch and toss,
And lose, and start again at your beginnings
　　And never breathe a word about your loss;
If you can force your heart and nerve and sinew
　　To serve your turn long after they are gone,
And so hold on when there is nothing in you
　　Except the Will which says to them: "Hold on";

If you can talk with crowds and keep your virtue,
　　Or walk with kings—nor lose the common touch;
If neither foes nor loving friends can hurt you;
　　If all men count with you, but none too much;
If you can fill the unforgiving minute
　　With sixty seconds' worth of distance run—
Yours is the Earth and everything that's in it,
　　And—which is more—you'll be a Man, my son!

　　　　　　　—RUDYARD KIPLING, *If—*

(AUTHOR'S NOTE: And what is even more—you'll also be an ideal
single-handed ocean voyager. In fact, you'll be such a paragon of
goodness and such a self-righteous bore that everyone in port will
surely rejoice to see your eventual departure.)

219

List of Recommended Books

Books about single-handed and crewed ocean passages in small sailing craft

BARDIEUX, MARCEL. *4 Winds of Adventure.* New York: John de Graff, 1961.

BARTON, HUMPHREY. *Atlantic Adventures.* London: Adlard Coles, 1953.

BLEWITT, MARY. *Celestial Navigation for Yachtsmen.* Date unknown.

———. *Navigation for Yachtsmen.* New York: McKay, 1964.

BOMBARD, ALAIN. *The Voyage of the* Heretique. New York: Simon and Schuster, 1954.

BOWKER, R.M. *Make Your Own Sails.* New York: St. Martin's, 1957.

CALDWELL, JOHN. *Desperate Voyage.* New York: Ballantine, 1949.

COOKE, FRANCIS B. *Single Handed Cruising.* London: Arnold, 1924.

DUMAS, VITO. *Alone through the Roaring Forties.* New York: John de Graff, 1960.

GERBAULT, ALAN. *The Fight of the Firecrest.* London: Hart-Davis, 1955.

———. *In Quest of the Sun.* New York: Doubleday, 1955.

GUZZWELL, JOHN. *Trekka around the World.* London: Adlard Coles, 1963.

HENDERSON, RICHARD. *Singlehanded Sailing.* Maine: International Marine, 1972.

HISCOCK, ERIC. *Voyaging Under Sail.* London: Oxford University Press, 1959.

HOLM, DONALD. *The Circumnavigators.* Englewood Cliffs, New Jersey: Prentice-Hall, 1974.

LEWIS, DAVID. *The Ship would not sail Due West.* New York: St. Martin's, 1976.

MARIN-MARIE. *Wind Aloft, Wind Alow.* New York: Scribner's, 1947.

MOITESSIER, BERNARD. *The First Voyage of the Joshua.* New York: Morrow, 1973.

———. *The Long Way.* New York: Doubleday, 1975.

PIDGEON, HARRY. *Around the World Single Handed.* New York: Appleton & Co., 1933.

RIDLER, DONALD. *Eric the Red.* London: William Kimber, 1972.

SLOCUM, JOSHUA. *Sailing Alone Around the World.* First published in 1899, Blue Ribbon Books, New York. It is now available in a number of paperback editions.

TANGVALD, PETER. *Sea Gypsy.* New York: Dutton & Co., 1966.